JOB-SAVING STRATEGIES

WORKER BUYOUTS

AND

QWL

Arthur Hochner
Temple University

Cherlyn S. Granrose
Temple University

Judith Goode
Temple University

Elaine Simon
University of Pennsylvania

Eileen Appelbaum
Temple University

1988

W. E. UPJOHN INSTITUTE for Employment Research

Library of Congress Cataloging-in-Publication Data

Job-saving strategies : worker buyouts and QWL / Arthur Hochner . . .
  [et al.].
    p.   cm
  Bibliography: p.
  Includes index.
  ISBN 0-88099-069-4.   ISBN 0-88099-069-6 (pbk.)
    1. Supermarkets—Pennsylvania—Philadelphia—Management—Employee
  participation. 2. Management—Employee participation. 3. Employee
  ownership. 4. Quality of work life.   I. Hochner, Arthur.
  HD5658.G82U65 1988
  658.8'0683—dc19   88-39650
                                                                              CIP

∞

THE INSTITUTE, a nonprofit research organization, was established on July 1, 1945.
It is an activity of the W. E. Upjohn Unemployment Trustee Corporation, which was
formed in 1932 to administer a fund set aside by the late Dr. W. E. Upjohn for the
purpose of carrying on "research into the causes and effects of unemployment and
measures for the alleviation of unemployment."

The facts presented in this study and the observations and viewpoints expressed are
the sole responsibility of the author. They do not necessarily represent positions of
the W. E. Upjohn Institute for Employment Research.

Dedicated

to

the spirit of participation and collaboration

PREFACE

It was hard for the five co-authors to agree on a title for this book. It was not so much a disagreement among the members of our research group as it was a difficulty in coming up with a succinct title to convey the many aspects of the book and the study reported in it.

While this book is indeed an in-depth study of the effectiveness of two job-saving strategies used to reverse the shutdown of supermarkets in Philadelphia, we believe it is much more, too. It compares worker buyouts and QWL (quality of worklife) programs—two phenomena of great interest over the 1970s and '80s to the public, the mass media, and officials in business, labor, and government. It is a study that should prove interesting and useful to researchers in economics and other social sciences, to practitioners of management-labor relations, and to policymakers.

In the book, we attempt to break new ground both theoretically and empirically in the study of employee ownership and worker participation. Chapters 1 and 2 present a synthesis of previous research on these topics in order to develop a theoretical framework. We hypothesize and attempt to demonstrate in chapters 5, 6, and 7, in concrete terms, *how* employee ownership and worker participation are linked with economic outcomes for both workers and organizations. We link workers' attitudes to their firms' economic performance as we look at both the individual and organizational effects of innovative structures and operational practices.

This study adds to a small but growing body of literature showing the importance of ownership and participation for organizational performance. In fact, a very recent study by the United States General Accounting Office, which was released after the main text of this book was written, found that: ''Those ESOP (employee stock ownership plan) firms in which nonmanagerial employees have a role in making corporate decisions through work groups or committees showed more improvement in our measure of productivity than firms without such participation'' (USGAO 1987, p. 3).

Though we wanted to reflect the multiple focuses of the study in the title, we eventually settled on the primary theme of job-saving strategies. Not only was job-saving the initial and overwhelming motivation of the workers, union leaders, consultants, and managers who dealt with the shutdown supermarkets and the innovative structures, but it is also a significant social, economic, and policy issue of our time.

How can our society and economy deal with the pervasive restructuring and dislocation which affects so many workers? That question loomed very large in the early 1980s when the events recounted and analyzed in this book took

v

place. In Philadelphia, the scene of the O&O worker buyouts and the creation of Super Fresh with its programs of worker involvement in decisions and profits, the late '70s and early '80s brought month after month of shutdowns, layoffs, and job loss.

Was it just a short-term crisis? The acuteness of the problem in 1982, when the Great Atlantic and Pacific Tea Co. (A&P) announced the closing of its Philadelphia stores, was highlighted by the context of a deep national economic recession. Labor force statistics, however, showed a long-term pattern of dislocation and change, especially in the manufacturing sector where an average net reduction of 1,000 jobs a month had taken place over a 10-year period.

Even now in the late 1980s, with the Philadelphia economy relatively robust and the unemployment rate lower, corporate restructuring and interregional and international competition continually threaten the jobs of those in formerly well-established industries. The question of dislocation and unemployment may not get so much mass media attention as it once did, but it has not gone away. In 1988 the U.S. Congress passed a bill, which President Reagan opposed but did not veto, calling for prenotifiation to workers and communities by firms considering shutdowns or large layoffs.

Regardless of which political party is in power, a major issue in coming years will be how to prepare for the economy of the future. We hope that a major thrust of the emerging debate will be how to better use our human resources. We must ask: What kinds of management skills and structures will be suited to maintaining prosperity and productivity? What role will workers and their union representatives have in maintaining workplace conditions and enhancing the fair distribution of income and wealth? How will we ensure that basic democratic principles do not get lost in the drive for efficiency and profitability?

These questions are not restricted to the context of job-saving, but cover a whole range of management, labor, and economic development themes, even in the context of economic expansion. In the few years since their initiation, both innovations reported in this book have been expanded to other organizations. Two original O&Os, which were worker buyouts, have now spawned experience with four other O&O supermarkets, as described briefly in chapter 4. The Super Fresh experiment started in Philadelphia has now spread too. At the 1987 A&P shareholders meeting, chairman James Woods praised Super Fresh as a model for the entire retail grocery chain. The model has been extended companywide to 243 stores (Palley 1987).

The stories of the O&O and Super Fresh supermarkets, humble and limited as they might be, help in the emerging discussion of the issues. Other pieces of evidence are being gathered in studies of the results of alternative forms of work organization (Rosow 1986), of the role of unions in raising productivity and fighting mismanagement (Freeman and Medoff 1984; LeRoy 1987), and of the changing global context of American industrial relations and the importance of worker participation to industrial change (Kochan 1985). Together, these studies share the view that labor-management cooperation is indeed required for the future economy, but they warn of the dangers of unbalanced and nonreciprocated acts of cooperation. Power sharing between labor and management is called for, but is much more easily advocated than accomplished.

This study was also, significantly, an interdisciplinary one. In the field of employee ownership and worker participation, such an approach is often advocated but rarely put into practice. Dialogue among behavioral scientists and economists is often difficult, owing to differing definitions of theoretical "modeling," differing methods, differing approaches to statistical methods and differing degrees of reliance on them, and differing standards of proof. For example, economists often seem to favor systems of equations based on variables that can be measured with high degrees of reliability and accuracy. On the other hand, behavioral scientists, looking for patterns of behaviors and social interactions, often construct models for heuristic as contrasted with predictive purposes. Behavioral scientists look at measures of structures and behaviors as desirable, but are willing to accept the messiness of human perceptions, attitudes, and self-reports, with all of their potential error, bias, and unreliability. Even among social scientists, differences in theoretical orientations and methods between, say, anthropologists and psychologists may inhibit cross-fertilization of thinking and research.

These obstacles may have been minimized in this study because, like the worker/owners we studied, we can together in this group in part through interpersonal linkages. That is, some of us were drawn in because of mutual friendships, acquaintanceships, and prior experience with each other in other types of activities. Working together strengthened these bonds and developed them in other directions as well. For instance, several of us became more active in our faculty union together, partly as a result of informal discussions at our research group meetings.

Nevertheless, we still had to struggle to understand each other and to integrate our perspectives. The reader will have to judge how well we accomplished a kind of synthesis.

To study a set of workplaces based on democratic principles, we set up a democratic research group. That way we experienced both the agonies and the ecstasies our research subjects told us about. For us, speed was sacrificed, but the multidisciplinary effort we made was profitable and productive. Some of the time we had to struggle and fight about our philosophies, our methods, and most particularly, our differing abilities to work towards a common deadline.

vii

Most of the time, however, we enjoyed the challenge of working with people bringing different perspectives to bear on a complex problem. We had researchers trained and practicing as social psychologists, industrial relations specialists, urban anthropologists, and labor economists. At the time we began, three of us were nontenured (one in a nontenure-track position) and two tenured. Our group was composed of four females and one male. Differing personality traits and quirks entered into the mixture. It was not possible for us to rely on common habits, professional jargons, traditional role relationships, or hierarchical ranks for guidance in making decisions.

Though it was a group job throughout, we each took on special areas of responsibility. Art Hochner took primary responsibility for writing chapters 1, 2, and 8, and for integating the final product. Cherry Granrose had primary responsibility for the analysis of data from the workers' survey and for writing chapters 3 and 6. Judy Goode supervised the interviewing of the workers, analyzed the interviews and wrote chapter 5. Elaine Simon also worked on the interviews, put together the codebook which was invaluable for analyzing those interviews, and was primarily responsible for writing chapter 4. Eileen Appelbaum took primary responsibility for the analysis of data from the shop stewards and store managers, as well as data obtained at the corporate level, and for writing chapter 7.

After the initial drafts of chapters were submitted to the group, comments and criticisms were forthcoming, and members of the group participated in rewriting each other's chapters for later drafts. In the end, the book was the product of the entire group, with both the benefits and costs of group work.

Acknowledgements

A number of others, whose names do not appear on the title page, also worked hard to conduct the research and assist in the writing and production of this book. They all deserve credit for this study's accomplishment, but of course bear no burden of its mistakes, which are inalienably those of the co-authors.

Our supporting case was large and their talent and hard work were much appreciated, even if at times undercompensated. Special thanks must be given to Michael Blim, whose contribution was nearly that of a sixth co-author. Mike conducted many interviews himself, helped write the codebooks for analyzing all our interviews, and coded most of the data used in chapter 5. Besides all this, Mike wrote a paper for a session we organized at the American Anthropological Association (cited in our references) which proved very important for our thoughts on the labor process in the retail grocery industry, especially in chapters 4, 5, 7, and 8.

Julia R. Dobrow, Catherine S. Einhaus, Lynn W. Gregory, Patricia A. McBroom, Wesley Shumar, and Michael J. Willmorth conducted most of the interviews of workers, along with the co-authors and Mike Blim. Jo Anne Schneider entered the interview data into the computer and conducted analyses of those data. Catherine M. Rishar keypunched the data from the surveys of workers, shop stewards, and store managers. Ron Proudford and Virendra Singh performed programming and data analysis for those survey data. William A. Kleintop and Cynthia Craig Olds provided general research assistance. Sandra Simmons supplied general administrative and other research support. Virtually all of the typing and word processing was done by Gloria Basmajian, Pamela Bennett, Shelah Burgess, Janet Evans, and Ernestine Hopson.

We would surely be remiss if we did not acknowledge the invaluable aid given to this study by its subjects, the consultants, managers, union leaders, and workers involved. Staff members of the Philadelphia Association for Cooperative Enterprise, Inc. (PACE)—particularly Adina Abramowitz, Sherman Kreiner, and Andrew Lamas—helped us in working with the O&O stores in ways too numerous to mention. We are grateful for the cooperation of A&P, Super Fresh, and the United Food and Commercial Workers (UFCW) locals 56 and 1357. We especially want to thank "Bud" Lewis from A&P, Gerald Good, Jim Varian, and Jack Defiore from Super Fresh, Leo Cinaglia from UFCW local 56, and Wendell W. Young III, Charles Gentile, and Bob Wolper from UFCW local 1357. Without their help we would never have been able to collect the data we analyze and report here. The workers at the O&O and Super Fresh stores who put up with our intrusions into their jobs and lives deserve a very hearty thank you. We hope that our findings are meaningful and helpful to all parties involved.

Finally, we want to thank the Upjohn Institute and our other funding sources (especially the Samuel S. Fels Fund and Temple University) for their support. In particular, we want to express our deep appreciation that a private institution like the Upjohn Institute devotes so much keen attention to the central problems of work and nonwork in our society.

Philadelphia, PA
December 1987

CONTENTS

xi

TABLES

FIGURES

xvi

1

Using Worker Participation and Buyouts to Save Jobs

I had been at Food Fair in 1979 when it closed, then joined as part-time at A&P. I saw the writing on the wall as far as chains were concerned.—a former A&P worker.

It was a tough period . . . you didn't know what the heck was happening before the lay-off, it was a bad time. People were bumping all over the place. Still, it was a big shock. January 31 and all of a sudden you're out of a job. There's nothing. At the time most everyone was gone other than high seniority people—over 14 years. I don't think it really dawned on them that they were going to lose their jobs. We were in a store that was doing well, and didn't think it would close.—a former A&P worker.

I closed three stores, kept bumping around. It was very, very sad, a lot of tears. It had been a very closeknit store, like a family.—a former A&P worker.

It wouldn't make any difference if I never got the $5,000 back. Just the experience was worth it. Here, you have a chance at possibly making some money, but also to have some control over your destiny.—a worker/owner.

In late February 1982, during a national recession, the Great Atlantic & Pacific Tea Company (A&P) announced, as required in its local union contract, that it was closing its 29 remaining Philadelphia supermarkets in 20 days (see table 1.1 for chronology). A&P had been closing Philadelphia area supermarkets gradually over the preceding decade, but closings had accelerated in the last months and the announcement of a complete shutdown of A&P's Philadelphia operations meant that suddenly 2,000 people would be thrown out of work.

One of the affected unions, local 1357 of the United Food and Commercial Workers (UFCW), was primed to respond. Less than a week after A&P announced the final store closings 20 days away, the union made a buyout proposal that eventually led to the establishment of the O&O stores. The union originally proposed that A&P workers-to-be-laid-off purchase 21 of the closed stores. News got around among the A&P workers that there was an alternative to unemployment or looking for another job, and meetings about the buyout plan began at the union hall. About 600 union members showed up for the initial meetings. Each potential worker/owner would have to contribute $5,000 and a $200 downpayment would hold a place. The union's credit union would make arrangements for loans. Newspaper accounts reported that about 600 workers signed pledges worth $3 million within the next three weeks.

New Relationships in the Workplace

During the past decade, a great deal of public attention has been paid to worker buyouts. To save their jobs, workers have contemplated or launched into buyouts of firms threatened with shutdowns. These firms range in size from the large 7,000-worker integrated National Steel Mill in Weirton, West Virginia to the two small A&P supermarkets in the Philadelphia area converted to O&O supermarkets with about 50 workers each. Worker buyouts have occurred in a variety of industries in addition to steel and supermarkets, including furniture, machine tools, frozen foods, mining, shoes, trucking, printing, meat packing, taxicabs, railroads, garments, and wood products. According to the records of the National Center for Employee Ownership (NCEO), about 60 firms threatened with shutdown or massive layoffs have been bought by their employees since 1975. Moreover, it appears that about 90 percent of these bought-out firms have survived thus far.

Employee ownership and worker cooperatives have a tradition stretching back to the mid-nineteenth century. Workers in recent years have rediscovered employee ownership in the midst of crisis and found for themselves a new way to work. Furthermore, the current rediscovery has been occurring not only in the United States, but in most western industrial nations (Jones and Svejnar 1982).

The worker buyout is one path taken in the search for ways to change relationships between workers and their workplaces. Currently, various means of including workers in the ownership and control of work organizations are being explored. The most widespread forms are employee stock ownership plans (ESOPs) and quality of worklife (QWL) programs.

Quality of worklife is a vague term that means many things to many people. The kinds of activities it includes often take many other names too, such as "employee involvement."

> [QWL] is used interchangeably with "humanization of work," "work reform," "work redesign," and "work improvement." It is too frequently used loosely to characterize almost any joint [labor-management] program that requires a committee, but it ought to be confined to joint ventures that in the first instance aim at satisfying workers' desires or needs for restructuring of the workplace. This restructuring should allow greater participation in decisionmaking on the job, constructive interaction with one's fellows, and opportunity for personal development and self-realization.
>
> . . . All things considered, perhaps a sound enough guide to what QWL means is provided in a definition included in a news report of an international conference that ended in Toronto in early September 1981: "many forms of new work organizations . . . involving workers in shop-floor decisions through problem-solving committees" (Siegel and Weinberg 1982, 140-142).

The General Accounting Office estimates that about 4,800 firms have ESOPs with various degrees of ownership in each (USGAO 1986). A New York Stock Exchange study conducted in 1982 found that 14 percent of firms employing 500 or more people had quality circles, 13 percent had employee suggestion systems, 11 percent had employee task forces, 8 percent had profit sharing plans, and 8 percent had labor-management committees. Overall, "one fourth [of corporations with 500 or more employees] have at least made a start toward the less-adversarial environment associated with QWL'' (Freund and Epstein 1984, p. 129).

This trend toward experimentation has emerged for a number of loosely connected reasons. Structural changes in the economy have put pressure on manufacturing industries, on unions, and on the Frost Belt. The process of change has been exacerbated by corporate strategies that promote deindustrialization, by conglomerate mergers, and by intensified foreign competition. Economic stagnation, deep and frequent recessions, and a recovery that left elevated unemployment rates resulted in severe economic dislocation—that is, massive layoffs and worsened structural unemployment.

At the same time, there have been institutional and cultural changes affecting workplaces. The quality of working life has become a concern, not only of white-collar workers, but also of blue-collar employees. Participation by workers in decisionmaking has been lauded as a keystone of the Japanese economic achievement, as well as a necessary element for reversing declining labor productivity. Union-management relations have staggered from management hostility, union concessions, and union membership decline to union-management cooperation. In this confusing context, some workers have sought to take their job security into their own hands.

There are smaller numbers of worker buyouts compared to other forms of employee ownership and worker participation. Despite this, the drama of saving jobs, the mystery of rescuing seemingly failing firms, and the paradox of workers taking managerial responsibilities in worker buyouts have combined to fascinate both the popular and theoretical imagination. Aside from emotional appeal, however, worker buyouts seem to be more full-fledged attempts to implement employee ownership and worker participation. Observers of ESOPs often criticize them for giving workers mere paper ownership without control (Slott, 1985a, 1985b). Meanwhile, critics of QWL programs distrust so-called participation without a genuine redistribution of power (Parker 1985). In theory, worker buyouts possess the potential to release workers' energies and to reforge the organization on a more effective and more egalitarian basis.

Creation of Innovative Structures in Philadelphia Supermarkets

The buyout proposal and other union efforts spurred lengthy union-management negotiations between A&P and local 1357, which continued through the spring of 1982. In May, the UFCW and A&P agreed to a landmark contract which would save many jobs through the creation of two innovative business structures. First of all, two stores would be sold to groups of employees, who would independently own and operate them as employee-owned businesses. The second innovation was Super Fresh, a new subsidiary of A&P, which would reopen many of the remaining stores. Super Fresh would incorporate new methods of management, a quality of worklife program to provide employee participation in decisionmaking, and a revenue-based bonus plan as an incentive for workers. A&P promised to open 20 Super Fresh stores eventually and to give preference to former A&P workers in hiring. In exchange, the UFCW agreed to wage cuts of 20 percent and concessions on some benefits.

Even though announcement of plans for the employee-owned stores preceded the announcement of the Super Fresh plan, Super Fresh stores opened first. The first Super Fresh store opened in July 1982. Super Fresh engaged consultants from the Busch Center at the Wharton School of the University of Pennsylvania to establish the first QWL programs and to conduct the training of "associates" and "store directors" (the new terms for workers and store managers, respectively). Super Fresh stores were set up with a decentralized philosophy, so that the store director would have more autonomy than under A&P.

The information meetings on the worker buyout plan were held for a time, while union-A&P negotiations dragged on. After May, however, most workers dropped out of the buyout scheme, expecting to be recalled at Super Fresh.

The remaining prospective worker/owners met over the summer for planning and research. The first O&O store opened with 24 worker/owners in Roslyn, Pennsylvania, a northwestern suburb of Philadelphia, on October 13, 1982—about seven months after the A&P shutdown announcement. The second O&O store, with 17 (later reduced to 14) worker/owners, opened the following month in the far northeast section of Philadelphia, in a neighborhood called Parkwood Manor. Each O&O store established bylaws calling for substantial worker/owner control over a hired store manager.

This case of worker buyout, in contrast to many that have been reported in the news media, occurred in an urban context where a shutdown did not threaten the sole employment opportunity in town for displaced workers. The A&P workers found themselves out of a job at a time when the economy was slumping and employers all over the country were calling for union concessions. Even though these workers had slim prospects of finding a job with another super-supermarket chain, former A&P employees did have two options they could take to keep supermarket jobs. Eventually, 38 became worker/owners in the two O&O supermarkets. Over 1,500 of the displaced A&P workers became Super Fresh employees.

As a result of the March 1982 shutdown, 29 A&P stores were actually closed. Twenty-six of these eventually became Super Fresh stores; two became O&O stores; and one was closed permanently because of structural flaws in the foundation.

The Super Fresh chain was later to convert all remaining A&P stores in southeastern Pennsylvania, southern New Jersey, and northern Delaware to the new subsidiary. Many were changed over by the end of 1982, and by mid-1983 there were over 50 Super Fresh stores in the region. These stores had been minimally affected by the shutdown threat in 1982 and were represented by other UFCW union

Table 1.1 Chronology

Feb. 1982	A&P announcement of closings.
March 1982	UFCW proposes employee buyouts and holds meetings to get pledges from workers.
May 1982	A&P/UFCW agreement to sell two stores to workers, reopen most others as Super Fresh.
July 1982	First Super Fresh openings.
October 1982	First O&O store opens.
November 1982	Second O&O store opens.

locals not actively seeking QWL or employee ownership and not enthusiastic about the agreement between local 1357 and A&P, to say
the least. QWL training was not instituted as early nor was training
conducted as fully as in the stores in Philadelphia, which had been
involved in the shutdown. These employees had thus not participated
in the discussions about employee ownership and QWL conducted by
UFCW 1357 at the time of the shutdown.

The Study

Despite increasing openness by workers to the idea of buyouts and
some apparent survivability of bought-out firms, little is actually
known about the effectiveness of buyouts. That is, though jobs are
saved, how do worker buyouts compare with other job saving methods? Do they generate new jobs or merely slow the onset of unemployment? Do they open up new sources of organizational efficiency
or survive through employee subsidies and painful sacrifices? Do
they redistribute power in meaningful ways? Do they substitute one
set of worries for another, financial risk for job insecurity?

This book looks at how worker buyouts function and how successfully they meet the goals of saving jobs and increasing worker control. It studies the two O&O supermarkets created from former A&P
stores in Philadelphia in 1982 and compares the effectiveness of
these buyouts to another method of job-saving—labor-management
concessions which included productivity bonuses and a QWL program in the Super Fresh stores. Since both of these situations
emerged from the same labor negotiations between A&P and locals
56 and 1357 of the UFCW, the setting provides a natural field comparison and contrast. It allows for clear and controlled explorations
of employee ownership and worker participation.

The research began when the shutdown was announced and
UFCW local 1357 proposed worker buyouts. Members of a study
group at Temple University investigating plant closings and job loss
contacted UFCW locals 1357 (retail clerks) and 56 (meatcutters),
A&P, and the consultants working with them and asked to study this

experience. The research group conducting the overall study was multidisciplinary, drawn from the fields of industrial relations, organizational behavior, psychology, sociology, anthropology, urban studies, political science, and economics. The group drew upon many perspectives and methodologies in conducting the study. There were three major data collection phases, as shown in table 1.2.

This book covers results from Phases II and III. It is divided into eight chapters. First, here in chapter 1, we place worker buyouts in the context of employee ownership and worker participation, theoretically, historically, and practically. In chapter 2, we present a theoretical framework of the organizational processes involved in employee-owned firms and the expected outcomes for organizations and individual workers. The framework will attempt to explain in theory how worker buyouts function and how they affect the organizations' operations and the individuals in them. Chapter 3 presents the research design and methods of data collection used, namely semistructured interviews and systematic questionnaire surveys. In chapter 4, the formal structures of the O&O and Super Fresh stores are described. Chapter 5 reports data primarily from interviews concerning the personal experiences of the workers and the informal social structures of the stores. Chapters 6 and 7 present quantitative tests of hypotheses derived from theoretical framework. Worker-level perceptions, attitudes, and economic outcomes are included in Chapter 6. Store-level functioning and outcomes are examined in chapter

Table 1.2 Research Phases

July 1982	Phase I: Worker survey.
Summer 1983	Phase IIa: Interviews with O&O worker owners.
Fall 1983	Phase IIb: Interviews with former A&P workers at two Super Fresh stores in Philadelphia.
Fall 1984	Phase IIc: Interviews with former A&P workers in two Super Fresh stores outside Philadelphia.
Fall 1984	Phase IIIa: Survey of workers interviewed in Phase II.
Winter to Summer 1985	Phase IIIb: Shop steward and store manager surveys.

7. The final chapter, 8, draws conclusions and translates them into policy-relevant recommendations for future research and practice.

Varieties of Participative Firms and Buyouts

To understand the importance of the recent wave of worker buyouts, it is necessary to put them in historical, practical, and theoretical focus. Where do these 60 or so firms fit? In particular, why study the case of the O&O Supermarkets? These buyouts are less well known than larger ones, such as Weirton Steel, South Bend Lathe, or Rath Packing. Moreover, the O&O stores are in a retail industry as contrasted with the more familiar and "typical" manufacturing buyout. However, the O&O case allows for the investigation of concerns of practitioners and theorists accumulated over the past decade which emphasize not only employee ownership but also worker control. Furthermore, the unique setting of the O&O case provides an unusually rich example of employee ownership and worker participation.

There are many types of employee ownership. The generic term, employee ownership, is used to refer to most forms of ownership by jobholders in a company, both workers and managers. Employee ownership is usually associated with the ESOP, only one of the many forms and hybrids that employee-owned firms take. The diversity of types is often highly confusing.

Two researchers have offered typologies of employee-owned firms in attempts to clarify the important similarities and differences among them. One typology depends primarily on the three legal forms in which employee ownership is found: ESOPs, direct employee ownership, and worker cooperatives (Toscano 1983b). The ESOP is defined in the tax code as a type of employee benefit program which invests in its own company's stock and which is eligible for certain tax breaks. There are ESOPs with tiny amounts of stock in the company, such as at AT&T and Mobil, others with substantial stock, such as Eastern Airlines, still others with majority ownership, such as Rath, and a few with 100 percent ownership, such as Weirton Steel. ESOPs are often an indirect form of ownership for workers because stocks are held in trust—through an Employee Stock Ownership Trust (ESOT)—which may or may not be controlled by nonsupervisory employees. Some of these ESOPs resulted from buyouts, but most did not. Worker buyouts number only about 1 percent of the estimated number of ESOPs.

Direct ownership is share ownership by workers without the legal and tax standing of an ESOP and without the indirect ownership device of the ESOT. Worker cooperatives, the oldest form of employee ownership, tend to involve equal share ownership and equal voice in management for all members or owners of the firm. The O&O stores were set up as worker cooperatives, but while all owners are workers, not all workers are owners.

Each of the three forms has legal and operational advantages and disadvantages. Moreover, they each include so many variations that they often may not be operationally distinguishable. For instance, there are so-called democratic or cooperative ESOPs, which resemble worker cooperatives in the distribution of ownership and control.

A second typology of employee-owned firms, developed in England, distinguishes employee-owned firms on the basis of the reasons for their origins (Cornforth 1983): (1) cooperatives "endowed" by the original capitalist owners, (2) worker buyouts, (3) defensive (job-saving) cooperatives, (4) alternatives (i.e., counter-cultural) cooperatives, and (5) job creation cooperatives using government money to combat high unemployment. Because this typology was derived in England, it ignores ESOPs, which form a large group here, but were virtually absent in the U.K. in the early 1980s.

More important, though reasons for establishment may be classifiable, firms in a particular category do not inevitably have similar characteristics or objectives. As Blasi and Whyte (1981) have pointed out, while job-saving worker buyouts in the 1970s and 1980s are similar in origin, they differ in key characteristics and behaviors. In the 1970s buyouts, unions were either hostile or passive and rarely was management structure changed. In contrast, in 1980s buyouts, unions took initiatives to shape the terms, and workers have sought and obtained more say in the firms' day to day operations.

While legal forms and origins are important, they tend to reflect historical and legal trends and do not clarify how different organizations function. A more precise typology is necessary.

For theoretical and practical importance there seem to be two main dimensions. These are (1) the *amount of employee ownership* in the firm and (2) the *degree of worker participation* in decisions about policies and day to day management. These dimensions are complex and not easily reducible to quantitative scales. Amount of employee ownership should take into account not only the percentage of equity owned by employees, but also the distribution of shares among owners, the dispersion of shares among employees, and the percent of equity owned by managers compared to that owned by nonsupervisory employees (Conte, Tannenbaum and McCulloch 1981). Likewise, degree of worker participation is actually multidimensional, involving the degree of worker influence, the range of decisions influenced, the extent of participation among workers, whether participation is direct or representative, and other aspects (Dachler and Wilpert 1978).

Some rough subdivision of these dimensions does allow us to make meaningful distinctions among categories of employee-owned and worker-participative firms. The following table (1.3) splits amount of employee ownership into three segments: no employee ownership, minority employee ownership (employees own less than 50 percent of the shares), and majority employee ownership (more than 50 percent of the workers own more than 50 percent of the shares). The other main dimension is dichotomized into low worker participation and high worker participation. High worker participation involves such things as (a) restructured hierarchy and control systems, changed role of supervisors, worker input to decisions; (b) worker representatives on the board of directors and/or on the ESOT, worker voting rights on shares; and (c) union involvement in collectively bargaining for the ownership and/or participation plans, promoting the plan, and seeking a changed role for workers and/or the union. Low worker participation means workers and unions have not been involved in these issues. Table 1.3 illustrates this typology.

Though some of these categories are self-explanatory, others are not. The first two categories involve garden-variety capitalist firms and are included here for contrast with forms of employee ownership. (1) Conventional firms, probably the largest category, includes those with no employee ownership and minimal worker participation. (2) Firms with QWL or other participatory programs, but with no employee ownership belong to an apparently growing group. Some well-known examples include Ford Motor with its EI (Employee Involvement) programs developed in cooperation with the United Auto Workers (UAW), General Foods with its Topeka pet food plant, and, one of the subjects of this study, Super Fresh Food Markets.

The remaining four categories comprise the forms usually lumped indiscriminately together and called employee ownership. (3) Most ESOPs involve a minority of company equity and minimal worker participation. According to a survey by Marsh and McAllister (1981) of ESOPs of at least three years of age, only 13 percent held greater than 50 percent of company stock, the average ESOP holding being 28 percent. Moreover, the survey found that 69 percent of ESOPs granted no voting rights on the stock plan participants, and that more than one-half of ESOP companies report no effects of the ESOP on worker-management communications, cooperation among employees, or employee suggestions. Furthermore, the chief motives

Table 1.3 Typology of Employee Ownership and Worker Participation

		Amount of employee ownership		
		None	**Minority**	**Majority**
	High	(2) QWL and participation programs	(4) Concessionary buy-ins	(6) Worker co-ops and worker buyouts
Degree of worker participation	Low	(1) Conventional firms	(3) Most ESOPs	(5) Employee/ manager buyouts

for adoption of ESOPs were, in rank order, providing an employee benefit, increasing productivity, and taking advantage of available tax breaks. (4) Concessionary buy-ins form a relatively small category, though an important one, and are particularly a product of the 1981-83 recession and its aftermath. Companies in which workers and unions have given wage concessions in return for company stock and, in some cases, seats on the board of directors include Pan American Airways (including the Airline Pilots Association, known as ALPA), Eastern Airlines (including a number of unions, such as International Association of Machinists [IAM], ALPA, and others), Chrysler (with UAW), and Consolidated Rail Corporation (Conrail) (including a number of railway unions). This category, the subject of heated debate in labor circles (e.g., Metzgar 1984; Compa and Baicich 1984a, 1984b; Barber and Banks 1984) has never been identified as a special subtype of employee ownership, though it is neither a typical ESOP nor a full-fledged buyout.

The final two categories, (5) the employee/manager buyout and (6) the worker buyout have also not been distinguished before. In this study, the term employee/manager buyout implies majority employee ownership with conventional management control. Such firms include those turned over by idealistic owners ("endowed cooperatives" from Cornforth 1983) and those bought by both managers and workers, with stock distribution weighted toward higher-paid management employees. Often these employee/manager buyouts are structured as ESOPs, but almost always control of the stock is in the hands of the manager group and/or the financiers of the deal, and the typically hierarchical authority structure of the firm is unchanged. Employee/manager buyouts tend to conform to what Blasi and Whyte (1981) called "1970s buyouts." They include such firms as South Bend Lathe (with the cooperation of a United Steelworkers local union), Bates Fabrics, and Dan River Textiles.

In contrast is category (6), worker cooperatives and worker buyouts. These firms involve both majority employee ownership and high levels of participation in decisions by management, workers, and/or unions. Older cooperatives include the plywood firms of the Pacific northwest (Berman 1967). Relatively new worker cooperatives include numerous countercultural organizations (Rothschild-Whitt 1979). The buyouts tend to be of the "1980s variety" (Blasi and Whyte 1981) with union involvement and attempts at restructuring the hierarchy. The O&O supermarkets, the main focus of this study, fit into this final category.

In sum, the six categories outline different types of firms with differing qualities based on the amount of employee ownership and worker participation they contain. We expect that the goals they set, the methods they use, the problems they face, the solutions they devise, and the effectiveness which results may differ fundamentally from one category to the next. For instance, the expectations of workers concerning their input to decisions may depend on the degree of employee ownership, such that levels of input adequate in a QWL program may be frustrating to those in worker buyouts. Similarly, motivation and productivity gains in ESOPs may be related more to stock prices than they would be in worker cooperatives where independence from managerial control may be more important.

The focus of this study, worker buyouts, has broad significance, despite its narrow focus on few firms. Worker buyouts are one of the most theoretically interesting forms of participation. Workers and unions seem to have noticed limitations of previous cases which included less ownership and participation, and recent establishment of concessionary buy-ins shows the tendency to mix ownership with participation. Future buyouts and buy-ins may continue these patterns. Along with our focus on worker buyouts, we compare the O&O stores to Super Fresh Stores, some of which have implemented QWL. Thus, we can compare employee ownership with participation to participation alone. This enables us to see more clearly the relative effectiveness of worker buyouts.

Past and Recent History of Employee Ownership

The various forms of employee ownership have had a long history in the United States dating back to the 1790s in the case of worker cooperatives and to the 1920s in the case of ESOPs. Employee ownership did not always enjoy as much notice or as much success as in the last few decades. In fact, this history has often been used to criticize employee ownership. Lessons can be learned from past experience on the importance of cooperatives and ESOPs within past labor-capital wars, on employee ownership's feasibility and viability in the present, and on its likely place in the future. The prevailing wisdom, according to critics, claims that:

(1) worker cooperatives failed as an anticapitalist labor strategy;

(2) worker cooperatives are doomed to sink as socialist islands in the capitalist sea or as anarchic and undisciplined, hence inefficient, businesses;

(3) ESOPs are historic manifestations of management hostility to unions;

(4) employee ownership is a sidetrack from either conventional collective bargaining or from "Theory Z" type corporate human relations policies;

(5) at best, worker buyouts are moderators of structural economic dislocation, and at worst, they are a stick of financial burden attached to a paper carrot of stock ownership.

Without denying the validity of criticisms of many aspects of past performance and practice, it is possible to see recent experience with employee ownership as a break from the past. While some motives for establishing worker cooperatives and ESOPs have remained constant, the ideological, economic, institutional, and legal environments have shifted. Thus, employee ownership need not be heavily tarred with the brush of past failure and past criticism.

Two separate streams (at times, trickles) of development—of worker cooperatives and of ESOPs—have been joined at the contemporary wave of employee ownership. They had quite different origins: worker cooperatives in the early labor movement of the mid-nineteenth century; ESOPs in the antiunion welfare capitalism of the 1920s.

Worker Cooperatives

Since the 1830s, workers have formed cooperatives during strikes, lockouts, and depressions. Some histories trace them back to the 1790s (Jones 1984; Curl 1980). Early cooperatives were also part of "alternative" or socialist movements, including those stimulated by the thoughts of men like Robert Owen and Horace Greeley and by Communitarian settlements like Brook Farm. By the 1860s, they had become an integral part of the platform of the short-lived National Labor Union (NLU) led by William Sylvis. Sylvis and the NLU helped found a number of worker cooperatives, but these soon began to fail or be dominated by a few worker/shareholders or outsiders. Subsequent labor organizations, such as the Knights of Labor (KOL), continued to promote cooperatives as the solution to industrial conflict between labor and capital. In fact, Jones (1984) credits the KOL with establishing about 200 worker cooperatives in the 1880s at the height of that union's influence. The next large wave took place in the 1930s, when unemployed workers formed "self-help" cooperatives during the Great Depression.

As the American Federation of Labor (AFL) gained hegemony over the U.S. labor movement in the late nineteenth century, however, its leaders turned toward collective bargaining through business unionism and disdained worker cooperatives as impractical. Worker cooperatives became dissociated from the labor movement. Furthermore, as observers and theorists of the labor movement emerged in middle-class intellectual circles, critiques of worker cooperatives and defense of collective bargaining buttressed the AFL's case. John Commons in the U.S. (Derber 1970) and Sidney and Beatrice Webb (1920), Fabian Socialists in Great Britain, discredited worker cooperatives as inevitably unstable forms of organization, and as inferior to collective bargaining in promoting equality of power between labor and capital.

Were the labor officials and intellectuals correct in their pessimism? The verdict on worker cooperatives by subsequent observers has frequently been just as negative (Shirom 1972). Generally, worker cooperatives have been found to be difficult to organize, undercapitalized, concentrated in craft industries and/or those threatened by structural and technological changes, handicapped by weak management and weak commitment to cooperative ideals, beset by hostility from business and labor, and short-lived (Aldrich and Stern 1983). However, recent studies by Jones (1984) have shown the record of worker cooperatives not to be "as overwhelmingly bleak as some critics contend" (p. 51). Worker cooperatives with the most cooperative features (i.e., equal share ownership, work requirements for members, and participation in decisionmaking) have had the best success in viability, longevity, and integrity of democratic governance structure, Jones finds.

Nevertheless, worker cooperatives have never been more than a marginal economic force. Currently, some of them are important in a few industries, for example, high grade plywood manufacture in the Pacific northwest or refuse collection in the San Francisco Bay area (Perry 1978). However, for the largest number of currently existing cooperatives, those formed out of the social upheavals of the 1960s and 1970s, economic marginality is a fact. Jackall and Crain (1984) estimate that in 1980 approximately 1,000 small worker cooperatives existed. The origins of these firms seem to be motivated mainly by opposition to corporate America and a desire to create alternative institutions. Most operate in the service sector, food production, distribution, and sales, with very few in manufacturing, primarily in printing and publishing. These cooperatives are small, with about 10 members on average and about $200,000 in sales per year. Their worker/owners are young, educated, white, and low-paid. Indeed, until the recent wave of interest in employee/manager and worker buyouts, even sympathetic observers of worker cooperatives deemed them anachronistic, idealistic, and/or marginal.

Employee Stock Ownership Plans

At about the same time the labor movement cut its ties with the employee ownership movement, capitalists and managers became interested in stock ownership for workers. In the 1870s, Abram

Hewitt, then congressman and later mayor of New York City, advocated worker stock ownership and profit sharing as the solution to industrial evils (Derber 1970). In fact, Patard (1982) traces the roots of the idea back to the 1840s. However, it was not until the post-World War I period that employee stock ownership flourished, through employer-initiated savings plans, stock purchase options, profit sharing, and employee benefit plans. Patard describes the employee stock ownership movement of the 1920s as bigger in proportion to the number of shares outstanding than the contemporary ESOP movement in 1980. Employee stock ownership was often promoted by management in connection with employer-dominated company unions. Unionists and leftists denounced these plans as union-busting, co-optation devices, giving workers big financial risks without any genuine participation in decisions. The stock market crash of 1929 destroyed and discredited this movement. Subsequent stock ownership plans tended to be limited to highly-paid executives.

In the 1950s, a visionary investment banker, Louis Kelso, took up the banner of employee stock ownership in the *Capitalist Manifesto* (Kelso and Adler 1958) and in his *Two Factor Theory* (Kelso and Hetter 1967). Despite sharp critiques of his theories by eminent economists, Kelso was persistent in promoting his views. His efforts and those of his students, associates, and converts to his ideas have created the contemporary ESOP movement. Kelso's pragmatic thrust has been to take advantage of features in the Internal Revenue Code that allow qualified employee benefit trusts to borrow money to buy the employer's stocks or other securities. Kelso hailed ESOPs as an instrument of corporate finance, of hostile takeover prevention, of wealth redistribution, of productivity improvement, and a number of other boons to capitalists, workers and the economy in general.

ESOPs have been enhanced by virtually every federal tax change since the early 1970s.[1] The Employee Retirement Income Security Act of 1974 (ERISA) and the Tax Reduction Act of 1975 drew increased attention to the tax benefits to corporations of establishing ESOPs. Kelso's chief convert in Congress and the most powerful and active proponent of ESOPs has been Senator Russell Long (D., La.), son of Louisiana's late populist governor, Huey Long. Sen. Long was the chairman of the Senate Finance Committee in the 1970s and was the committee's ranking Democrat until his retirement in 1986.

Under ESOPs employers establish ESOTs for their employees to give or sell stock in their own company as a benefit, somewhat similar to a pension fund. Tax breaks to the employer issue from this transaction; for instance, social security tax is not paid on contributions to the trust, employer contributions are tax deductible, and a tax credit might be claimed as well. Employees get a tax-exempt benefit and receive vested stock when they leave the firm. The ESOT can borrow money to purchase stock and use the employer's contribution to pay off the loan. The ESOP particularly attracts employers because of its usefulness to: (a) raise investment capital; (b) pass a company on to employees; and (c) provide a special type of pension plan, exempt from several important ERISA protections. However, for workers the ESOP is generally not seen as a suitable substitute for a fully protected pension plan.

Business journals emphasize the advantage to management of allowing employee ownership: quick capital formation, tax breaks, avoidance of pension fund obligations, union avoidance, improved worker motivation and discipline, etc. Fears of management manipulation of ESOPs and of lack of worker control over stock voting rights have led many unionists to be very wary of employee ownership.

While their primary appeal has been to employers, ESOPs have sometimes been used to effect employee/manager and worker buyouts. The first such employee/manager buyout using an ESOP for job saving occurred at South Bend Lathe in 1975. Despite the predominance of management control, ESOPs have been used by some unions to gain a say in management decisions through concessionary buy-ins. In fact, the rise of the ESOP seems to have revived the idea of spreading stock ownership or making workers into capitalists. Ironically, the rise of the ESOP may have helped to resuscitate labor movement interest in employee ownership. In addition, the worker cooperative movement has been transformed by lessons learned in employee/manager buyouts—those which granted little control to workers or unions.

Current Environment of Employee Ownership

The growth of interest in employee ownership has been stimulated by other factors in addition to legislative benevolence to ESOPs. Societal changes over the last few decades also motivate the study and practice of employee ownership. These changes reflect popular ideology, the economy, legislative approaches to current problems, and institutional rearrangements.

Ideology

Ideological currents in politics, business, and interpersonal relations in the western industrial nations may be said to have contributed to a desire for powersharing. Sandwiched in with movements such as decentralization and accountability in government and self-determination through feminism, since the early 1970s there has been a drive for greater worker participation in decisionmaking. The Lordstown strike and the book *Work in America* (1973) led to calls for job enrichment and the humanization of work. The rising awareness of foreign competition has given long tenures on the best seller list to books advocating forms of corporate powersharing, such as *Theory Z* (Ouchi 1981) and *In Search of Excellence* (Peters and Waterman 1982). Academic interest in powersharing at work has also been stirred by examination of socialist alternatives to Soviet bureaucratic centralism, most notably by the Yugoslav system of self-managed enterprises. The Solidarity union in Poland renewed this interest through placing self-management high on its now-repressed agenda of societal change. Although it has been considered quite radical at times, the concern for powersharing has pushed into many areas of the mainstream and lends legitimacy to forms of worker participation and ownership. Even the wave of conservative ideology resulting in the Reagan presidency stressed self-help and entrepreneurship, which have been used to justify employee ownership.

Economics

Economic changes, particularly structural ones, have given the greatest impetus to both worker participation and employee ownership. Several forces have combined to shut down many workplaces, to force millions to the unemployment lines, and to change the power balance between labor and capital. The conglomerate merger movement from the late 1960s to the present, together with corporate disinvestment policies, and deindustrialization closed factories, offices, and stores that had become unprofitable or not profitable enough for corporate financial analysts (Bluestone and Harrison 1982). Population migration to the Sun Belt, the shift of employment from manufacturing to so-called postindustrial sectors, and a rapid series of recessions compounded the economic dislocation. Business sought solutions for its decline in competitiveness and productivity, taking advantage of unions' political and economic weaknesses. Management initiated QWL and participative programs and bargained for labor concessions.

Many workers faced with these pressures and the loss of job security had to come up with new coping responses. Some accepted concessionary buy-ins, while some others engaged in employee/manager and worker buyouts.

International Developments

Workers in other countries pursued similar paths as well. In Western Europe, interest in employee ownership as an answer to recession and unemployment grew. Employee-owned companies more than doubled in number in both Great Britain and France between 1975 and 1983. In 1983, the Wales Trade Unions Congress (TUC) made employee ownership an integral part of its overall strategy for Welsh economic recovery. In Italy, the number of employee-owned firms topped 18,000 by 1981, ranging in size from tiny firms to those employing thousands of workers. Most of these firms belong to cooperative leagues affiliated with the major trade union federations. Increasing numbers of worker cooperatives have arisen in Holland,

Belgium, and Denmark, too. Finally, Spain boasts a rapidly growing employee-owned sector, including the famed Mondragon cooperatives of the Basque country, employing over 18,000 in more than 85 employee-owned firms. The Mondragon cooperatives are extremely well-integrated, featuring their own central bank, a technical university, and the largest manufacturer/exporter of household appliances in Spain (EEC 1981).

Employee ownership took on an entirely new meaning in Sweden and Denmark during the 1970s and 1980s. The Social Democratic parties of those nations proposed a series of plans for "economic democracy," in which ownership of private sector firms would, over a few decades, pass over to union and/or worker control through accumulated employer contributions to "wage-earner funds." Although these proposals were stalled and watered down in the Scandinavian parliaments, this idea of employee ownership is part of a much larger tendency in northern European countries toward worker participation and co-determination.

Legislation

The movement towards expanded employee ownership in the U.S. has also gained momentum from a variety of legislative initiatives. Aside from the various changes in the tax code over the years that favor the formation of ESOPs, attempts to aid communities distressed by unemployment, shutdowns, and poverty have increased awareness of the opportunities for employee ownership. For instance, legislation was introduced in a number of states, several cities (including Philadelphia), and Congress over the past decade to mitigate the impact of plant closings. Though these bills primarily focused on prenotification of layoffs and shutdowns, most also included provisions to encourage employee/manager and worker buyouts. Arguments used by advocates of plant closing legislation often emphasized that a minimum of six months prenotification was necessary if a buyout was even to be contemplated.

On another front, Congress established in 1979 a National Consumer Cooperative Bank, which can reserve up to 10 percent of its funds to aid worker cooperatives, employee/manager and worker buyouts, and even ESOPs. The Economic Development Administration (EDA), the Small Business Administration (SBA), and the Farmers Home Administration (FmHA), among other agencies, have been involved in assisting employee-owned firms, particularly through buyouts. Their involvement stems from either broad interpretations of their legal mandates or explicit mandates to work with employee-owned firms. Innumerable state and local initiatives and agencies have directed attention, money, and other aid to employee ownership. Recently, Massachusetts passed a new worker cooperative statute that aids in the formation of democratically-owned and operated businesses.

In Pennsylvania, an Employee Ownership Assistance Program was established by a state statute in June 1984. The act provided for a fund of $15 million to be used over a three-year period: (a) $1 million per year was set aside for technical assistance and professional services, including the funding of feasibility studies. It was initially set up as a "forgivable" loan program, but this later became a grant program with the requirement that 10 percent of the grant be matched by some other source. (b) $4 million per year was devoted to a revolving loan fund for debt financing (or for "gap" equity loans while worker/owner investors came up with their own personal contributions).[2]

Support Networks

The establishment of a developing network of support organizations to advance, encourage, and aid employee ownership demonstrates an important institutional shift from the past. The legislation passed in Massachusetts was drafted by staffers of the Industrial Cooperative Association (ICA) of Somerville, Massachusetts. The ICA is one of a growing number of institutions that have sprung up in the past decade to support the employee ownership movement. In the past, employee-owned firms often operated in total isolation. Now, organizations such as ICA, the Philadelphia Association for Cooperative Enterprise (PACE),[3] the O&O Investment Fund, and the North

Carolina Center for Community Self-Help give several types of technical and financial assistance to worker cooperatives, buyouts, and new start-ups. Educational and advocacy organizations like the National Center for Employee Ownership (NCEO), the Employee Stock Ownership Association, and the Association for Workplace Democracy (AWD) encourage, conduct, and publish research, disseminate information, and even lobby the government (in the case of the ESOP Association) to promote employee ownership.

Furthermore, in colleges and universities, ongoing research, education, and training have led to established centers of expertise on employee ownership at such places as Cornell University, Boston College, the University of Michigan, Brigham Young University, Stanford University, Guilford College, and Temple University, among others. While the support network is growing, it is still quite loose. Thus far, no superstructure has been able to knit together the diverse, disparate, and dispersed set of employee-owned firms.

Considerations in Establishing Worker Buyouts

Despite a few cases that have achieved major media attention, actual experience with worker buyouts is limited. As stated earlier, about 60 firms have undergone employee/manager or worker buyouts, and most have survived. Yet no one knows in how many cases buyouts were contemplated but never started or were proposed but never consummated. Many potentially interested participants may have been deterred by lack of knowledge, by fears, by lack of leadership, or by discovering that their dreams could not be transformed into workable plans. It may be useful here to briefly outline some issues respecting the forms, feasibility, and union-management relations of worker and employee/manager buyouts in order to understand some of the stumbling blocks.

There are two main legal forms, the worker cooperative and the ESOP. In a traditional worker cooperative, each member invests an equal amount of money, which forms the basis of the firm's capital.

In traditional cooperatives, a major problem can be that as the value of the company rises, the value of individual shares rises, too. After a while, success can be a golden handcuff. If share values rise too high for potential new members to afford, this may lead to hiring of nonowning workers or selling out to a larger, capitalist firm. These problems occurred in the San Francisco Bay scavenger firms and also in the plywood cooperatives of the Pacific northwest. However, recently ICA and PACE developed a new model of worker cooperatives based on the experience of the Mondragon cooperatives in Spain. ICA's model of worker cooperatives gets around this problem by drastically lowering the cost to be a member (to about $100). Members have equal voting rights, and they share in the profits. But the members' profit shares are distributed, not in the form of stock, but to what are called "internal savings accounts," which operate like internal pension funds.

The ESOP form provides a clear model of employee ownership that gives substantial incentives to employers for agreeing to a buyout. Probably the major advantage of the ESOP, especially when compared to the typical cooperative, is its flexibility. This flexibility involves several important issues: who buys stock; the distribution of ownership; the degree of overall employee ownership; financing; and the rights and privileges of ownership. However, the flexibility reflects vagueness and also leaves the ESOP form open to manipulation. The popularity of the ESOP in buyouts, particularly in what we call employee/manager buyouts, leaves unionists skeptical of its advantages.

There has been a trend, as workers and unions gain experience, to combine many of the advantages of the two main forms of employee ownership into a hybrid form. Olson (1982) calls these cooperative ESOPs. These hybrids take the major feature of worker cooperatives, commitment to democratic control, and join it to the major feature of ESOPs, flexibility in financing and taxation. Creatively structured cooperative ESOPs have been initiated at Rath Packing, Hyatt-Clark, and Atlas Chain. These worker buyouts provide for worker control over management through democratically structured, one-member-one-vote ESOPs. The cooperative ESOP owes its genesis to the active involvement of local unions, which fought to protect worker interests and to avoid serious pitfalls of previous efforts, such as South Bend Lathe, which the worker/owners struck in 1980, and Vermont Asbestos Group, where worker/owners, disgruntled over lack of worker input into decisions, sold a controlling interest to a businessman. However, it has proven difficult to convert firms to this new form because of problems in sustaining cooperative involvement by workers and managers in struggling firms.

In general, would we expect employee ownership to be a feasible path to save jobs? Or, as some critics claim, are plant closure buy-outs examples of "lemon capitalism" for workers? If the corporate owner cannot make it, why should anyone expect the worker/owners, lacking entrepreneurial experience and expertise, to revive dead firms? Questions about the viability of employee/owned firms worry even those predisposed to favor them.

The "lemon capitalism" argument implies that plant closings are caused by the inescapable, invisible hand of market forces. That is, competition, technological change, population shifts, educational ex-pansion, cultural upheaval, and other such seemingly impersonal forces cause the closure. And if workers buy it out to save jobs, they are just swimming against the tide.

This is the conventional wisdom of yesteryear, which has been overturned by observation of companies closing profitable plants (Bluestone and Harrison 1982; Whyte 1984). Such was the case of the O&O supermarkets in Philadelphia. A&P threatened to shut down all its stores in the region (and many others in other regions) to satisfy its corporate goals, not because each store was unprofitable. Furthermore, there are numerous plants threatened with shutdown that could in theory be profitable if some of their operating proce-dures were changed instead of closing them.

Not every plant closing is an appropriate target for employee own-ership, however. Successful buyouts have several characteristics: good timing, planning, adequate resources, technical assistance, and organization, as well as luck (Stern and Hammer 1978). The key element is an objective feasibility study, or as Woodworth (1982a) puts it, "a cold, hard look at the facts." Virtually all of the successful employee/manager and worker buyouts involved one or more feasibility studies.

In addition to these elements, successful worker and employee/manager buyouts have good sources of finance, a governance structure involving workers, competent management, and increasingly, union support. Adequate financing is crucial, for many failures of employee-owned firms, particularly in the nineteenth century, have been traced to undercapitalization. The governance structure may assume greater operational importance only after the buyout is established.

Managerial expertise can be a problem, but is not an inevitable one. Most researchers agree that managerial expertise is crucial, and sometimes it is hard to recruit or keep. However, as Long (1978a) reported, managers in one employee/manager buyout were more likely to cite advantages than disadvantages for themselves. Advantages included greater worker input in decisions, greater worker interest in doing a good job, and better cooperation between workers and managers. Disadvantages for managers included workers overrating their importance and demanding too much say, loss of managerial authority, and managers needing to work harder and perform better under employee ownership. As Bellas (1972) noted in a study of worker cooperatives: "The manager must be an educator and a motivator, knowing full well that his autonomy will diminish as he increases the capability of his employees."

Unions have been skeptical about employee ownership. Some commentators see no role for unions once workers are owners. However, others believe the role of the union will be preserved and made easier through reduced labor-management conflict. In practice, the impact on collective bargaining is mixed, but there is still a significant and necessary role for the union at employee-owned companies (Sockell 1982; Stern and O'Brien 1977; Hochner 1983a, 1983b). Where unions take leading roles to facilitate the buyout, they often push for participative changes in management and organizational culture. This may require them to take on new roles and question some traditional values, as well as to learn how to run and finance businesses. These new roles require education.

Employee Ownership's Role in Policy

The potential uses of employee ownership are many, according to its advocates. Overall, there is much to be found in employee ownership for those of all political stripes. While the implications of our particular findings for policy will be elaborated in the final chapter, a brief general picture of some potential goals for worker buyouts can be given here.

Three overall sets of goals can be identified in increasing order of scope (or grandiosity). First, worker buyouts can be used to save jobs threatened by structural unemployment and by corporate strategic shifts. As Bradley and Gelb (1983) point out, one of the main thrusts of buyouts has been to moderate the velocity of economic change and decline of certain industries. Buyouts not only help workers avoid the pain of job loss, but also have other ameliorative functions. Communities can be spared sudden ruptures in their social and economic fabric and can encourage buyouts as a way to preserve other local business and the taxbase.

Second, from broader perspective, buyouts and employee ownership may support a strategy of economic decentralization. Employee ownership and ESOPs have been perceived as tools for achieving a number of political and social goals, such as (1) spreading ownership in the face of increased economic concentration of power (e.g., U.S. Joint Economic Committee 1975); (2) shifting responsibility for dealing with economic dislocation to private initiatives; (3) providing alternatives to government welfare policies and nationalization strategies; (4) opening up options for the development and preservation of a strong small business sector; and (5) leading to some type of radical restructuring and democratizing of the economy, i.e., economic democracy.

Finally, buyouts and employee ownership appeal to those interested in expanding the economy and providing it with new engines of growth. As Louis Kelso asserts, opening up ownership may increase the number of sources of capital. Furthermore, if employee ownership indeed is a key motivational tool, it may be useful for elevating general productivity.

So far, we have attempted to introduce the issues relevant to job-saving through worker buyouts and to discuss even more briefly the role of QWL programs. In the following chapters, the story of the particular job-saving attempts, the issues in evaluating the success of the innovations, the methods we used to conduct our research, and our research results are treated much more thoroughly. First, in chapter 2 we present a theoretical framework for evaluating employee ownership and worker participation as job-saving strategies.

NOTES

1. Very recent and up-to-date summaries of this legislative history and references to the actual changes in the tax code, including the Tax Reform Act of 1986, can be found in Rosen (1987) and BNA (1987).

2. In 1987, the funding for technical assistance and professional services was reduced to $1/2 million per year, and the revolving loan fund received no allocation because the larger amounts of funding had not been used much in the previous three years. Some observers believe that the Pennsylvania Employee Ownership Assistance Program was not marketed aggressively by the state government.

3. PACE worked on developing the initial legislation and the guidelines for the Pennsylvania Employee Ownership Assistance Program.

2

Worker Participation, Employee Ownership, and Job-Saving Efforts
A Theoretical Framework for Gauging Effectiveness

How do we judge the effectiveness of worker buyouts and labor-management cooperation to save jobs? On the simplest level, we want to know how many jobs were saved and whether or not the bought-out firms are viable and profitable. In fact, these concerns seem to be the basis for claims that worker buyouts are a proven job-saving method. One can point to numbers cited by the U.S. Senate Select Committee on Small Business (1980) that between 50,000 and 100,000 jobs were saved through employee ownership during the 1970s. "As a job creation program alone, employee ownership would compare very favorably to government funded public works jobs" (p. 18). Similarly, one can point to the fact that of approximately 60 buyouts during that time period, about 90 percent have apparently succeeded (Whyte et al. 1983).

There may have been factors other than employee ownership that contributed to the successes, however. The fortunes of the Vermont Asbestos Group, for example, rose soon after the buyout by workers from the GAF Corporation in the mid-1970s because of sudden shifts in the worldwide asbestos market. Similarly, some observers point to the failures of some prominent buyouts, such as at Rath Packing, as evidence that employee ownership does not work. However, to what degree did employee ownership contribute to the failure? Close observers and participants (Redmon, Mueller, and Daniels 1985), believe, in fact, that the seeds of Rath's failure were planted long before the buyout, and that jobs *were* saved, though only for four or five years.

To look at effectiveness, we have to ask: how does employee ownership work? Specifically, we need to look at the operations of worker buyouts, which we defined in the previous chapter's typology as combining employee ownership with worker participation. It seems that the operations of worker buyouts would work differently from the other employee ownership types.

While a number of researchers and observers of employee ownership have theorized about its nature and what makes it effective, none have differentiated clearly among the types. Thus, some insist that worker participation is a necessary ingredient for success in employee-owned firms (Whyte et al. 1983). Some others argue that the effectiveness of employe ownership depends much more on the value and size of ownership stakes than on worker participation (Rosen, Klein, and Young 1985). Still others claim that worker participation does not need employee ownership in order to be fully effective (Bernstein 1976). Each position has its share of supportive evidence. However, the positions may be based on evaluation of different types of employee ownership.

According to our typology, different organizational features may contribute to organizational effectiveness in each of the types. In conventional employee-owned firms, most ESOPs (category 3), the degree of worker participation is minimal and the amount of employee ownership is minor. In these firms, the value and size of employee owners' shares may be most relevant in motivating employees to effective performance (Rosen, Klein, and Young 1985). In employee/manager buyouts, those with majority employee ownership but minimal worker participation (category 5), ownership stakes may lead to high expectations of worker control, which may not be fulfilled (Whyte et al. 1983). In firms with QWL-type participation programs and in those with concessionary buy-ins by workers (categories 2 and 4) worker participation is predominant over ownership stakes. Thus, changes in the social and decisional structure of the firm may be necessary for effective performance (Bernstein 1976).

To answer the question of how effective are employee ownership and worker participation, we have to look at the features that go into a worker buyout or into a participative organization and how they function. Based on a review of theoretical and empirical literature on employee ownership and worker participation, we have developed a theoretical framework to look at the worker buyout. Despite general interest in them, there is relatively little written from a systematic perspective about what we call worker buyouts, (or even about QWL programs), so we have relied on writings about a variety of related topics. The literature reviewed is culled from many nooks and crannies in several disciplines. It is hoped that this method will increase the relevance of our framework for other combinations of employee ownership and worker participation. In fact, the theoretical framework was devised to take into account comparisons of worker buyouts, such as the O&O supermarkets, to job-saving through joint labor-management concessions, which was the case with Super Fresh supermarkets.

Theoretical Framework

The theoretical framework comprises three parts: (1) the ingredients that led to or existed at the time of the worker buyout, termed here Basic Input Features; (2) the functioning of the firm, specifically aspects having to do with employee ownership and worker participation, termed here Organizational Processes; and (3) how effective the firm is, termed here Outcomes. With these three parts, we can look at the processes and features that contribute to the effectiveness of the worker buyout as a job-saving strategy.

Basic Input Features of Worker Buyouts

A number of sources seem to agree that for buyouts—whether employee/manager or worker buyouts—to take place, several key ingredients are necessary. These ingredients involve characteristics of the actual and potential worker/owners, of the organization they work in and acquire, and of the environment in which the firm operates. These ingredients would also presumably be important for the functioning of organizations in which worker participation takes place.

Worker Characteristics

Usually in the initial stages of buyouts, the decision to go ahead depends on the motivations, willingness, and resources of a group of workers. These workers may be motivated by pragmatic job-saving desires, by desires for a piece of the "American dream," i.e., entrepreneurship, by desires for a more participative workplace, or by a combination of some or all of these (Granrose and Hochner 1985; Hochner and Granrose 1985). These motivations may color the expectations workers have for their buyout. Other observers point to the importance of workers' willingness and resources (Bradley and Gelb 1983; Oliver 1984; Cosyns and Loveridge 1981). That is, a self-selection process is at work. Not all workers affected by an impending shutdown, not even all of those interested in the idea of a buyout, will participate in a buyout attempt. Those who do participate need to be not only willing, but also able, because in most cases workers either have to pay directly or to sacrifice something, such as a portion of future wages or a pension plan, to get ownership stakes.

Worker characteristics influence both organizational processes and outcomes for workers. For instance, workers inclined toward participation may help increase the participativeness of an organization, and workers' gains or losses from the buyout will depend partly on the degree of hardship the buyout imposes on their resources.

Organization Type

The way the buyout or the participation programs is legally and organizationally structured, its organization type, tends to determine how decisionmaking will be handled, who will have which legitimate rights, and what opportunities there will be for workers to participate. The structure will affect the type of internal processes that will be expected and that will occur. As the Industrial Democracy in Europe International Research Group (IDE 1981) puts it, legal participative structure tends to lead to actual participative practice. If laws or by-laws governing the firm's operations mandate equal ownership stakes and democratic forms of management, as in worker cooperatives, the firm is more likely to be run participatively. If

those laws or rules tend to mandate distribution of shares to ꝓ.ᴗy-
ees according to their incomes and say nothing about management
procedures, as in most ESOPs, the firm is more likely to be run in a
conventional hierarchical way. With respect to participative structures, some organizational theorists hold the position that to be effective, participation has to be a key organizing principle and must
be thoroughly integrated into the organization at all levels to be truly
effective (Hochner 1978).

Role of Consultants and Unions

A number of observers (Stern and Hammer 1978; Parzen, Squire,
and Kieschnick 1982) describe the importance of a number of other
features and conditions surrounding buyout attempts. Buyouts need
legal, technical, and financial help, supportive (or nonhostile) union
attitudes, cooperation from the current owner of the plant, and an
assessment of the feasibility of profitable operation, based on past
and projected performance in the firm's markets. Similarly, participative programs such as QWL need well-rounded support from all
levels of management and from the union (Zager and Rosow 1982).
However, Parker (1985) expresses the fear that even strong union
support for QWL programs can backfire and undermine the union
itself.

The role of consultants and unions is an important determinant of
feasibility, of sources of finance, and of actual participativeness. For
instance, in the Weirton Steel buyout, consultants from Wall Street
financial firms and conventional ESOP lawyers insisted on a fairly
conventional ESOP structure with limited worker input to management decisions for a number of years. In another case, at Atlas
Chain, the union and the consultants agreed that a very democratic
ESOP structure was possible and desirable. In both cases the structures recommended by the outside experts were adopted.

Even the lack of support by experts and unions, among others, can
be a strong influence on the success or failure of employee-owned
firms. Studies by Aldrich and Stern (1983) and Jones (1984) conclude that the persistent economic marginality of employee-owned
firms over the past century-and-a-half in the U.S. is linked to the

attitudes and actions of potential support institutions. Moral, financial, political, and institutional opposition from such groups as lawmakers, labor unions, bankers, and educators contributed to a hostile environment for employee-owned businesses to grow in. Studies by Blasi, Mehrling, and Whyte (1983, 1984) demonstrate the importance of this environmental opposition by contrasting American experience with that in other countries, notably Israel's kibbutzim, Spain's Mondragon cooperative sector, and Yugoslavia's worker-managed economy. In these other countries, worker-owned and -managed firms have been supported by a number of popular customs and social institutions as well as by government support or neutrality.

Business Environment

The business environment involves the context within which the job saving effort takes place. Sociological and historical studies have identified several factors conditioning the formation and success of employee-owned firms. For instance, socioeconomic forces, such as business cycles, structural industrial change, and structural unemployment have been said to induce workers to form employee-owned firms, through buyouts or formation of new worker cooperatives (Jones 1984; Shirom 1972).

The relation of the worker buyout to other firms, such as suppliers of essentials and competitors, can also be crucial to its success or failure. The degree of competition among firms in the product and labor markets in which the bought-out firm will operate determines such things as potential market share, pricing policies, and profit margins. For instance, Russell (1985) points out that the viability of the worker-owned refuse collection companies of the San Francisco Bay area is enhanced by the near-total monopoly granted them to collect residential refuse by the cities they serve.

Similarly, the availability of debt capital for the buyout will be important if the capital requirements of the firm outstrip the resources of the workers contributing. Several observers have pointed to the hostility of banks and also of shutting-down employers as a key factor in failures of worker-owned business in American history (Jones 1984).

Furthermore, many commentators have pointed to the shortcircuiting of worker participation in cooperatives and participative experiments by the exigencies of the marketplace (Parker 1985). Worker cooperatives are said to "degenerate," i.e., fail outright or fail as democratic cooperatives, because they are isolated islands in the capitalist sea (Clarke 1984). Even in conventional organizations, crises brought on by turbulent environments may lead to increased centralization of power in the hands of managers and elites (Mintzberg 1979). Thus, the environment may impact internal processes and decisions of the organization. Moreover, the environment—including such conditions as economic boom or recession, expanding or depressed markets, and relations to external institutions, all of which affect firms of any type—may directly impact outcomes for job saving efforts.

Organizational Characteristics

The final basic input feature of worker buyouts and participative programs to be taken into consideration is the organization's characteristics. This feature reflects the past history and present capacities of the plant to be bought out or restructured. These factors plus projections of the future, based on assumptions about how the firm will operate, comprise important aspects of a market feasibility study. Often, consultants play a large role in evaluating this factor. Sometimes they may recommend against a potential buyout. Or they may recommend key changes in the firm, such as downsizing the workforce or even, in one case, moving to a nonunion plant (Hochner 1983b). In addition, the past fortunes of a firm may partly determine the decisions that will be made in the future and how well the firm can do. For instance, Hyatt-Clark Industries was troubled during its life as a worker buyout by the decline of its basic product market, wheel bearings for rear-wheel drive vehicles. In fact, this problem led GM to consider a plant shutdown and brought about the worker buyout in the first place. Similarly, Rath Packing was forced to do something about its declining product quality and declining marketing efforts.

Furthermore, cultural practices and customs in firms have been said to contribute to or detract from the development of employee ownership. Sometimes, successful employee ownership has been fostered by ethnic enclaves, such as at the Norwegian-American plywood cooperatives of Oregon and Washington, the Italian-American scavenger firms of San Francisco, and the Russian-American taxi cooperatives of Los Angeles (Russell 1985). Conversely, the American traditions of individualism and mobility may contribute to the small number of employee-owned start-up firms (Blasi, Mehrling, and Whyte 1983, 1984).

Organizational Processes

The basic input features are essentially "givens" at the time of or prior to the job-saving attempt. Once operations begin, organizational processes start to play a role. In many firms, these would include purchasing and marketing efforts, among others. Here, however, the emphasis is on organizational processes and practices related to the participative and employee-owned nature of worker buyouts. These processes include the governance of organizational decisionmaking (participativeness) and specific managerial decisions made concerning the deployment of resources (organizational functioning and labor strategy).

Our view of organizational processes distinguishes this theoretical framework from those of many other students of employee ownership. We see these processes playing a vital role in translating plans into actions. A number of other frameworks that have appeared in the literature tend to confuse process with outcome, though it is admittedly true that sometimes in organizational change strategies the institutionalization of the process is a primary desired outcome (Kanter 1983). For instance, workplace democratization is the outcome Bernstein's (1976) theory was established to explain.

On the one hand, to establish what is *unique* about the worker buyout as a job-saving method, it is important to show in which operating aspects worker buyouts differ from conventional firms or from labor-management cooperative efforts. However, to convince interested parties that worker buyouts are or are not *effective* ways to save jobs, it is necessary to show more than that employee ownership and worker participation change attitudes and behavior in the firm and that the buyout operates under some different principles than the conventional firm. Theory and research must both (a) demonstrate the results for workers and the organization of doing things by means of a buyout and (b) account for the sources of these results.

Participativeness

Participativeness and its effects on individual and organizational performance have received much attention in the literature on worker participation and employee ownership. Social psychologists have tended to look at the advantages of participation as a means of improving attitudes, communication, and organizational effectiveness (Likert 1961; Tannenbaum 1966).

However, we are also concerned about the impact of participativeness on organizations. Some, but very few, studies have focused on the mediatory role of participation on organizational outcomes. A report of a study of the economic performance of employee-owned firms stated, "Participation is the key" (NCEO 1986).

In our terminology, participation refers to actions of individuals, while participativeness is an organizational process reflected by perceptions, structures, and practices. Increased individual participation may lead to certain outcomes for the organization as well as for individuals, such as greater effort and less downtime through absenteeism. However, these outcomes may be more properly seen, according to our framework, as either additional aspects of organizational processes or by-products of outcomes such as profit, income, and job security. Increased organizational participativeness, on the other hand, is related to overall organizational functioning, such as decisions concerning the deployment of resources. Both types of organizational processes affect individual and organizational outcomes which result from organizational effectiveness.

Worker participation is often defined by a variety of terms, such as involvement, influence, control, or power, which tend to be ambiguous. However, Bernstein (1976) identifies three key dimensions of participation, which we include in our term participativeness: (1) the *degree* of influence exerted;

(2) the *range* of issues over which influence occurs; and

(3) the organizational *level* at which influence occurs.

Dachler and Wilpert (1978) add the dimension of *form,* i.e., whether participation is formal or informal and whether it is direct or thorough representatives. In general, the more of each of Bernstein's three dimensions an organization has, the more participative it is.

Participativeness is theorized to affect processes and outcomes at several organizational levels. At the level of the individual worker, theorists hypothesize that participation reduces alienation, while enriching job design and increasing effort, productivity, commitment to organizational goals, self-esteem, and mental health (Argyris 1957; Blumberg 1968; Conte 1982; Long 1978b; Nightingale 1982; Rhodes and Steers 1981; Tannenbaum et al. 1974). Moreover, labor costs related to absenteeism and turnover are hypothesized to decrease.

Furthermore, participativeness affects the group and overall organizational levels. Participation is linked to greater teamwork, group cohesion, self-policing behavior, information flow between hierarchical levels, less need of direct supervision, reduction of hierarchical power distinctions (while expanding the total amount of power and influence available), fewer adversarial conflicts, and more adaptiveness and flexibility (Bradley 1980; Lammers 1967; Tannenbaum 1968, 1983).

These hypotheses about the positive effects of participation are not accepted by all. Perrow, for one, likens the participative model to a "boy scout creed for organizations" (1982, p. 125). A number of conditions, contingencies, and contradictions are said to diminish the effectiveness of participation. For individual workers, participation may require increased education as well as a need for influence (Singer 1974; Vroom 1959). Strauss (1963) questions the impact that unattainably high expectations for participation have on its effectiveness. The type of technology used and the design of jobs also may be seen as a limit on the ability to spread participation. Furthermore, some argue that democratic decisionmaking is slower and less efficient by increasing "transaction costs" (Williamson 1975). Finally, some commentators point out that the effects of participation (and, we extrapolate, participativeness) are tempered by the nature of the organization's external environment (Mintzberg 1979).

Whether employee-owned firms are indeed participative is a matter of some debate and cannot be taken for granted. However, studies of long-established employee-owned firms, such as the plywood cooperatives and the San Francisco Scavengers, find high levels of participativeness. Relative to managers, line workers in these firms tend to have high degrees of influence in both informal and formal ways over both shop floor and strategic decisions (Greenberg 1980, 1984; Russell, Hochner, and Perry 1979). In some recent buyouts, relatively high levels of participativeness were found—i.e., voting rights on stock or high worker influence relative to managers (Conte, Tannenbaum, and McCulloch 1981; Long 1978b). However, in some other buyouts, which we would call employee/manager buyouts (see chapter 1), workers' influence had either not increased or had actually diminished since the takeover (Long 1982; Hammer and Stern 1980).

The evidence on the impact of participation on workers and organizations fills volumes and defies clear summary. However, general reviews (e.g., Locke and Schweiger 1979) conclude that participation tends to have positive effects on job attitudes and mildly positive or neutral impacts on performance. A comprehensive review by Strauss (1982) of worker participation studies in a variety of countries and organizational forms concludes its success depends on the criteria chosen by the observer. Nevertheless, Strauss notes that the evidence on economic impacts is "somewhat spotty" (p. 244).

Organizational Functioning and Labor Strategy

Our theoretical framework posits that participativeness is important primarily to the degree that it has effects on Organizational Functioning and Labor Strategy. That is, to have an impact on most organizational and worker outcomes (e.g., profits, income), organizational democracy must have an effect on management decisions on deployment of resources.

However, the role of resource deployment and ways of allocating labor has hardly received much explicit attention in prior literature. In this framework, we hope to help correct this deficiency. Most of the attention paid to the types of decisions made in employee-owned and -managed firms has been by economists. Sometimes social psychological issues have been looked at concerning the relation of participation to organizational functioning. A few researchers (e.g., Conte 1982) try to bridge the gaps among the potential links of employee ownership and worker participation to performance. Often, the literature has the following deficiencies.

(1) Worker attitudes, such as job satisfaction or commitment, become a dead end. That is, they either *are* the outcome to be derived or are merely *assumed* to be related to other, ultimate outcomes, such as job security, income, productivity, and profit.

For instance, Long (1978) developed a framework for looking at the effects of employee ownership in a buyout. However, both the framework and the empirical research he reports devote most attention to worker attitudes and tend to neglect the link even to behaviors like absenteeism. Rosen, Klein, and Young (1985) similarly analyzed the causes of job attitudes in employee-owned firms, with little analysis of their link to performance.

(2) Worker attitudes are related to weak measures of organizational performance such as absenteeism, rather than directly to productivity and profit.

Both the models presented by Conte (1982) and by Rhodes and Steers (1981) tie in worker ownership and participation to individual worker behaviors, but do not go much further to discuss the relationship of these and other features of employee-owned firms to overall performance. Even when researchers try to establish the notion that worker ownership indirectly affects performance through the social system of the firm (Tannenbaum 1983), they focus on individual performance, rather than that of the overall organization.

(3) Organizational features special to employee-owned and -managed firms, such as increased participativeness, nonhierarchical authority structures, and reduced job specializations, are identified but are not connected to comparative organizational performance. Rothschild-Whitt (1979) does a fine job of dissecting the differing arrangements of organizational structures and practices between collective-democratic firms and bureaucratic ones. But her theoreti-

cal framework does not explain what difference the different structures make in comparative performance, save on what goals are important to each. Similarly, Nightingale (1982) presents a theoretical model emphasizing that the congruence of organizational values, structures, processes, and outcomes in participative firms makes them a qualitatively different type of organization from conventional bureaucracy. However, the outcomes he discusses never get beyond worker attitudes.

(4) Assumptions are made about how participation affects entrepreneurial and managerial decisions in the firm without a clear understanding of the true costs and benefits of democratic, participative management practice. This problem occurs most often in the economics literature on employee-owned and -managed firms.

For instance, economic theory assumes a model of motivation in which individuals maximize their individual gains. Thus, worker/owners are assumed to be maximizing their own individual gains, rather than the gains of the entire group based on majority rule.

(5) In fact, the focus of most literature on employee ownership and worker participation, whether from an economic or a social psychological perspective tends to be the individual, rather than the group or the organization, where attention should more often be directed. However, recently a few studies have been directed toward the issue of organizational processes and organizational outcomes (Katz 1985; NCEO 1986).

Many positions exist on the issue of what kind of managerial decisions are made in employee-owned firms. In fact, early observers, such as Sidney and Beatrice Webb (1920) believed that the quality of managerial decisionmaking in employee-owned firms was seriously handicapped by an inability to recruit competent managers and by the impossibility of managing a group of owners.

The economics literature on labor-managed firms originates with the assumption that employee-owned and participative firms, in contrast to their "capitalist twins" whose main goal is profit maximization, tend to maximize income per worker (Ward 1958; Meade 1972; Vanek 1970). Economists then derive a number of characteristic entrepreneurial and managerial decisions that would seem to flow from the initial assumption. For instance, worker/owners would be expected to pay themselves high wages now, rather than invest for the future. Similarly, they would tend to try to reduce the number of worker/owners when profits were being made rather than to increase the number as one might expect. That is, they would rather increase their own relative shares than to have more worker/owners with whom to share the profits.

Other economists challenge this pessimism (Ellerman 1982; McCain 1982, Sertel 1982). Some argue that employee-owned and participative firms have operational advantages over conventional ones, such as: (a) an ability to tap human resources, i.e., teamwork, consensus, commitment, involvement, and communication; (b) less need for supervision; and (c) reduced labor costs and increased productivity (Conte 1982; Levin 1984). Pryor (1983), in a review of theoretical literature, concludes that the original assumption of income maximization per worker as the firm's objective function is easily modified, which changes all subsequent derivations and predictions of behavior.

As Batstone (1982) asserts, such a starting point assumes that employee-owned firms are democracies of small capitalists, rather than collectives of solidaristic workers with other objectives, such as collective income maximization, worker satisfaction, group maintenance, or even "the reduction, if not the eradication, of the role of the conventional capitalist or shareholder" (p. 100). Moreover, the objectives of potential and actual worker/owners may be a complex mixture of pragmatism (saving jobs), entrepreneurial values (for ownership and profits), as well as collective values (worker participation in decisions), as pointed out in our earlier studies of the workers involved in the Philadelphia-area A&P shutdown of 1982. (Granrose and Hochner 1985; Hochner and Granrose 1985). Such mixed motives may have great effects on managerial decisions.

Our theoretical framework emphasizes that participative processes should make worker buyouts do things differently from conventional firms and the other types identified in chapter 1 (Batstone 1982; Jones 1984; Levin 1984; Nightingale 1982; Rothschild-Whitt 1979;

Tannenbaum, Cook, and Lohmann 1984). Organizations with more participative forms of employee ownership are hypothesized to:
- use less supervision,
- give more responsibility to workers,
- increase communication of information to all levels,
- reduce internal wage differentials,
- employ job rotation and job redesign,
- invest less in capital and more in workers through wages and training,
- hire higher quality labor, i.e., be less inclined to save on labor costs by hiring low-paid, part-time, unskilled workers,
- get higher effort levels and less downtime from their workforces,
- rely more on work method innovations, though less on technological modernization, and
- have a lower level of adversarial conflict, e.g., strikes and grievances.

The evidence for these hypotheses comes from a variety of sources concerning employee-owned and -managed firms. What evidence there is tends to support the hypotheses, though there are some contradictory findings. In studying the plywood cooperatives, Greenberg (1984) found considerably less use of supervision than in conventional firms. In fact, he reported that when an employee-owned firm was bought out by a conventional firm, one of the first things the new owners did "was to quadruple the number of line managers and foremen" (p.193). Similarly, Nightingale (1982), who compared 10 participative firms—some of which were employee-owned—with 10 conventional firms, found that workers perceived significantly fewer bureaucratic rules, less supervision, more opportunities to take initiative, and less hierarchy in the participative firms. On the other hand, neither studies by Hochner (1978) on the scavenger cooperatives nor by Long (1978a, 1978b) on an employer/manager buyout at a trucking company found that work groups were more cohesive. Yet international studies by Tannenbaum et al. (1974) had found that the opinions of the work group tended to be more important to workers than the opinions of supervisors in organizations with greater worker participation, such as the Israeli kibbutzim.

Nightingale also reports increased communication at the rank-and-file level in his sample of participative firms. However, again neither Hochner (1978) nor Long (1978a, 1978b) found more communication between management and workers or greater information flow. Perhaps these findings on communication reflect the already simple and flat hierarchies of refuse collection and trucking firms. This may have implications for the current study of supermarkets, which have similarly simple and flat hierarchies.

Concerning wage differentials there is little direct evidence for American firms with worker ownership and participation. The scavenger cooperatives historically had a policy of equal wages for all worker owners, but began to abandon that policy in the 1960s to keep and attract managerial talent (Perry 1978; Russell 1985). We are not aware of other reports of wage policies in employee and worker buyouts. However, the example of the Mondragon system in Spain's Basque region, where a ratio of 4.5:1 from the highest-paid to the lowest-paid has been established, has received wide attention. In the U.S., where wages are a matter of union-management negotiation in unionized firms, wage policies in employee-owned firms may vary more widely. If employee-owned and -managed firms do hire more skilled labor, than wages for worker/owners may be at the top of the pay scale. Considering that researchers on employee ownership often tend to be concerned about such benefits to workers as job satisfaction, it is somewhat odd that wages have been relatively neglected.

There is also evidence that organizational resource deployment in worker-owned and -managed firms is more flexible than in conventional firms. For instance, Nightingale (1982) reports that in participative firms, a number of job design features have been altered, such as the amount of task variety, of autonomy, of required interaction with others, and the number of conflicting demands. It may be that job design itself is not altered outright by participativeness, but that a reduction of the kind of detailed job specialization that is often found in conventional bureaucracies takes place by more workers being aware of the requirements of other workers' jobs, either through cross-training or job rotation. Moreover, it is possible that the participative process itself, while changing nothing directly about a worker's job tasks, adds new tasks associated with discussions at meetings, for instance. The degree of actual job redesign may be a function of organizational characteristics, such as the prior amount of specialization and hierarchy.

A recent study by Tannenbaum et al. (1984) found that while employee-owned firms were less technologically adaptive than conventional firms (in their adoption of new technology), they tended to have a higher rate of survival during the recession of the early 1980s, probably because of greater flexibility and adaptiveness in their use of human resources. In fact, Berman (1967) reports that the plywood cooperatives adjusted worker/owners' wages downward to cope with business downturns, rather than lay off workers as is typical in conventional plywood mills.

Concerning effort and downtime, the evidence is mixed. On the one hand, most studies find that commitment of workers to organizational goals is more positive in employee-owned and/or participative firms. Worker participation, in fact, seems more strongly related to commitment than does ownership in the scavenger companies and in the employee/manager buyout of a trucking company (Hochner 1978; Long 1978b). The importance of participation seems to explain the findings of Kruse (1984), who measured employee job attitudes in two employee/manager buyouts that had little provision for worker participation and found few improvements after the buyouts.

It is hypothesized that increased commitment would be related to lowered absenteeism and turnover. However, a study by Rhodes and Steers (1981) of the plywood cooperatives found that, though perceived commitment was higher than in conventional plywood mills, absenteeism did not differ significantly. Hammer, Landau, and Stern (1981) studied patterns of absenteeism following an employee/manager buyout. They found that while overall absenteeism did not decline, the reasons for absenteeism shifted. This is, voluntary absenteeism (not legitimately excusable for illness, death in family, etc.) increased. Perhaps, the commitment of workers to this firm led to a felt need to follow its rules. A more straightforward link of worker participation and absenteeism was found by Katz, Kochan, and Weber (1985). They found that absenteeism was significantly negatively related to worker participation in suggestion programs and to worker involvement in QWL programs.

Nevertheless, the mixed relationships of commitment to performance measures such as absenteeism suggest that performance in employee-owned and -managed firms may be only slightly affected by changes in worker attitudes. Our framework suggests that absenteeism rates are only one part of organizational functioning that is affected by participation and ownership. Organizational performance may be more generally related to larger changes in resource deployment.

The final aspect of organizational functioning and labor strategy to be considered here involves adversarial conflict. Again, the evidence is mixed. Much was made in the media about the irony of worker/owners striking their own company when in 1980 there was a strike at South Bend Lathe, which had undergone an employee/manager buyout in 1973. Furthermore, labor-management conflict at Rath Packing (a worker buyout in 1980 which filed for bankruptcy in 1984) and at Hyatt-Clark Industries (a worker buyout in 1981 which has been reported to be seeking an external buyer) seems to have been a continual problem. Even some empirical studies, as opposed to media accounts, give little apparent support for our hypothesis. Sockell (1981) studied aspects of labor-management relations at several employee/manager buyouts. She found that labor relations neither worsened nor improved based on incidence of strikes and grievances.

All of the cases cited in the media, however, were cases in which what conflict did occur was about the withholding of decision involvement from workers by management. Furthermore, the cases studied by Sockell tended to be ones in which there was little worker participation, i.e., the union did not get involved with the buyout, preferring to be a passive observer, and there were few if any provisions for worker input into everyday managerial decisions.

In fact, evidence from organizations with substantial amounts of worker participation indicates the positive side of participation for labor-management relations and conflict. In a historical study of worker cooperatives and employee-owned firms from the 1840s to the 1970s, Jones (1984) reports that strikes have tended to occur in firms with high numbers of nonowning workers, i.e., in which not all workers participate in ownership and, presumably, in decision-making. Katz (1985) reports that in QWL programs at General Motors from 1977-80, even limited worker involvement can be causally linked by statistical methods to lower grievance and discipline rates and smoother collective bargaining. Moreover, worker participation has been successful in Europe, particularly West Germany and Yugoslavia, in toning down adversarial labor relations (Strauss 1982).

It may be that worker participation and employee ownership do not merely reduce conflict, but actually change its nature. That is, some types of conflict, such as those concerning strategic direction of the firm and allocation of resources, may be brought to the surface more readily in employee-owned and -managed firms. According to the 12-nation study of industrial democracy in Europe (IDE 1981), frequency of conflicts is positively correlated with the power of participatory bodies representing workers directly or indirectly. This should not be surprising, for increased information flow and the involvement of more people in decisionmaking, such as in matrix organizational structures adopted by many conventional firms over the past 20 or so years, tends to surface conflicts and to require that employees have greater tolerance for ambiguity and learn to practice diplomacy (Mintzberg 1979). However, as Strauss (1982) points out in his review of literature on worker participation, while participation may slow down the decisionmaking process, it seems to make implementation smoother.

Outcomes for Organizations and Workers

The final part of our theoretical framework involves the outcomes of worker ownership and participation in a worker buyout. We posit that the performance of the firm (organizational outcomes), such as viability, productivity, and profitability, are influenced by organizational functioning and labor strategy, as well as by the business environment and organizational characteristics. Furthermore, the performance of the organization will directly influence what the workers get out of the buyout experience (worker outcomes). That is, worker income, job security, job and life satisfaction, and family well-being are all results which are evaluated based on how well the firm does. However, worker outcomes may also be independently affected by organizational resource deployment, i.e., by what wage rates are set, by aspects of job design, and by other conditions of work. Similarly, the degree of participativeness may affect workers' evaluation of tradeoffs, if any, between job satisfaction and economic outcomes. Finally, workers' outcomes are influenced by their motivations, their resources, and the expectations they have about what their results should be. This part of our theoretical framework is perhaps the most difficult to support, because so little direct evidence on worker buyouts has been collected.

Organizational Outcomes

Prior evidence for these hypotheses, particularly concerning economic results, which is a major concern in our study of the effectiveness of worker buyouts, is mixed and scarce. For instance, Jones (1984) has studied the historical record of over 750 American worker cooperatives and employee-owned firms from the 1840s to the 1970s to examine their viability and efficiency. He found that worker cooperatives were often viable (i.e., able to survive more than 10 years), that they tended to do more poorly as they aged, and that efficiency was highly variable. Viability and performance were better in firms with "the *most* cooperative features" (1984 p: 52). These are firms adhering most closely with the following features: (a) restriction of ownership to those working in the firm; (b) control and management on a one-owner, one-vote basis; and (c) distribution of profits based on labor contributed, rather than on capital.

Tannenbaum and his colleagues have done two broad studies of large samples of employee-owned firms in business in the 1970s and 1980s to look at aspects of economic functioning (Conte, Tannenbaum, and McCulloch 1981; Tannenbaum, Cook, and Lohmann 1984). However, the two studies came up with contradictory results, even though their samples of firms overlapped considerably. The first study looked at 98 employee-owned firms—including ESOPs, employee/manager and worker buyouts, and long-established worker cooperatives. The second study expanded the sample of employee-owned firms to 200. Neither sample appears to be representative of the population of such firms, but at this time they are the only data bases containing significant amounts of information about economic results. Conte, Tannenbaum, and McCulloch (1981) found the 98 employee-owned firms to be more profitable than a matched set of conventional firms. Moreover, the percent of equity owned by workers was the highest and only significant predictor of profitability in a regression analysis. However, Tannenbaum, Cook, and Lohmann (1984) did not replicate the earlier study's findings. The 200 employee-owned firms studied did not score higher either on a ratio of profit-to-sales or on growth over a five-year period. Moreover, this time there was a small negative correlation of percent of equity owned by workers to growth. Despite these neutral findings, employee-owned firms *did* have a higher rate of survival between 1976 and 1982, a turbulent period in the overall economy. From these studies, the effect of employee ownership on economic results is unclear. Nevertheless, employee ownership appears to have at least neutral if not positive effects, and may give added strength to a firm in adverse times.

Another study of growth in employee-owned firms concerned the number of jobs created (Rosen and Klein 1983), finding that employee-owned firms created three times as many jobs as the typical firms in their industries. However, employee-owned firms that pass on stock voting rights to employees (rather than exercising these rights through trustees) did not show quite the superiority over conventional firms in employment growth. Rosen and Klein imply that this means that democracy in the firm leads to slower growth. Stock voting rights are a very small part of worker participation, however. Moreover, alternative explanations are possible, e.g., that fast-growing firms are more likely to adopt ESOPs as an employee benefit program and that those firms passing on voting rights may have tended to be in trouble even before employee ownership.

In fact, the research findings of Rosen and Klein, which came out of a study for the National Center for Employee Ownership, were contradicted by a subsequent study by NCEO (1986). As mentioned earlier, this study found that worker participation in employee-owned companies "is the key." Compared to a matched sample of 164 conventional companies, a sample of 30 employee-owned firms not only performed better, but job-level worker participation was the explanatory factor most consistently significant in predicting economic success—i.e., job growth, sales growth, and growth in the ratio of sales-per-employee.

Few in-depth studies of the economic results of particular employee-owned firms have been conducted. Long (1977) found evidence of increased quality after an employee/manager buyout at a trucking company in Canada. A few studies looked at results in the plywood cooperatives. Berman (1967) found productivity 30 percent higher than in conventional plywood mills. Bellas (1972) confirmed Berman's findings and extended them. Taking a complex measure of worker participativeness in the firm, Bellas found it to be the highest and only significant correlate of performance, defined by change in the value of an ownership share.

The relationship of participativeness to economic results, which was raised in Bellas' study, has rarely been looked at in employee ownership studies. However, a few studies of QWL and labor-management cooperative programs show positive impacts of the programs on performance. Macy (1979) conducted a longitudinal assessment of the Bolivar QWL project in Tennessee. He found worker participation associated with increased job security, job safety, and productivity. Schuster (1984) conducted a study of several forms of labor-management cooperation at a variety of firms. He found that both employment and productivity either increased or remained the same for the majority of cases in his sample. More recently, Katz (1985) analyzed the impact of QWL programs at GM between 1977 and 1980 and reported that they had a slight positive impact on measures of quality and labor productivity, with an even larger indirect effect on these outcomes through their effect on industrial conflict.

Worker Outcomes

Economic outcomes for workers involved in worker buyouts have been rarely if ever studied. Some evidence from other employee-owned and -managed firms does exist, however. Jones (1984) concludes that over the 140-odd years of experience with worker ownership in the U.S., workers in firms with the most cooperative features (equal ownership, democratic management, and profit sharing based on labor contribution) tended to make higher incomes than workers in other employee-owned firms. Similarly, Berman (1967) found that worker/owners' wages at the plywood cooperatives were 21 percent higher than the industry average. Similarly, Russell, Hochner, and Perry (1979) found that the income of worker/owners at the San Francisco scavenger companies in 1976 was approximately 50 percent higher than income of refuse collectors at comparable private firms or municipal departments in the same region. Both the plywood cooperatives and the scavenger firms tend also to conform to Jones' definition of firms having cooperative features.

The potential for diminished economic well-being for workers in buyouts does exist, nevertheless. For instance, the workers at South Bend Lathe gave up their pension plan to gain ownership through an ESOP. Similarly, workers at Weirton Steel, Rath Packing, and Hyatt-Clark Industries took wage concessions, agreed to or had imposed on them dismantlement of their pension plan, and/or waived severance benefits. The workers at the O&O stores examined in this study took a pay cut to achieve their buyouts, as did their fellow former A&P co-workers as part of the deal to create Super Fresh with its QWL program.

In some of these cases, however, the initial cuts or concessions may have been a kind of investment which may or may not pay a return. The present study is an evaluation of such costs and benefits to workers of the O&O buyouts compared to workers taking the Super Fresh route to save their jobs.

Other types of worker outcomes, such as job satisfaction and mental health, have received some attention in the literature on employee ownership and worker buyouts. Tannenbaum (1983) sums up the research results as being reasonably consistent with the hypothesis that ownership is a source of satisfaction at work. However, the studies he cites sometimes found a negative effect on the job satisfaction of managers.

Studies measuring mental health are about as close as anyone has gotten to looking at life satisfaction for worker/owners. The findings do not indicate a simple positive effect of employee ownership and worker participation. Nightingale (1982), for instance, found a significantly higher level of overall mental health and a lower level of alienation at the rank-and-file level in his sample of participative firms. However, in studying the San Francisco scavenger firms, Hochner (1978) found lower levels of perceived powerlessness among worker/owners, while Russell, Hochner, and Perry (1979) reported them complaining of a greater incidence of nervous tension, worry, and anxiety compared to other refuse collectors. In retrospect, such mixed findings are not surprising, since increased power also leads to increased responsibility.

Summary of the Theoretical Framework

Organizational and worker outcomes in worker buyouts are highly variable. To understand the sources of this variation, it is necessary to look at several factors at once. Assuming that the outcomes result directly from employee ownership and worker participation misses the real story behind the ways that worker buyouts and labor-management cooperative efforts are put together and function over time. Our framework emphasizes that outcomes result from organizational processes, which in turn result from basic input features.

This framework does not imply that employee ownership and worker participation are either the cure-all for ailing firms or the villains if and when the firm fails, just as managerial practice is not necessarily the cause of good or bad performance in organizations. For instance, the worker buyout at Rath Packing led to a substantial effort to change the organizational culture from management autocracy and labor adverarialism to participative labor-management cooperation at several levels (Whyte et al. 1983). Nevertheless, the firm is in bankruptcy today. Such a case serves as a reminder that employee ownership and worker participation may not be as effective as theory would have it, or more likely, that they are not always potent enough to overcome the effects of the business environment and organizational characteristics.

The following set of equations sums up the diagram shown as figure 2-1:

Participativeness = f (worker characteristics, organization type, role of consultants and unions);

Organizational functioning and labor strategy = f (participativeness, business environment, organizational characteristics);

Organizational outcomes = f (organizational functioning and labor strategy, business environment, organizational characteristics); and

Worker outcomes = f (organizational outcomes, worker characteristics, participativeness, organizational functioning and labor strategy).

In the case under examination here, as we shall see in chapter 3, several aspects of this framework will require modification. For instance, because the business environment facing the O&O buyouts and the Super Fresh stores at the time of the A&P shutdown was basically the same, and because the stores being studied still operate under very much the same regional and local market conditions, this basic input feature is considered as a constant. Furthermore, some aspects of the business environment, such as the availability of capital, may indeed differ for the O&O buyouts compared to Super Fresh (still wholly owned by A&P). Yet these differences may be too difficult to measure, and thus, impossible to factor in.

Similarly, many of the constructs, as indicated by the contents of the boxes in figure 2-1, are complex and multidimensional. Thus, this framework and the quasi-equations above do not match the precise equations used in analyzing the data we collected. While we quantify as many relationships as possible, a great deal of qualitative data is needed for clarification. In the next chapter, the actual methods used to test the theoretical framework are described. The chapter following that describes the complexities of the A&P shutdown and the circumstances and actions leading to the O&O buyouts and the creation of Super Fresh.

Figure 2.1
Theoretical Framework of Employee Ownership and Worker Participation

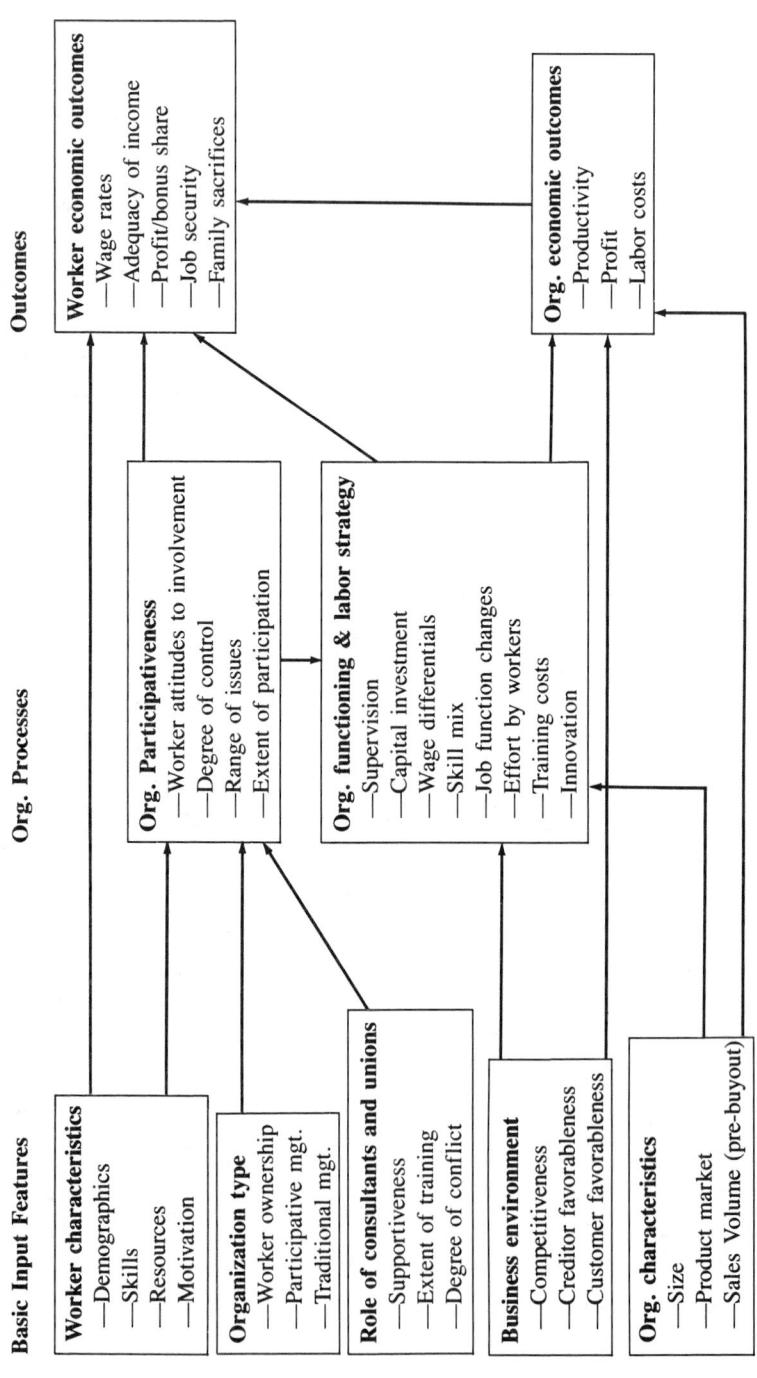

3

Research Design and Methods

In previous chapters we introduced the 1982 Philadelphia A&P shutdown and subsequent job-saving efforts through worker buyouts and labor-management cooperation (see chapter 4 for further detail), and presented a theoretical framework for looking at their comparative effectiveness. This chapter deals with research issues emerging from the theoretical framework set forth in chapter 2. The issues include finding a situation to study, selecting a sample, operationalizing constructs, conducting measurements, and testing hypotheses. We describe the research strategy followed and the methods by which we gathered our data. We also present an overview of the research project, discuss the objectives of our research design, review general methodological issues, and report our procedures in collecting data.

We begin with a description of the three major phases of the longitudinal research project:

Phase I: First Worker Survey

With financial support from the unions, the A&P, Super Fresh, and Temple University, the research group sent a mail survey questionnaire during the summer of 1982 to members of locals 56 and 1357 employed by A&P. This survey focused on perceptions of the workers' former and current situation as well as opinions about the opportunity to become worker/owners or to have a QWL program. The findings of this phase are not reported here. For details, see Hochner & Granrose (1985) and Granrose & Hochner (1985). This survey was important because it began a long research relationship and yielded information about worker expectations for the new situations. The data were helpful in formulating subsequent research instruments and interpreting data collected after the new stores had opened.

Phase II: Semistructured Interviews

During the summer of 1983, one year after the initial survey, employee/owners in two O&O stores agreed to participate in individual interviews. This phase of the project was guided by a developing theoretical framework, which eventually evolved into the one presented in chapter 2. The primary focus, however, was on organizational processes and individual motivations. The interviews asked employees their reasons for becoming owners, their views on how it was working out, and the utility of their training. The interviews were partially supported by a grant from Temple University. Also, one member of the team, Cindy Coker, was supported by the Ford Foundation to evaluate the training the owners had received from PACE and Grey Areas, two consulting groups (see chapter 4). She helped coordinate the two research efforts into a single interview format and gained cooperation from the worker/owners.

By the fall of 1983, further support from the Samuel S. Fels Fund enabled us to conduct a similar set of interviews with former A&P workers from two Super Fresh stores in Philadelphia. In these stores, workers and managers had undergone extensive formal training in operation of a QWL program to increase employee participation in decisionmaking. The aim of these interviews was to provide a data set for comparison with the O&O workers and stores. They focused on worker experiences in the new setting and the new QWL system of worker participation in the organizations. This group of workers was asked why they had *not* chosen to become worker owners and what conditions were like in Super Fresh after training in QWL.

In the fall of 1984, support from the Upjohn Institute enabled us to conduct similar interviews with former A&P workers in two Super Fresh stores outside Philadelphia. These stores had been minimally affected by the shutdown threat in 1982 and were represented by union locals (UFCW 27 and 56) not actively seeking QWL or employee ownership. QWL training was not instituted as early in these stores as it had been in the other stores in which interviews took place. These employees had not participated in the discussion about employee ownership and QWL conducted by UFCW 1357 at the time of the shutdown.

Phase III: Structured Questionnaire Surveys of Workers, Shop Stewards and Store Managers

The Upjohn Institute funding also enabled the focus of the project to be extended more explicitly to economic issues for individuals and stores. During the fall of 1984, a written questionnaire asking about current conditions in the stores and personal financial welfare was given to every Super Fresh employee and O&O worker/owner who had been interviewed. Similar questionnaires were sent to shop stewards representing these six stores and the other 19 Super Fresh stores in Super Fresh's Philadelphia zone.

Managers from every O&O and Super Fresh store whose workers or shop stewards had contributed data, also filled out a written questionnaire about the store as a whole. Data on the stores' financial condition were obtained from the Super Fresh corporate headquarters, from the O&O store boards, and from available published sources.

Study Objectives

The research design was guided by two major objectives: to document an important and unique case in which worker buyouts and labor-management concessions were used to save jobs; and to examine and test the proposed theoretical framework in order to compare the effectiveness of the two innovations for workers and their stores (see chapter 2).

Longitudinal Documentation

The first major goal was to document longitudinally the consequences and the remedies established in this particular plant shutdown situation. By following this experience from the initial announcement, valuable new information on the process of adjusting to a shutdown could be gained. Another related goal was to explore in depth employee ownership in retail stores rather than in the manufacturing setting typical of past cases reported in the literature. Since buyouts in the trade and service sectors may occur more often in the future if employee ownership becomes more popular, this information could prove valuable. Furthermore, this worker buyout occurred in an urban context where a shutdown did not threaten the sole employment opportunity for displaced workers, in contrast to the typically studied buyout. Given these conditions, we believed it would be desirable for social policy to clarify whether and under what circumstances worker buyouts might be a beneficial alternative to job loss.

Theory Testing

A second, equally important objective was to study the linkages suggested by the theoretical framework presented in chapter 2. We aimed primarily to evaluate the influence of the basic input features on internal organizational processes and the influence of organizational processes on outcomes for individuals and organizations. Specifically, we wanted to compare (1) the efficacy of saving jobs through worker buyouts and labor-management concessions, and (2) how different organizational processes, namely employee ownership and worker participation, affect outcomes.

Comparative Efficacy of Saving Jobs Through Different Methods

As stated at the outset of chapter 2, to many observers the efficacy of job-saving may be judged only by the number of jobs saved. However, in this study the research design aimed to determine the type and level of economic outcomes occurring for both individuals and organizations. Economic objectives were broadly defined to include job and life satisfaction, as well as income and employment goals, i.e., both subjective and objective welfare. Economic outcomes were singled out because financial benefits are often advocated as the primary reason for undertaking a buyout. A broad definition of "economic" was adopted because there was concern not only for whether or not jobs were saved, but also what kinds of jobs and at what cost to other aspects of an employee's life.

This study addresses another issue not usually considered in previous research, namely, the issue of relative effectiveness. Unless results are compared to other alternatives these workers might have had, it would be difficult to interpret the economic consequences of an employee buyout. The comparison of the O&O stores to the Super Fresh stores enables us to determine the comparative ability of worker buyouts and QWL to provide jobs, income, well-being, and store profits.

Processes and Outcomes of Employee Ownership
and Worker Participation
The theoretical framework presented in chapter 2 differentiates employee ownership from employee participation. First of all, employee ownership and labor-management cooperation, as organizational types, operate within contexts that involve many factors: worker characteristics, consultants and unions, business environment and particular organizational characteristics. Second, the framework specifies that it is necessary to establish that worker buyouts and joint labor-management programs do indeed involve worker participation operationally. Third, the framework posits organizational functioning and labor strategy as a theoretical construct separate from participativeness and as a key input into organizational outcomes. Operationalizing organizational functioning and labor strategy is a key task in studies of worker participation in decision-making. Fourth, the framework hypothesizes that organizational and individual outcomes are influenced by a number of factors and require consideration of several sources of variation.

General Methodological Issues

Three major difficulties, which were considerations in the design and execution of this study, are inherent in studying employee ownership and worker participation. The first is the problem of defining and operationalizing important theoretical constructs. The second is taking into account the influence of contextual factors on the key variables in comparing employee-owned and participatory firms with more conventional ones. A third problem concerns who is a better source of information about the key variables in the theoretical framework: workers, managers, or union representatives?

Definition and Operationalization of Key Theoretical Constructs

Several of the boxes in our theoretical framework (chapter 2) involve difficult-to-define, multidimensional concepts having to do with ownership, participation, organizational functioning and labor strategy, worker motivations, effectiveness, and productivity.

Of particular importance are the nature and distribution of ownership and participation, which are covered in our constructs of organizational type and participativeness. Because we restricted our study to the worker buyout, which is a particular form of employee ownership, and to Super Fresh, which involves a particular form of cooperative labor-management agreement, the issue of organizational type is clearly defined here.

However, there are some major controversies in the study of worker participation, influence, power, and control, all of which contribute to the construct of participativeness (IDE 1981). First, there is a lack of agreement among researchers about definitions of the various terms. Similarly, there are inherent problems quantifying "soft" concepts such as participativeness. Second are potential problems of methodological errors and bias, such as the possible qualitative difference in participativeness between worker buyouts and forms of labor-management cooperation (e.g., through QWL programs). Another potential methodological problem occurs in the variety of approaches to the study of power and dimensions of participativeness. Walton (1970), in surveying the research on community power structures, found that choice of methods was significantly related to consequent results. For instance, the reputational method (asking respondents who has power) tends to find pyramidal structures, while the decisional method (analyzing the decision process) tends to find factional or coalitional structures.

To deal with the definition of participativeness, we follow the multidimensional definition given by Bernstein (1976), which includes (a) the degree of influence, (b) the range of issues involved, and (c) the organizational level where influence occurs. Measurement of these dimensions, using operationalizations developed by Hochner (1978), IDE (1981), and Tannenbaum et al. (1974), also gives us the ability to compare our results with those of other related studies.

To deal with method problems, our research strategy involved what Jick (1979) calls "triangulation," i.e., using different methodologies to study the same phenomenon. Both qualitative, semistructured interviews and quantitative structured surveys were conducted with workers in the various stores chosen for intensive study. This enabled us to get a better handle on measuring and evaluating internal processes in the organizations. The qualitative worker interview results are reported in chapter 5, while the quantitative worker survey results are reported in chapter 7. Integrating and reconciling these results, where different, is one of the tasks of the concluding chapter (8).

Other theoretical constructs, such as worker motivation (part of worker characteristics), organizational functioning and labor strategy, and worker outcomes, involve some of the same difficulties as participativeness. They are all hard to define, operationalize, and measure. Where possible, we chose measures derived from previous literature. Also, the use of triangulation permitted us to get two perspectives on the impact of these variables.

Effectiveness and other aspects of outcomes were also difficult to define. As noted above, a broad definition of worker economic outcomes was adopted because of our concern not only with the number of jobs saved, but also with what kinds of jobs and at what cost to other aspects of an employee's life. Thus, we looked at objective outcomes—whether the jobs are full time or part time and the amount of job income received—and at subjective outcomes—the degree of sacrifice imposed on workers by the shutdown and subsequent events and their satisfaction with their jobs, lives, and economic results.

Effectiveness at the organizational level is another important matter. A number of researchers on employee ownership and worker participation comment that conventional measures of profits may have limited applicability because cooperatives do not always keep their books and account for profits the same way conventional firms do. For instance, Thomas and Logan (1982), in their study of the Spanish Mondragon cooperatives, advocate measures of performance such as value added. According to Berman (1967), ownership leads to stability of employment, a primary outcome for both individuals and firms. (In this study, we were able to use comparable measures of profits from both worker-owned and conventional firms. See chapter 7.)

In theory, the objectives of employee-owned and participatory firms may differ from those of conventional firms. Instead of single-minded pursuit of profit, the objectives of employee-owned and participatory firms may be multiple: profit, employment security, high and steady worker income, and desirable work hours. In this study, we took a multidimensional approach to organizational outcomes. More detail on this approach will be forthcoming in chapter 7.

The Influence of Contextual Factors

In addition to employee ownership and worker participation, the literature discussed in chapter 2 strongly suggests the importance of certain contextual variables and organizational characteristics in determining worker and store outcomes. Control of the context is important for determination of the extent to which results can be generalized. That is, it will enable us to incorporate or rule out the particular context (depending on the degree to which contextual and organizational factors interact), suggest the circumstances under which other worker buyouts might have similar effects, and help indicate what can or cannot be done to enhance or promote successful buyouts. Levin (1982) favors an experimental analogy of control: "cooperative or labor-managed and traditional capitalist forms of organization would represent experimental treatments applied to productive enterprises to see which provides higher productivity" (p. 53). To approximate such experimental conditions, a study of employee-owned and participatory firms would be expected to find a sample which would hold constant the companies' resources, nature of the products, market prices, and external environments, including geographical area. Furthermore, it would be necessary to randomly assign employees to experimental treatments.

In reality, the experimental analogy is a false one. Firms are not created by some invisible experimental hand, allowing comparisons on only one key variable at a time, say employee ownership versus conventional ownership, while holding all other sources of variation constant. Instead, firms are formed for a variety of reasons at a variety of times. Historical forces and personal preferences predominate in determining which firms get developed, when they get started, what stages they go through, and who gets in what firms. There is no random assignment for either workers or firms.

Levin considers this may be a serious problem "if LMFs [labor-managed firms] are found predominantly among enterprises that are purchased by their workers as a last resort to maintain employment, after the capitalist owners have decided to terminate production and close the firms. That is, if LMFs are typically a product of worker takeovers of failing capitalist firms, a comparison of productivity will hardly be valid" (p. 54).

However, instead of bemoaning the imperfect actual conditions under which tests of hypotheses must take place, it is more useful to identify ways in which fair tests of employee ownership and worker participation can take place. Hochner (1978) provides a few key criteria for these fair tests: (1) comprehensive and multidimensional theories of participation and (2) selection of appropriate cases to study, which involve meaningful motivations for worker participation.

First, it is possible to use a comprehensive theoretical model of employee ownership and participation and a measurement model that is inclusive of background factors. Then at least contextual factors will be taken into account. This is part of the approach in this study.

Second, various sampling strategies can be adopted. Many previous studies have tried to control contextual variations through sampling. Some studies tried to maximize control over contextual variables, including business environment and organizational characteristics, by matching a sample of employee-owned firms in a variety of industries with a sample of conventional firms in the same industries, sometimes also using such criteria as size of workforce and type of technology (Nightingale 1982; Conte, Tannenbaum, and McCulloch 1981; Tannenbaum, Cook, and Lohmann 1984; Rosen and Klein 1983). Other researchers have tried to control for industry by sampling firms with employee ownership and conventional firms within one industry, one region, and with similar work methods (Rhodes and Steers 1981; Greenberg 1980; Berman 1967; Bellas 1972; Russell, Hochner, and Perry 1979). Neither of these strategies, however, can rule out variations in worker characteristics. Even when workers in employee-owned and conventional firms do similar jobs and have the same basic qualifications, there may be self-selection at work. Though it is not possible to rule out self-selection through an experimental design, this factor needs to be incorporated in research designs.

The establishment of the worker buyout O&Os and the Super Fresh stores simultaneously makes this situation seem to be a type of naturally occurring field quasi-experiment (Campbell and Stanley 1963). A&P workers and stores were threatened with shutdown. The workers were reemployed and stores reopened through two organizational innovations. Therefore, this situation seems to control for many industry and background factors.

Even here, however, a precise experimental control analogy is faulty. While industry is held constant, plant differences may be significant. For instance, the actual openings of the different stores did not occur at the same time, but rather took place over a period of time stretching from mid-1982 to late 1983. Some A&P stores that received the Super Fresh treatment either had not actually been threatened in the original shutdown announcement or were only closed briefly to allow for conversion. Moreover, the potential worker/owners had to choose sites for buyouts from a list presented to them by A&P corporate staff, so it is likely that A&P kept the best sites for itself; and not all A&P stores were reopened as Super Fresh. Furthermore, the worker/owners do not have many of the resources of the big chain, though they have affiliated their stores with a quasi-chain, IGA (Independent Grocers' Association), which provides them with some coordinated advertising, short-term financing, purchasing, and warehousing.

Similarly, worker background in this situation may not be well-controlled either. As reported in chapter 4, though the workers in the different settings do have a common previous employer, they selected which option they would go to. In chapters 5 and 6, the importance of self-selection becomes clear when we discuss the differences between the O&O and Super Fresh workers. Some A&P workers were never explicitly threatened with job loss and lost only a few weeks work during the conversion process. In addition, not all former A&P workers were called back to work at Super Fresh. Nor did they all have a chance to participate in the planning of the worker buyouts, particularly if they were members of union locals either unreceptive or hostile to the idea.

In the unique setting of the current study, we were able to adopt a variation of the single-industry sampling strategy. We concentrated on one industry, but in addition, the workers in both the O&O and Super Fresh stores originally came from the same pool of A&P workers and got sorted into the new structures at approximately the same time. Furthermore, most of the firms in the sample were threatened with shutdown at the same time, and then reopened. Thus, this sample provided unique opportunities for comparisons of workers and of firms. In this context, we could control for industry, geographical area, and to some degree, the length of time the innovation has been established. To control or take into account other sources of contextual variation, where possible, we examined some worker self-selection factors (such as worker motivations to choose either O&O or Super Fresh), and some differences in organizational characteristics, such as preshutdown profitability, resources, and local external environment.

Whose Perspective in Data Collection?

Complex and controversial topics such as employee ownership and worker participation, tend to entail disagreement among theorists about how to operationalize theoretical constructs (IDE 1981). In particular, with respect to participativeness, various arguments are made that the perceptions of either workers, managers, or objective observers are more valid representations of reality. Contrarily, participativeness is sometimes defined by legal or constitutional arrangements in the firms (IDE 1981; Jones 1984). In this study, similar contentions could be made over organizational functioning and labor strategy. How do we validly measure difficult constructs?

To some extent, it is possible to hedge this question in research design by using multiple methods and multiple measures of each construct. For instance, in this study, by using both qualitative and quantitative methods, we were able to compare workers' spontaneously-expressed cognitive categories with *a priori* theoretical constructs and measurements.

However, there is a larger question here. Are organizational processes best seen from the workers' perspective, or that of managers, or through some other means? In theory, this may be unresolvable. Nevertheless, we had to come up with an answer in this study, because we focused on both workers and their stores. Where possible, we measured perceptions of organizational processes from three sources—workers, store managers, and union shop stewards. Because we asked workers about their experiences and their outcomes in the stores, we decided to ask them about processes. Likewise, because we asked store managers about store outcomes, we decided to ask about processes as well. However, because we were limited in our budget and because we were unsure that store managers and workers would see things similarly, we asked shop stewards, as possible proxies for workers' perceptions. In part, we were interested in differences in perceptions among organizational levels. However, to strengthen our confidence in our measures, it was necessary not only to test these differences, but to construct measurement scales using items that all organizational levels agreed hung together.

Nevertheless, the major reason we were concerned about differing perspectives had to do with the limits of our sample. Only two employee-owned stores were established through worker buyouts. That fact limited the sample that could be used for comparison with the new worker/owners, despite the fact that the Super Fresh stores, with their QWL programs, eventually numbered over 55 and employed several thousand workers.

The small number of cases necessitated modifications in the theoretical framework, to apply this framework to the actual setting. This test was split into two levels of analysis: one for individual worker perceptions of processes and outcomes and one for store-level processes and outcomes. At each level, a specific research design was selected that would compare workers for stores in three situations: (1) employee ownership with worker participation (the O&O stores), (2) conventional ownership in which QWL had been fully implemented (QWL Super Fresh stores), and (3) conventional ownership in which QWL had been less fully implemented (non-QWL Super Fresh stores).

Sampling Procedures

The Worker Sample

To study worker outcomes, attitudes, and perceptions in depth, a sample of workers from six stores was chosen. Perceptions of organizational processes and reports of individual worker economic outcomes could be studied intensively in the six stores selected for comparison. We chose this approach because (a) we wanted to follow up former A&P workers in the new setting; (b) we wanted to know how QWL worked; and (c) most important, we wanted to know how these workers and their situations compared with the

O&Os. Because only two O&O stores had been started, two stores of each type were selected for the in-depth look at workers. Limited resources led us to limit the number of comparison cases and of workers. Consequently, we tried to match the Super Fresh stores with the O&Os, but as explained below, the matching was rather imperfect.

In the O&Os, every available worker/owner was included in the sample. Within each Super Fresh store, subjects were selected from a list of all former A&P employees provided by management. After stratification for department, department head status, and sex, selection was randomly made by the research team. In the two Super Fresh stores outside Philadelphia, the number of former A&P workers was sufficiently small that almost all of them were interviewed.

The sample of workers was chosen to be representative of former A&P workers, not of all workers in the stores, because the major focus of this study was on job-saving. Not all of the workers in the O&O stores are worker/owners; several are hired workers. But these hired workers tend not to be former A&P workers, whereas the worker/owners are. Similarly, in the Super Fresh stores, there are workers who we ruled out of eligibility for selection to the sample because they had not been former A&P workers.

The Store Sample

For testing hypotheses concerning store-level processes and outcomes, a six-store sample would be inadequate. It would be impossible to answer questions about the economic consequences to stores on the basis of such a small sample. It was necessary, therefore, to gather store-level data from a larger number—to put the six stores studied intensively into a broader context and to enable some inferences concerning the relationship of store organizational processes to store economic outcomes. Store-level data were collected from 19 other Super Fresh stores in Philadelphia itself, as well as from the six stores at which worker interviews took place. For store-level measurement of the role of consultants and unions, organizational environment, store functioning and labor strategy, operational char-

Table 3.1 Data Collection Summary

	Store managers	Shop stewards	O&O worker/ owners	QWL Super Fresh workers	Non-QWL Super Fresh workers
Personal Interviews					
Number Contacted	—	—	39	41	59
Number Responding	—	—	31	41	58
Number of Stores	—	—	2	2	2
Date Data Collected			9/83–3/84	3/84–1/85	3/84–1/85
Survey Questionnaire					
Number Contacted	25	48	39	41	59
Number Responding	25	47	27	36	53
Number of Stores	25	25	2	2	2
Date Data Collected	1/85	1/85	2/85	2/85	10/84–1/85

acteristics, and organizational economic outcomes, a survey of store managers was conducted.

Shop stewards as proxies for workers.

Though we needed to measure the worker perspective on the key variables of participativeness and store functioning, financial limitations prohibited contacting every worker in these stores. Instead, two shop stewards for each of the additional 19 stores as well as the six original ones—one representing retail clerks from local 1357 or from local 27 and the other representing meatcutters from local 56—completed a structured written questionnaire about their store, including information on the extent of QWL implementation and on participation in decisionmaking. Shop stewards were chosen as proxies to represent the perceptions of workers in their stores of overall store participation and functioning.

How good a proxy were the shop stewards' responses for workers' responses in the larger sample of stores? (See appendix for table.) After we categorized Super Fresh stores as being either QWL or non-QWL stores (see below), we compared the mean levels of shop steward characteristics, participativeness, and perceived store functioning variables reported by workers in the two stores in that category studied in depth.

Overall, the shop stewards' responses showed few if any significant differences from workers in their category. First, shop stewards were no different from workers in worker characteristics. Second, combining both categories, shop stewards' responses tended to fall roughly intermediate between the responses of full-time and part-time workers on all measures, though on some variables they differed from either full-time or part-time workers. Third, for the QWL Super Fresh stores, shop stewards seemed to be quite representative of both full-time and part-time workers. Fourth, for the larger sample of non-QWL Super Fresh stores (n = 8), shop stewards did perceive less worker influence in daily and intermediate decisionmaking, and less learning from their training session compared to workers in the two non-QWL stores studied in depth. This last finding, however, may be a function of the special nature of the stores selected for in-depth study, as discussed below.

It would have been desirable to interview and survey workers in a larger number of stores, but given financial and time constraints, it was not possible. It may have been possible to survey a larger group of workers in a larger number of stores by skipping the intensive interviewing, but that would have eliminated the triangulation of methods so desirable and so necessary for studying worker motivations and structures of participation and decisionmaking, as noted above.

Selection of stores for in-depth study

The Super Fresh stores studied in depth were selected jointly by the research team and Super Fresh corporate management. In selecting the initial two stores to study (expected to fit the label "QWL Super Fresh"), the research team requested that they be matched with the O&Os on the basis of size, location, and business volume. However, Super Fresh management strongly recommended two particular stores, which turned out to be larger than the O&Os and located in urban neighborhoods with higher density. This did not match the less urban setting of the O&Os. These two Super Fresh stores were part of the initial group of stores receiving QWL training. They were accepted by the research team because they were expected to be representative of stores in which QWL had been implemented and because they were stores represented by UFCW local 1357, which had been the original party to the innovative Super Fresh labor agreement.

The other two Super Fresh stores in this sample (expected to fit the label "non-QWL Super Fresh") were also selected jointly by the research team and Super Fresh management. We wanted stores most closely resembling, operationally, A&Ps before the shutdown and conversion. In addition to similar matching criteria, a particular concern was to select stores outside the jurisdiction of local 1357, which had initiated the worker buyouts, negotiated the QWL program and worker bonuses with Super Fresh, and was involved in extensive training programs likely to change workers' opinions to be less representative of the old A&P. Though the agreement between Super

Fresh and local 1357 became a pattern for contracts between the company and other UFCW locals in the area, the other locals were not enthusiastic about the agreement. The two Super Fresh stores chosen for the sample were south of Philadelphia, and the workers were represented by UFCW locals 27 and 56. They were supposed to have implemented a QWL program, but this had been initiated later than in Philadelphia, involved less extensive training, less union support, and the workers in these two stores had not faced a permanent shutdown in 1982. For these reasons we expected a low level of QWL implementation in these stores.

As a check on the degree to which stores had really implemented QWL, we also gathered data on the extent to which QWL was known and practiced in these stores. We had expected that our original sampling categories of QWL and non-QWL would be filled through taking two stores in Super Fresh's Philadelphia zone (where QWL was originally proposed and implemented) and two stores outside that zone (where QWL was formally implemented later, if at all). More details on the establishment of both the O&O worker-owned stores and the Super Fresh chain and its QWL program will be found in chapter 4.

Reclassification of stores to sampling categories

Data from our interviews, as reported in chapter 5, and the answers to some questions on the worker surveys, concerning the degree of QWL implementation in the stores led us to question our original assumptions. One store in the Philadelphia zone and one store outside had actually fully implemented QWL and the two other Super Fresh stores (one in Philadelphia and one outside) had either done an incomplete implementation or had not followed up the initial training. Thus, we reclassified the Super Fresh stores in the sample used in our in-depth study on the basis of the degree of actual implementation. Moreover, the stores in the larger sample were classified according to these new criteria, too.

Sampling biases in store samples.

A number of sampling biases need to be discussed to help interpret our findings. As mentioned above, despite our efforts to select four Super Fresh stores for the in-depth part of the study that would be matched with the O&O stores on the basis of size, location, and business volume, Super Fresh management recommended four particular stores.

To check on how representative these stores were, we compared the store-level data collected from managers and shop stewards at (a) the two QWL stores from the sample studied in depth with stores in the larger sample of 19 which we classified as QWL stores (n = 11) and (b) the two non-QWL stores from the in-depth study with non-QWL stores from the larger sample (n = 8). Specific findings of this analysis (see table in appendix for detail) revealed the two QWL stores studied in depth were larger in square footage, sales revenue, and payroll; had been more profitable in the year before the A&P shutdown; had significantly more worker influence, overall and in certain decisions; and had instituted more training programs for workers. There were fewer differences between the two non-QWL stores studied in depth and the others. For instance, the non-QWL stores did not differ in participativeness. Nevertheless, they did have significantly higher payroll costs, sales, current (1983) profits, more worker training programs, and higher worker bonuses than the non-QWL stores in the larger sample. In addition, it appears that the non-QWL stores in the larger sample have about the same levels of participativeness on many variables as do the QWL stores.

Overall, it seems that Super Fresh management chose "star" stores for us in the in-depth part of the study for comparison with the O&O stores. This may significantly bias the comparisons we make. However, if we find that workers in the O&O stores differ from those in the Super Fresh stores in ways predicted by the theoretical framework, we can be rather certain about confirmation of our hypotheses.

Procedures Used in the Collection of Data

Worker Interviews

This method asked respondents to describe current and recollected situations in depth, providing an insider's view of personal motives, informal social networks, informal systems of communication, and store operations. The semistructured worker interviews consisted of approximately one-and-one-half hours of conversation focused on:

Reasons for their choice of this work situation;
The nature of their former and current jobs;
Decisionmaking and supervisory practices in the store;
Social networks at the stores;
Career history and aspirations; and
Household circumstances.

The interviews were usually conducted in a back office at the store or in a nearby restaurant. The setting was reasonably private, but sometimes hot, cold, or noisy because of the loading and unloading of food going on in other parts of the back of the store. Most Super Fresh employees were given time off from work to be interviewed. The O&O employee/owners were paid $10 from Ford Foundation funds for coming in early or staying late in order to be interviewed. Interviews were conducted by the research team or by graduate anthropology students trained in the collection of ethnographic material.

Interviewers took notes in space provided on the interview questionnaires, and taped the conversation.[1] After the interview was completed, the interviewers refined their notes based on the tapes. Each completed interview protocol was then coded by three anthropologists. In coding the O&O interviews, the primary objective was to develop categories which fit the cognitive categories of the employees. If information in response to one question was elicited as an aside in a later question, the information was coded in both places.

Construction of the Super Fresh interviews benefited from the experience gained interviewing O&O employee/owners. Some questions were simplified and others made more specific or more structured, using the coding categories developed after the O&O interviews. Coding of the Super Fresh interviews conformed as much as possible to that of the O&O employees, but if different ideas were being expressed, preference was given to capturing the ideas of the employees rather than forcing responses into O&O-determined categories. A copy of the questionnaire used for each group is located in the appendix. The coding scheme will be discussed in conjunction with the explanation of the interview findings in chapter 5.

Worker Survey

Whereas the interviews occurred over a long time span in different stores, the survey gathered data from all employees concerning approximately the same time period. The questionnaires, which could be filled out in about a half hour, contained precoded questions on:

> Job experience;
> Training, particularly in the new setting;
> Perceptions of the amount and type of participation in decisionmaking;
> Perceptions of store functioning under QWL or worker ownership;
> Personal values;
> Aspects of job and life satisfaction;
> Household situation; and (for Super Fresh workers) the QWL system and worker's knowledge of it.

Some questions were selected or adapted from prior instruments, such as the survey administered in Phase I of the research project, Tannenbaum (1968), IDE (1981), and the Michigan Quality of Work Survey (Quinn and Staines 1977). Others were written specifically for this study using ideas gained from the completed interviews or from the theoretical constructs needed for model testing. All questions were structured or provided with precoded categories for response except the group of questions on the Super Fresh questionnaire that asked employees to define QWL and to describe its implementation in the store. A copy of this questionnaire is located in the appendix.

The questionnaires were distributed directly by interviewers in the last two stores studied. In other stores, questionnaires were delivered to workers at the stores by members of the research team or our assistants. A cover letter assured the employees of confidentiality and reinforced the message that the data were being returned to the

Temple research team, not to their store or union. They returned completed questionnaires by sealing them in provided envelopes and dropping them in a box in the store. Those employees who did not return their questionnaires immediately were contacted by phone if needed and personal follow-up was continued until a response or a refusal was received. After the completed questionnaires were received, a research team member assigned code numbers, checked them for completeness, and coded the QWL questions. Data was then keypunched directly from the questionnaire.

Shop Steward Survey

Since all stores but the O&Os were represented by two unions, one for retail clerks and one for meatcutters, both shop stewards in each store were surveyed, partly to make sure there would be at least one response from each store.[2] The survey of shop stewards was distributed and returned by mail, since these stores were widely dispersed geographically. Names and addresses were provided by Super Fresh management. The questions on the shop steward survey were identical to those in the employees' written questionnaire except that in some questions the steward was directed to respond based on her or his perception of the workers' general situation in their store rather than her or his own particular situation or belief. Specifically, the shop steward was asked about:

> Personal background (similar to worker survey job experience);
> Participation (questions similar to worker survey but asking about all workers, not just this individual); and
> Training (again, concerning the whole store not just this individual).

A copy of this questionnaire is located in the appendix.

If responses to this survey were not received immediately, a follow-up postcard was sent. Telephone reminders were then used to encourage stragglers to return their questionnaires. Because the sample size was small, a response was needed from virtually all in the sample. If the data were not returned by mail after several phone calls, the responses were collected by telephone interview. All questions were precoded and were punched directly from the questionnaire.

Shop stewards from both the retail clerks local and the meatcutters local in the store were surveyed. However, we actually used the responses of the retail clerks steward, unless we were not able to obtain his or her response from a particular store. In those cases (n = 4), we used the responses of the meatcutters steward. These meatcutters stewards' responses did not differ significantly from those of the retail clerk stewards used. Retail clerks rather than meatcutters stewards were our first choice because of the greater support of the new Super Fresh arrangements by the main retail clerks local (1357).

Store Manager Survey

Similar to the shop stewards survey, store managers' (called store directors at Super Fresh) questionnaires were sent and returned by mail. The questionnaire covered:

> Characteristics of the store;
> Participation in decisionmaking (similar to shop steward questions, but covering all levels in the store—manager, department heads, and workers;
> Methods being used in the organizational innovations;
> Store financial information, including strategy for tough times; and
> Amount of consulting and training programs received, plus what workers have learned.

In all cases, we had to collect store financial data which (1) were available from the stores and corporate management and (2) were comparable to the data we were getting from the other sources. In most cases, store managers were reluctant to provide the detailed economic data requested. For the Super Fresh stores, financial information was then obtained from Super Fresh corporate headquarters.

At one of the O&O stores, the manager filled out most of the questionnaire, but wouldn't divulge financial information. The board of directors and the worker/owners as a whole also refused to release the information, though they had been cooperative up to then. For that one store, we had to use information from key informants cross-checked with published data about the industry and about the stores. We have every reason to believe that it reliably represents figures comparable to those obtained for the other stores.

Table 3.2
Sources of Measures of Theoretical Constructs

Variable or construct	Sources of data
I. Basic input features	
Worker characteristics	Worker interviews and survey.
Store type	Sampling (also shop steward and manager survey).
Role of consultants & unions	Store manager survey.
Business environment	Sampling or manager survey.
Store characteristics	Store manager, corporate archives, and published sources.
II. Organizational processes	
Participativeness	Worker, shop steward, and manager survey, and worker interviews.
Store functioning and labor strategy	Worker, shop steward, and manager survey, and worker interviews.
III. Outcomes	
Worker level	Worker survey and interviews.
Store Level	Manager survey and corporate archives.

Limitations of the Study Design

There were several possible limitations which need to be taken into account when results of this study are interpreted. The small number of stores and workers increases the probability that particular cases are not representative of stores in general. Of course, it would also have been better to have had more than two employee-owned stores, but having at least two alerted the research team to possible store idiosyncracies.

Concerning individual data, self-report data were used, although several sources were used for many of the key variables. Self-report data always are subject to bias due to the difficulty people have in objectively perceiving their world and reporting it honestly to others. It also would have been desirable to obtain data from all of the workers involved, instead of using the proxy measurement of key informant shop stewards used for testing the store-level analysis. However, the shop steward data, as reported above, appear to be representative, based on the six stores studied in depth.

Conducting the store-level analysis on a sample of just 25 stores means that few variables can be used in quantitative tests. Thus, less detail is available than can be used in the analysis of the individual level. However, the qualitative information collected in semistructured interviews should help in interpreting both the worker-level and the store-level analyses.

Controlling for industry, region, and organizational type meant that some generalizability was sacrificed. By carefully documenting the circumstances of this buyout, the nature of jobs, and the definition of constructs in ways comparable to other studies, however, it is possible to determine when the findings of this research project can realistically be applied to other settings.

Despite the uniqueness of the setting, our sample may be representative of employee buyouts, even if not representative of the supermarket industry. The O&O worker buyouts tend to share several characteristics of previous employee buyouts (Whyte et al. 1983). (1) Profitable units were closed by the parent company, so economic viability was possible. (2) Management delayed notification of a shutdown, though the union had anticipated it. (3) Plant management practices could be improved and several strategies for improvement were available. (4) Financial, managerial, and organizing leadership were available to the potential worker/owners through the union and consultants. (5) Complex financial arrangements, including both secured bank notes and individual capital investment, were needed to fund the buyout. (6) The degree of participation in decisionmaking to accompany ownership was identified as a crucial issue affecting economic viability of the firm.

Conclusion

In this chapter, we reviewed the overall research project, our objectives in the current phase, and our strategy and procedures in collecting data. Overall, the setting provided a unique opportunity to compare job saving in worker buyouts to labor-management cooperation and to test theoretically meaningful hypotheses. Our research design was developed to focus on both worker- and store-level processes and outcomes.

In the next chapter (4), we go into detail on the context which led to the establishment of the O&O and Super Fresh stores and the formal implementation of the worker buyouts and the labor-management cooperative programs. The following chapters present the findings of our qualitative and quantitative explorations of the hypotheses suggested by our theoretical framework.

NOTES

1. The employees were assured that the tapes would only be heard by the interviewers or senior researchers. They were also assured that identification of their individual responses would not be revealed to anyone at the store, the company, or the union. If someone objected to being taped, their wishes were honored.

2. The meatcutters local did not want to get involved in the worker buyout, so the meat workers in the O&Os were made part of the retail clerks local.

4

Context of the Closings and Implementation of Alternatives

A&P took down its last few red and white logos in the Philadelphia area in 1982. In their place, two new logos appeared on the fronts of some former A&P stores. O&O stores had a crisp blue and white logo with the name in classic lettering. Super Fresh raised a green and white sign to convey freshness. About all the general public saw was the exchange of signs. The public held (and still holds) many misconceptions about what happened to A&P and what kind of business structures characterize the new Super Fresh and O&O stores. This chapter describes what lay behind the series of events leading up to the establishment of the stores bearing those new logos. The first half of the chapter explores the national, industrial, and corporate context of the 1982 A&P closings in Philadelphia and the response of the local union. The rest of the chapter explains each of the two alternatives that emerged in the attempt to save supermarket workers' jobs: the O&O and Super Fresh stores. The second part of the chapter focuses on the formal labor agreement, training programs, and organizational structures that were planned and on the actual developments (planned and unplanned) occurring in the implementation of the two alternatives.

Using the terms of our theoretical framework, this chapter contains primarily descriptive information about most of the basic input features. The contextual description of the economy and the company is important background information on the business environment in which both job-saving attempts occurred. Similarly, the description of A&P corporate decisions and actions provides a general understanding of the organizational characteristics and past history that those creating new organizational forms had to contend with. The details of the actual store types are thoroughly rendered, including some sense of the differences between plan and realization. The roles played by consultant and union support are at the heart of the story of the establishment of the job-saving alternatives told in this chapter. The story of the implementation of the types gives some basic indications of how the organizational processes are expected to work, but that part of our framework will be examined in depth in chapters 5-7. Likewise, there is no discussion of the characteristics of the workers, which will be dealt with in those later chapters.

In a more basic sense, this chapter should enable the reader to understand events from the point of view of the various categories of insiders. What contributed to A&P management's decision to close its Philadelphia stores, gradually over a number of years, and then all at once in 1982? What did the A&P workers experience in the years and especially the months before the final announcement of store closings? Why did the union offer to buy and operate a number of stores as worker-owned? What were the motivations of A&P and workers' to go the route of Super Fresh? What were former A&P workers' expectations of each setting and what preparation did they have? The next chapter takes up the reality of implementation of the new businesses.

As stated earlier, a strength of this study is that the structure of the situation we describe has some of the qualities of an experimental research design. Nevertheless, the reader should keep in mind that the development of the businesses was not exactly parallel. This chapter also discusses the circumstances of development that account for these differences. For example, the amount and timing of training for working out the store structures differed for the two store types and training occurred not only before the stores opened but after stores started up. These differences in training affected how the stores evolved and led to a redefinition in this study of store types among Super Fresh stores based on amount and quality of on-the-job experience with QWL.

The Economy

Early 1982 was a period of deep recession in the economy as a whole. The national unemployment rate reached 8.8 percent in February, the month A&P announced the impending shutdown of its Philadelphia stores. Unemployment climbed steadily through the year, going up to 10.8 percent in November, when both O&O stores had opened. In this context, unions were negotiating relatively unprecedented contracts, agreeing to wage cuts and other concessions. Major contracts (covering at least 1,000 workers) negotiated in the first quarter of 1982 provided for first-year wage increases of 3.0 percent on average, compared to 9.0 percent for contracts negotiated in the fourth quarter of 1981 (Ruben 1983). The situation faced by the Philadelphia A&P workforce was in many respects duplicated throughout the country.

The Food Retailing Industry

The cyclical problem of plant closings and unemployment brought on in the recession exacerbated economic dislocation that structural shifts had been causing for several years. That is, industries undergoing profound changes in consumer demand, in technology, in plant location, and in competitive pressures, such as automobiles and steel, were among the hardest hit and accounted for much of the increase in unemployment.

Structural and strategic changes were occurring in other industries as well, however, even in relatively stable ones such as food retailing. Increasing suburbanization, sophisticated marketing strategies, and changes in cash register and warehouse technologies led food retailers to sharpen their competitive edges. A key management coping strategy in this environment has been to cut costs, particularly labor costs.

For workers in food retailing, this effort, by the late 1970s,

> had yielded mixed results. The automated check-out counter, with its scanners and pre-coded inventories, had reduced the need for labor. Product specialists in meats, vegetables, fruits and dairy had already been deskilled. Only meatcutters, as Braverman (1974, p. 371) notes,

"retain any semblance of skill, and none requires any general knowledge of retail trade." (Blim 1985).

The deskilling process also led to the bifurcation of the food retailing labor force (Doeringer and Piore 1971).

. . . [E]ach supermarket giant developed, in effect, its own internal labor market, through which the maintenance of the full-time, labor core of the organization was subsidized by a segment of the firm's labor force that best was characterized as less-well-paid, part-time, young and subject to high turnover (Blim 1985).

This trend was to be a key reason for problems A&P encountered as it shut down stores around the country in an attempt to remain competitive. Ironically, shutdowns led to the retention of a unionized, "full-time labor core" who bumped less senior workers. This meant higher, rather than lower, labor costs. However, the Philadelphia shutdown enabled A&P to leapfrog over its competitors, to introduce an even more fully developed version of the bifurcated internal labor market, as we shall see below.

A&P Corporate Context

There has been much speculation on the reasons for A&P's decline from the largest and most successful supermarket chain to one of the most troubled (Hartley 1983; Steiner 1982; "A&Ps Busy Boss"; Barmash 1982). Partly, massive store closings can be attributed to general trends in the industry toward fewer, bigger stores and increased competition. Yet, there is no shortage of internal reasons cited for A&P's long slide into financial difficulties. The history of A&P provides a key to understanding the decision to close the Philadelphia region.

A&P's biggest enemy may have been its history of success. By 1930, A&P had been in business for over 70 years, having pioneered the retail cash and carry food market chain structure (Dirlam 1977).

A&P was the biggest chain, with 19,422 stores in 1930 and sales of a billion dollars (Hartley 1983).

Although A&P had established stores across the country, management remained centralized until the 1920s when the company instituted a regional management structure. Even then, real power remained centralized. Founded by George Huntington Hartford in 1859, management remained in the family until George Jr. died in 1957. Until 1974, leadership of the company was elected from inside.

By the 1930s, A&P was a smug and complacent company, making it slow to respond to changes in the industry, in the geographical distribution of the population, and in the public's food buying preferences. The first challenge A&P failed to meet was the supermarket. The average size of a 1930 food market was only about 500-600 square feet and weekly sales about $500-$600. Michael Cullen's "King Kullen" chain, started in 1930, initially had stores of at least 6,400 square feet, with a weekly sales volume of $12,500 (Dirlam 1977). These stores could offer lower prices during the depression and offered free parking at a time when the car was becoming increasingly important. A&P was slow to follow the trend. The average A&P store in the 1960s was 14,000 square feet, compared with an average of 20,000 square feet in the other major chains (Hartley 1983).

After World War II, when the flight to suburbia was at its height, A&P failed to make adjustments. By the time A&P began moving out to the suburbs, the best locations were already taken by other chains. Further, A&P did not modernize its remaining stores, leaving them dimly lit, shabby, and small.

A&P was slow to pick up on new merchandising trends also, such as carrying nonfood items and trading stamps. Furthermore, A&P held on to the idea of selling its own brands, made in expensive food-processing plants, and failed to engage in mergers during the two periods of intense merger activity in the industry—between 1920 and 1930 and between 1949 and 1964. By the late 1960s, A&P found it had an image problem (Hartley 1983; Steiner 1982; Barmash 1982). A&P had become known for its dingy, poorly maintained stores, poor customer service and stodgy, old-fashioned management styles.

A&P Corporate Strategy: 1970s

In 1974, for the first time since the depression, A&P had a net loss—of $157 million. Although profits had been declining for several years, this devastating loss led the company to recruit Jonathan Scott as chairman and chief executive, the first outsider to head the company. He made strategic cuts in A&P's operations, eliminating unprofitable stores and food-processing units.

Reductions in the number of stores a chain operated was a general trend in the industry, and had accelerated during the last decade as companies moved toward bigger and bigger stores. When Scott entered the scene in 1974, there were 3,680 A&P stores and 125,000 employees. By 1980, there were only 1,542 stores and 63,000 employees. Scott also discontinued 36 food-processing plants (Steiner 1982; Barmash 1982).

After the devastating 1974 losses, the company made a slight comeback and actually had a modest profit of $18.7 million in 1976. Even though A&P continued to cut back stores and employees, the losses started again. In 1978, despite a record high in sales, A&P suffered a net loss of $52.2 million, and fell to the number three spot behind Kroger. Losses for 1979 matched the earlier high of $157 million. That same year, Tenglemann, a family-controlled German-based retail group with extensive food market holdings bought a controlling share of A&P stock of 42 percent ("A&P Looks Like Tenglemann's Vietnam"; Steiner 1982). Scott resigned in 1980.

Several analysts see the critical flaw as Scott's decision to close individual stores rather than entire regions ("A&P Looks Like Tenglemann's Vietnam" Barmash 1982; Hartley 1983). Savings realized by closing an unprofitable store were cancelled out by maintaining the overhead costs of distribution within a region (Hartley 1983, p. 137). This strategy not only failed to reduce costs, but also "drove up overhead and turned profitable stores into losers" ("A&P Looks Like Tenglemann's Vietnam"). Even with fewer stores, A&P became weaker (Steiner 1982).

Most merchandising decisions still were not sensitive to regional tastes and preferences. Scott left the highly centralized and top-heavy corporate structure unchanged, again failing to reduce overhead costs. Continued high overhead costs prevented investments in modernizing and building stores.

The cutbacks had caused labor problems as well. First of all, the drastic reduction in the number of employees meant that the remaining employees tended to be the oldest, highest-seniority, and highest-paid workers. Wage costs and workers' length of service were twice as high at A&P as at any of its competitors (Barmash 1982; Ackoff, Broholm, and Snow 1984; "Local Unions . . . "). Job histories of former A&P workers document a high frequency of transferring from store to store in the last few years, as senior workers "bumped" (i.e., displaced through contractual seniority provisions) less senior employees as stores were shut and positions cut. These transfers often entailed a loss of job status, loss of hours, or concern that it was only a matter of time before the job would be lost altogether. In addition, each time stores were closed A&P was forced to engage in local labor contract renegotiations, further weakening employee morale (Hartley 1983).

A&P Corporate Strategy: 1980s

Very few of the early observers of Tengelmann's purchase saw the wisdom in it, as exemplified by the title of one article, "A&P looks like Tengelmann's Vietnam." Hoping to restore A&P's health, Tengelmann replaced Scott with James Wood, who had been CEO at Grand Union, the country's second oldest chain. Wood, unlike his predecessor, consciously followed a strategy to reduce overhead costs, calling it a "revitalization" program (Barmash 1982), by closing entire regions rather than individual stores. When Wood came on, there were only 1,542 stores still open. He continued to cut the number of stores, but at a slower rate. However, during one six-month period in 1982, A&P announced 400 store closings (Ruben 1983). In addition, on April 1, 1982, A&P closed its huge food-processing plant at Horseheads, New York "Local Unions . . . ").

Wood also made significant cuts in central management. In his first year, he eliminated 100 of the 550 jobs at A&P headquarters in Montvale, New Jersey (Steiner 1982). He began a program to restructure procedures that would give store managers more responsibility, thereby reducing the need for central management. In 1982, the company reported a quarterly profit for the first time in two years.

To reduce labor costs, Wood began a campaign to get union concessions in various regions. Wood also intended to reopen or purchase new stores after the earlier round of closings in order to "dilute the number of senior employees" ("Local Unions . . . "). In New York City, A&P halted store closures after union locals agreed to introduce an early-retirement program. At this point, the Super Fresh model had not yet been proposed and analysts were not sanguine about the possibility of A&P being able to extract other union concessions in New York after years of A&P layoffs ("Local Unions . . . "). However, during 1982, wage concessions were given by a 300-member UFCW local to A&P in Norfolk, Virginia and by a 1,700-member UFCW local in Baltimore. Also, 13,000 UFCW workers took a wage freeze at A&P and two other grocery chains in Detroit (Ruben 1983).

To counteract A&P's image problems, Wood hoped to re-establish a competitive identity. For one thing, he wanted to focus on service, widening the range of products and emphasizing fresh produce and meats. Wood also intended to modernize existing stores and begin a building campaign, but the company did not bounce back quickly enough for him to direct resources to such a program. Although Wood was able to cut losses drastically, he continued the policy of shutdowns in his first years as chairman.

The 1982 Philadelphia A&P Shutdown

The phase-out of 79 stores in the Philadelphia region clearly reflects the implementation of Wood's regional strategy. From 1979 to 1981, A&P's share of supermarket sales in the Philadelphia metropolitan area dropped from 17 percent to 6 percent, while the number of stores was more than cut in half (*Supermarket News* 1981, 1983).

From employees' and customers' points of view, the rationale for closing the entire Philadelphia region was not clear. Although A&P had been closing stores in Philadelphia for years, the stores that had been disappearing during the 1970s were generally among the oldest and least profitable. In this new round of regional cutting, however, employees and customers saw that store profitability and a good competitive edge made no difference. A&P was vague about its motives, insisting that the decision was based on the profitability of stores and the competitive nature of the Philadelphia market. The behavior of A&P corporate decisionmakers made little sense to employees, who had a difficult time believing A&P would really close stores they knew to be viable.

Many employees attributed the moves to management incompetence. In a study comparing management practices at A&P and other food retailers in the Philadelphia area, Nicholson (1985) came to the conclusion that "A&P was a poorly managed corporation . . . at every level." Its chief competitors, both large national chains and independent, locally-owned, "had never experienced many of these problems [that A&P had]" (Nicholson 1985, pp. 147-148). Other companies were found to be more flexible and modern than A&P.

In late February 1982, when A&P announced they would close the remaining Philadelphia stores by March 20, there were only 11 stores still open in the city and 8 in the near suburbs. These were among the 29 to go. Warehouses in the area were also slated for closure. About one week later, in an inexplicable reversal, A&P announced that it would keep 6 of the 29 stores open, 3 of which were in Philadelphia and the remaining 3 in the surrounding Pennsylvania and New Jersey suburbs. Wendell Young, President of UFCW local 1357, immediately accused A&P of closing some of its better stores and keeping open some with a particularly low overhead and lower payroll costs: "Everyone that they're closing is a good store" (Schaffer 1982a). According to one chronicler of this event, James Wood actually admitted that high wages were a factor in closing stores, but the strategy also was clearly in line with his idea that it was important to save overhead costs by closing an entire region. Young suspected that A&P decided to keep a few stores open to save itself from having to meet pension obligations to employees (Lin 1982).

The Local Economic Situation

This shutdown of a major retail food chain in the Philadelphia area was just one in a long line of business closings that had been occurring at a high rate over the previous decade. In the national context of three recessions in the 1970s and early 1980s and a structural economic shift from basic manufacturing towards service industries, Philadelphia fared poorly. During the 1970s, Philadelphia lost employment in every sector but services, and its gain in services was not as strong as the rest of the nation's. The biggest losses were in manufacturing jobs, about 150,000 jobs lost from 1970-80, and that sector lost another 30,000 jobs during the 1982-83 recession (BLS 1982). Even finance and insurance jobs were lost in the Philadelphia metropolitan area during the early 1980s recession. Both the city and the suburbs lost about 20 percent of the jobs in wholesale and retail trade over the decade from 1970 to 1980. Two department stores, two large discount department store chains, and two major food chains closed their operations in Philadelphia. Altogether, 10 major retailers left Philadelphia, accounting for a loss of 10,000 retail jobs (Steiner 1982; Moberg 1982).

Several recent shutdowns weighed on workers in the Philadelphia area in early 1982. For instance, the venerable *Bulletin* newspaper, once the nation's largest daily in circulation, shut its doors in January 1982, despite its unions having agreed to concessions in negotiations the previous fall. Similarly, the Philadelphia *Journal,* a fairly new paper concentrating on sports, stopped publishing early in the year.

The Union Context

The Philadelphia area's weak economy and A&P's continuing decline confronted the leadership of UFCW local 1357 when they learned of A&P's 1982 closing announcement. By various calculations, this closing would mean a loss of membership of at least 2,000 to a local union that had undergone other recent losses and threats of losses.

According to some sources, the union had lost 5,000 members since 1976, but through aggressive organization of new employers the membership had been kept fairly stable at 12,000 for the four or five years prior to A&P's closing announcement in March 1982 (Steiner 1982; "Local Unions . . . "). Local 1357 had been struggling to keep up its membership over the years, and the loss of more than 2,000 jobs from A&P was significant, not only in numbers, but also in the nature of the members being lost. The A&P loss "represents a severe blow to the union. . . . Food-store members have the highest salaries in the local and contribute the highest member dues" (Hochner and Bennett 1982). About a year before, the governor of Pennsylvania had proposed privatization of the state liquor store system, which would have meant the loss of another major portion of local 1357's membership.

The current president of local 1357, Wendell Young, was first elected in 1963 at the age of 22. As a student at St. Joseph's College working part time in supermarkets, he saw the way companies exploited the lowest-paid, unorganized clerks. He sought the presidency and immediately led a strike against Food Fair, a now-defunct Philadelphia grocery chain that was opening new stores with non-union workers (Clark and Guben 1983).

Young characterizes his tenure in office as filled with examples of last minute announcements of store or chain closings. He notes that the usual few hours or even few days notice was insufficient for him to mount a meaningful response in light of the length of time regular negotiations took. He had been feeling frustrated and helpless to really do anything (Young 1984).

Young had begun working on the closing long before A&P made their February 1982 announcement. Although the threatened state liquor store closing never materialized, the continuing A&P store closings prompted Young to keep up his exploration for ways that the union could save jobs, and to consult with individuals from various points of view. These included Jay Guben, a successful entrepreneur in the restaurant business who had recently been working as a consultant to business for start-ups, and PACE (Philadelphia Association for Cooperative Enterprise), a local group with expertise in worker-owned business headed by Sherman Kreiner and Andrew Lamas. When the November 1981 round of A&P store closings began, information was leaked to Young that A&P's ultimate intention was to shut down all the Philadelphia area stores (Clark and Guben 1983). The union hired a food industry consultant to do preliminary feasibility studies on A&P stores. In January 1982, Guben contracted with PACE to enter into partnership to assist worker buyouts of several former A&P markets.[1]

During this period of consultation, Young was exploring other options, as well. He consulted the Busch Center of the Wharton School of the University of Pennsylvania, which advocated a quality of worklife program that restructured management. In the interest of saving jobs, he also went to other food store chains trying to interest them in buying some of the stores (Schaffer 1982b).

The Negotiation

On March 2, a few days after A&P gave the 20-day notice required in the union contract that it was closing its remaining Philadelphia stores, the union made a bid to purchase 21 of the to-be-abandoned stores. Immediately, local 1357 president Young held a meeting to explain to A&P-employed union members the idea of saving jobs through worker ownership. He announced that to buy in, each potential worker/owner would have to contribute $5,000, and asked for pledges of $200 to hold a place. Young told attendees that they would be able to make arrangements with the union's credit union to borrow the $5,000. By mid-March, orientation sessions began for the 500-600 workers who were interested in pledging. Jay and Merry Guben and Sherman Kreiner and Andrew Lamas of PACE jointly developed these planning and information sessions, with PACE concentrating on the cooperative structure and the Gubens focusing on business management topics.

By the time the stores actually shut down on March 20, A&P had still not responded to the buyout bid. Nevertheless, meeting and planning for the worker-owned stores proceeded. The reason for the delay was that Tengelmann, the West German parent company, had raised questions about the wisdom of moving out of the Philadelphia region (Kreiner and Lamas 1983). Perhaps domestic A&P management saw an opportunity to extract wage concessions as well. During March and April, A&P and UFCW locals 1357 (representing clerks) and 56 (representing meatcutters) began a round of talks. The unions, particularly local 1357, wanted to obtain options for workers to buy some stores and to get the right of first refusal to buy other stores A&P might decide to close in the future. A&P wanted wage and benefit concessions in exchange for restructured management and a reopened form of A&P.

At the end of April, slightly more than a month after 500-600 had pledged to become worker/owners and begun attending training sessions, the union announced an agreement with A&P, which provided for reopening stores as Super Fresh and granting options to former A&P workers to purchase up to four of the stores. A&P took the lead in establishing the Super Fresh identity, rehiring managers and workers, and beginning to design the quality of worklife program in cooperation with the Busch Center. The first Super Fresh stores actually opened in July 1982. Some former A&P workers were called back to begin working at Super Fresh, even while still attending worker/owner training meetings. Two stores were bought later that year by those still interested in worker ownership, and were opened under the O&O name in October and November.

Union-Management Concessions

In both O&O and Super Fresh, workers made concessions to save jobs. First, total compensation was cut in a number of ways. Both sets of workers lost about 20 percent of their hourly wage, although the meatcutters lost somewhat less. A clerk, for example, went from about $10 to $8 an hour (Whyte 1983). The starting wage for new hires, particularly in the unskilled "utility clerk" category, dropped to the federal minimum wage, $3.35 per hour. Overtime pay would begin after 10 hours per day instead of after eight as it had at A&P. The Sunday overtime rate was reduced from double to time-and-a-half, and the Saturday night overtime rate went from time-and-a-half to straight time. Workers in both settings gave up vacation time; senior employees entitled to four weeks of vacation lost three weeks for the first year of the contract. They also lost personal days and one holiday (Steiner 1982).

In many ways, these changes added up to

> a permanent two-tiered wage system, whereby new hires receive lower wages and fewer benefits for work equivalent to that performed by higher-paid existing employees-. . . . (Bureau of National Affairs 1985a; 1985b). New hires, depending on the job title, at one-half to three-quarters of the already reduced hourly rate of old A&P employees. In a word, new hires could never catch up with old hands, despite the fact that old A&P employees would only catch up to their prior hourly wage in the third year of the contract. (Blim 1985)

Third, the old A&P internal labor market was dismantled and reassembled. Concessions on seniority and staffing were sold as paths to flexibility and competitive efficiency. Super Fresh workers got single-store seniority, i.e., they could no longer transfer their seniority across stores. Essentially, this reduced A&P's high wage problem caused by senior workers bumping into other Super Fresh stores. Seniority was also lost in long-term layoffs. Moreover, because A&P chose to reopen fewer stores than it had closed, it effectively won the right to selectively call back old A&P employees (Blim 1985).

Fourth, work rule changes to save on labor costs, particularly on the assignment of hours, were instituted. Night crew workers were no longer promised two consecutive nights off. To workers, the most important changes may have been those with respect to the assignment of full-time jobs. The contract limited full-time jobs to 60 percent of the total number of jobs, determined on a store-by-store basis. In practice, most of the senior former A&P workers have had to settle for part-time jobs. Further, minimum hours of part-timers were cut in the interest of maintaining a low labor rate, i.e., the ratio of labor costs-to-revenues.

Together, these changes reinforce the tendency in service industries in general and in the grocery industry in particular toward bifurcation of the labor force into a small higher-paid, established, and protected senior component and a larger lower-paid, newer, and insecure junior component (Blim 1985). In 1984, for instance, two-tiered wage settlements were included in 35 percent of all airline contracts, 32 percent of contracts in the wholesale/retail sector, and 17 percent of agreements in both nonmanufacturing industries and motorized transportation (Salpukis 1985). In the food industry in 1984, three-fourths of the 400,000 members of the United Food and Commercial Workers were employed under two-tiered contracts (Ross 1985).

Two further contract provisions were presented as management concessions: a revenue-based bonus fund and a quality of worklife program. The bonus was envisioned as both a way for workers to gain back some of what they had given up in wages and as an incentive to keep labor costs low. It was to work as follows: Each store that kept its yearly labor costs below 10 percent of gross sales would receive at least 1 percent of the store's gross sales to be put into a fund. For every fraction of a percent store labor costs exceed 10 percent, the 1 percent bonus would be reduced by a fraction. For every fraction of a percent under 10 percent, the 1 percent bonus would be increased by a fraction. Part of the fund was to be an investment pool for workers to draw from in case they wanted to buy out any Super Fresh stores to close in the future. The other part was to be apportioned among employees within the particular stores according to the number of hours each worked in the course of the year and awarded annually.

The QWL program was to "provide a mutual basis for problem-solving." It was to be a joint labor-management set of arrangements to cooperate on methods and financial issues. Management was to be more flexible than in the past, with more autonomy given to store managers than under the traditionally centralized A&P system. Provision was made for involvement of managers, employees, and union representatives at the store and corporate levels. More information on the QWL arrangements will come later in this chapter.

How did these contract provisions compare with conditions at other markets? First, if Super Fresh kept wage costs below 10 percent of sales, they would be reducing by one-third the 15 percent labor cost A&P had before the shutdown. This would bring them below the industry average of 12 percent (Steiner 1982; "Worker Ownership . . . ''). Competitors have complained that the concessions gave Super Fresh an unfair advantage—a 20 percent lower wage than most of their competitors (Diamond 1983).

The lowered wage rate for Super Fresh has prompted other supermarkets in the area to try to extract similar concessions, although without restructuring management and increasing worker participation in decisionmaking as at Super Fresh. However, Nicholson (1985) makes a point that reinforces the conclusion reached earlier, namely, that A&P has been slow in adapting to change,

> [M]any of the changes in management attributed to the Super Fresh QWL Program had been implemented at Acme [a major rival chain, also organized by UFCW Local 1357] through more traditional methods (p. 147).

> [The effects of earlier Acme corporate decisions] are similar to those created by Super Fresh's redesign. These were reductions in the number of managers and management levels, decision making was pushed to lower levels of management, and an emphasis is placed on increased training and exchange of information between management levels (p. 149).

Continuing Efforts on the O&O Buyouts

Those A&P workers who wanted to stay in the O&O process after the establishment of Super Fresh had to come up with their $200 cash by the end of June and demonstrate that they could produce the remaining $4,800 by the first week in July. Local 1357 offered to lend them the money from the local's credit union. By this point, after Super Fresh stores opened, the number of prospective owners had dwindled to about 40.

Based on the feasibility studies done early in 1982, the Roslyn and Parkwood stores were highly rated among those the consultants recommended for bids. Recognizing the Roslyn store as having been very successful in the past, A&P offered two other stores at no cost in exchange for retaining the Roslyn store. The worker/owners-to-be at the Roslyn store rejected the offer.

The Parkwood store was, in fact, a second choice for the worker/ owners-to-be. Another store had been chosen, but physical problems with the foundation were discovered at the site. The group then decided to bid on the Parkwood store, which slowed their progress in starting up and actually opening their venture.

In the meantime, the union and consultants had been investigating various avenues for financing. They approached two national level financing sources required by law to consider worker cooperatives, the Small Business Administration (SBA) and the National Cooperative Bank (NCB). The NCB did not even go as far as to entertain a proposal. The SBA turned down an initial proposal for a 90 percent loan guarantee, but allowed submission of a revised proposal at the urging of Senator John Heinz (R) of Pennsylvania. The SBA's approval enabled the stores to get loans from Continental Bank in Philadelphia (Whyte 1983). The bank loans were not fully approved until after both stores actually began operating. The stores opened in the fall of 1982, Roslyn in mid-October and Parkwood a month later.

How did the owners match themselves up with stores? According to our interviews with them, the selection process was not complex. Their choice was primarily a matter of two factors—residential proximity and a judgment about what type of "personality" was best suited to each of the stores. Each of the owners had moved from one A&P store to another during A&P's last years, so they knew how stores differed, and they developed preferences for particular ones.

Though both stores are about the same distance from the center of the city in driving time, Parkwood is in the more urban Far Northeast section of Philadelphia, whereas the Roslyn store is located well outside the city limits. Immediately surrounding both stores are working class communities, but there are key differences in their locations. Roslyn itself is circled by several more affluent suburbs.

Parkwood draws mainly on the low-to-moderate income areas around it, including some public low-income housing, and local residents employed in nearby manufacturing industries. Residential structures near Parkwood are dominated by attached rows or apartment complexes of high density. The more uniformly single-family residential area surrounding Roslyn is dotted with commercial strips and malls. Chapter 5 will further discuss the ways in which social ties and former co-worker relations influenced recruiting for each store.

The Formal O&O Model

The banner across the front of the Roslyn O&O store reads, "We own it, We operate it, We care." This slogan describes the structure of the O&O supermarkets. As worker-owned cooperative businesses, the O&O markets are set up on the principle that each owner who has made the $5,000 investment has one share and one vote. Each member has equal participation in decisionmaking for the corporation. Profits are distributed based on "labor participation," that is, hours worked as a percentage of the total hours worked during a given period of time. Thus, when owners leave the cooperative for any reason, they are entitled to the return of their initial membership fee plus interest, and any profits allocated, minus losses (Kreiner and Lamas 1983). Their ownership share, however, would revert back to the cooperative, since the share is linked to the role of worker and not considered transferable or saleable (Clark and Guben 1983).

Participants in the O&O training program developed the by-laws jointly (so they were the same for both stores initially). The by-laws cover five areas of operations—corporate structure, membership, roles and responsibilities, profit allocation and distribution, and by-law amendments or changes. Membership essentially is defined as those who hold shares and work for the corporation. The store manager is not supposed to be a member of the cooperative, but is supposed to be hired from outside by the Board of Directors.

The entire membership is obligated to elect the Board of Directors annually. Reelection and rotation of board members has occurred in both stores more than once and more often than at annual intervals. The by-laws originally called for nine board members, although the Parkwood store lowered this number to five. (Parkwood dropped four slots because, with only 14 members, a nine-member board was considered too unwieldy).

The by-laws lay out the policies for authority and decisionmaking that define the roles of the manager, Board of Directors, and general membership. The scheme, referred to as the "Time Line, Money Line, and Member Line," provides criteria for evaluating decisions that determine what level in the organization—manager, Board or membership—has authority for any decision. The criteria include the immediacy of the decision, amount of money the decision would commit, and how many people would be affected by the decision (Whyte 1984). Those decisions involving amounts of money under $3,000, affecting fewer than seven members, or a daily time frame can be made by the store manager alone. Decisions concerning expenditures ranging from $3,000 to $10,000, affecting up to half of the members, or having a time frame of one to three years rest with the Board of Directors. Decisions involving over $10,000, affecting more than half the membership, or having a time frame of over three years are decided by the entire membership.

Members conduct business through meetings that occur regularly. The Board of Directors meets at least once a month or more frequently for specific issues as needed. In general, the board is responsible for setting goals and determining policies, overseeing the manager, and controlling finances. General meetings of the entire membership occur approximately once a month, although the by-laws require only one annual meeting. A member other than the Board president presides over the general membership meetings. Since the entire membership must vote on issues of wide impact, such as changing the Board of Directors or hiring and firing policies, these meetings are also called on an as-needed basis. Members can refer to an agenda posted before the store meetings and suggest additional agenda items for discussions. The membership has called for emergency or single-issue meetings on several occasions.

The by-laws detail the method of profit allocation to members and the corporation, policies for carrying out meetings and other procedures, and rules for changing the corporate structure. Changes in the by-laws have not been extensive and general operating procedures have evolved as the members gained experience in actually running the stores. The most significant change is that both stores currently have managers from within the ranks of the membership, for reasons which will be discussed later.

Implementation of the O&O Structure and Philosophy

The developers of training had no ready-made models or materials from which to prepare former A&P workers for operating worker-owned supermarkets. Devising the approach as they went along, the planners used three kinds of training settings. First, large orientation/news/announcement sessions were held periodically during the first two months, when the O&O idea was presented. Second, a series of substantive introductory sessions took place. Finally, the group formed into functional committees which met for the remainder of the training sessions. Union president Wendell Young convened the large meetings, but Sherman Kreiner and Andrew Lamas of PACE, with Jay and Merry Guben, created the training content, sometimes incrementally and disjointedly.

Training began as soon as the bid on the 21 stores was made. First, local 1357 called a large meeting. The consultants and union staffers explained the idea of O&O and recruited participants. PACE and the Gubens ran introductory sessions, repeated and scheduled at convenient times for interested former A&P employees, starting in the first week after the initial bid was made. These sessions were devoted to two topics, cooperative business structure and general business planning.

In the weeks that followed, Kreiner and the Gubens invited other consultants to involve the group in actively solving hypothetical cooperative business problems. At the introductory sessions, consultants from the Wharton School's Management and Behavioral Sciences Center encouraged participants to analyze problems encountered in their old jobs and to devise new systems.

Finally, the trainers divided the large group into functional committees for the remainder of the training period. The committees included the following:

By-laws and legal structure—to address self-management and worker co-operative law;

Governance—to allocate decisionmaking authority among the management, board of directors, and general assembly of worker/owners;

Union role and personnel policies—to discuss work rules, define the workers' relationship with the union, and outline the grievance procedure;

Worker selection and part-timers—to define the workers' roles and store staffing needs;

Umbrella association—to determine the feasibility of linking the stores in an association and to consider supplier affiliation;

Management selection—concerning store management, e.g., recruitment, selection criteria, training;

Financing and business planning—to acquire funding for start-up and to develop specific business plans for individual stores; and

Worker education—to put out a workers' newsletter, and to assume administrative duties such as public relations, organizing and scheduling meetings, etc.

In addition, one member from each committee was elected to a steering committee, which met weekly to coordinate information across committees. Participants gave the steering committee authority to make decisions for the group prior to the stores' start-up (*PACE News* 1982).

Although 500 people had originally expressed interest in the worker-ownership scheme in March 1982, as meetings progressed through April there were about 125 regular meeting attendees (Kreiner personal communication). A&P had still not responded to the bid so Kreiner's expectation was that there could be as many as 17 stores (the number was reduced from the original 21).

To accommodate the prospective worker/owners, meeting schedules were flexible, and most trainees came to the union hall for meetings two or three times a week. Individuals selected which committees they wanted to work on. They could participate in more than one committee and several switched committees during the training period. In later months, each store group formed a start-up committee for tasks necessary for getting the stores open (*PACE News* 1982). The functional committee meetings began in late April and continued for seven to eight months until the stores opened in the fall.

The attrition in the O&O group requires some further comment. The situation for the laid-off A&P workers in the spring and summer of 1982 was one of uncertainty and exploring possibilities. By the time the stores were identified and bids made, there were only 38 still involved.

Interviews with O&O owners revealed that few had made a commitment to worker-ownership right in the beginning. Many of them saw O&O as only one strategy to find work. A few continued to attend the meetings because of basic interest and time on their hands. Despite pledging in March, no cash changed hands until the end of June when the $200 pledge came due. The 500 early "pledgers" had not been financially committed. It seems plausible that many saw O&O as an "iron in the fire," but were attracted to Super Fresh, which suddenly materialized in late April. Furthermore, fewer worker/owner slots than originally anticipated were available. A&P's decision to reopen stores meant that no more than four stores would open as worker cooperatives. Many continued to attend O&O meetings anyway. They had no way of knowing whether they would actually be called to work at Super Fresh.

The fact that Super Fresh became a reality before O&O likely influenced workers' decisionmaking. The first Super Fresh store opened in July 1982, while the first O&O opening was not until fall. With job security foremost in their minds, and despite their negative view of A&P, dropouts probably doubted the O&O stores would ever open. Nevertheless, 38 met the $5,000 financial commitment and divided themselves up among the two stores, which were slated for bids by early June.

Differences Between the O&O Stores

Despite their legal and structural similarities, the development of the two O&O stores differed. As mentioned earlier, the Parkwood store had delays in opening. First, Parkwood became an alternative only when problems were found with another choice. Second, this switch affected the momentum of the group. Third, the delay in getting loan approval left members in a vulnerable financial position for the several months. The process went more smoothly at the Roslyn O&O store.

The stores also differed in basic physical characteristics. There is a significant size difference: 23,000 square feet and 24 owners for the Roslyn store compared to 13,500 square feet and 14 owners for Parkwood. Roslyn is a free-standing store on a heavily travelled suburban road. Two other supermarkets, each about two miles away, compete with the Roslyn O&O, since customers tend to shop within a three- to four-mile radius of home (Dirlam 1977). Parkwood, on the other hand, shares space with a variety of stores and a movie theater in an urban shopping center at a busy intersection. When it originally opened, there were no other supermarkets close by, but four stores later opened. Parkwood's location within the shopping center attracts shoppers who make small quantity purchases. Both stores changed their hours several times in adapting to the competition.

The two stores also had different experiences with their managers. The by-laws required experienced nonowner managers. One of the functional committees set up the hiring criteria, recruited, and narrowed the field of candidates. The committee members interviewed two finalists and tape recorded the interviews for the other owners. Both stores hired experienced former supermarket managers.

Only a few weeks after he started, the Roslyn manager had a heart attack. Once he returned, he and the Roslyn owners worked well together. He remained in the position until 1985 when he bought a food store of his own. The former assistant-manager, an owner, took over as manager. Seeing him as too much a product of the supermarket chains and not in tune with what they wanted for the store, the owner/workers came to believe they could run the store better themselves. After almost a year of operation, they let him go and appointed the president of their board as manager. He has held both positions since then.

A Third O&O Store

The Parkwood owners purchased an additional store (not a former A&P), located nearby in the small New Jersey town of Lambertville, near Trenton. The purchase came because of uncertainty whether the Parkwood O&O store would prove successful. Ironically, after the Lambertville purchase, Parkwood's performance improved. The 14 Parkwood owners are divided between the two stores, so fewer owners work in each of these stores than at the Roslyn O&O store.

Relationship Between the O&O Stores

No formal relationship exists between the Roslyn and Parkwood O&O stores; the proposed umbrella association to link the stores for mutual benefit was never formed. Both use IGA as their supplier. Occasionally, events and obligations bring owners together to represent the first worker-owned and -operated supermarkets.

The Formal Super Fresh Model

Super Fresh is a wholly-owned subsidiary of A&P. Major differences from its parent company, include: (1) a participatory management program(QWL); (2) a sales-based bonus plan; (3) an obligation to give workers the right of first refusal on buying any store to be closed; and (4) a single-store seniority system which restricts workers' mobility to a single store and eliminates the store-to-store "bumping."

Another unique structure established by the union at the time of the Super Fresh agreement was a fund for providing seed money for future worker-owned businesses. This fund, called the O&O Investment Fund, was to be financed by a percentage of the bonuses of

Super Fresh employees, and was intended to support the right-of-first-refusal clause in the Super Fresh agreement.

The new management structure adopted by Super Fresh was intended to increase worker participation in corporate decisionmaking, thereby increasing job satisfaction and productivity. Busch Center of the Wharton School of the University of Pennsylvania served as consultants in the design of their QWL program.

The consultants worked with a 30-member design team representing A&P/Super Fresh management, union staff, and full-time and part-time hourly employees (Steiner 1982; Ackoff 1984). Using the Busch Center's "Interactive Planning" method, the work of the team resulted in a design for the participation structure as described in the booklet, "Quality of Work Life for United Food and Commercial Workers Local 56 and Local 1357 with Super Fresh Food Markets."

Essentially, the approach sets up entities called "planning boards" for all levels or units of the corporation. The lowest level or smallest unit is the department, and the next levels are the store, region, and corporation. The exact content of decisions and concerns was not specified, although general guidelines for organizational strategies, policies and procedures were provided. The booklet describes planning boards as policymaking bodies, rather than "merely advisory committees," and it includes the proviso that "executive decisions will be left to respective managers." The booklet states that planning boards should meet regularly, but does not specify a schedule or minimum number of meetings.

Department planning boards include associates[2] within a department and the department manager. The store-level planning board consists of the store director, assistant directors, department managers, representatives of the Super Fresh president, two union representatives, and employees elected from each store department.

The corporate planning board consists of the Super Fresh president, the store directors, a representative associate from each supermarket selected by the store planning board, Super Fresh marketing directors, representatives from corporate support services units, the presidents of the union locals, representatives from A&P, and possibly outside shareholders. The regional planning boards are subunits of the corporate planning board for particular geographical units. The original design called for regional boards when enough stores began operating. Each regional board includes only those assigned to a particular region in addition to someone from Super Fresh corporate headquarters.

As the QWL handbook states, "Decision-making will be made at the lowest possible level where participation will be reflected by authority and responsibility." Participants at each level, then, set policy only for concerns that can be handled at that level or below, although they are encouraged to have input or make suggestions to higher levels.

The autonomy of each Super Fresh store is encouraged through a system of financing which incorporates sales incentives. The Super Fresh corporation receives all store sales minus direct costs. Super Fresh pays all indirect costs of corporate level services. Funds for business development at each store, however, are set aside as a percentage of each store's financial contribution to the Super Fresh corporation. All profits go to A&P, although Super Fresh can negotiate with A&P for reinvestment funds to use for expansion and renovation. Each store director has flexibility in pricing and product mix according to a four-category system, and although most inventory comes from A&P warehouses, individual store directors are allowed to use local vendors as well. In this way they are encouraged to try to tailor merchandise to customer tastes. Management also has an incentive fund, based on sales, employee satisfaction and the amount of financial contribution to Super Fresh.

As explained earlier, employee bonuses are tied to the stores' sales and labor costs. Employees get an annual bonus based on the hours they work, how well the store does, and the labor costs at that store. Each store has its own sales and labor cost incentives, and the bonuses vary across stores.

The O&O Investment Fund

UFCW local 1357 president Wendell Young conceived of the O&O Investment Fund as a mechanism to supplement financing of additional worker-owned businesses. The Fund was incorporated, had a director and Board of Directors. Young, who is generally recognized as the "architect" of the fund idea, sat on the 18-member board (Lin 1983). The Board included academics, business people, elected officials, and representatives from the two O&O supermarkets. Jay Guben, also president of a consulting firm called Grey Areas, served as acting director of the Fund until the spring of 1985, when PACE assumed the management role. The Investment Fund also established working committees which brought in others from the community to address specific issues related to business development and research.

Support for the Investment Fund was originally to come from a portion of Super Fresh employee bonuses. Under the Super Fresh agreement, the corporation was to contribute the amount employees pledged from their bonuses to a union-controlled "incentive and investment fund." The union would transfer the money to the O&O Investment Fund (Lin 1983). Initially, the employees were expected to pledge 60 percent of their bonus amounts to the Fund. The Fund directors assumed that the potential for becoming worker/owners would serve as the incentive for employees to pledge a portion of their bonus money. The first contributions to the fund would be made in the summer of 1983 after the first Super Fresh stores had been open for one year. The Fund's directors expected that the fund could receive as much as $750,000 in its first year, which they believed could leverage as much as $2.5 million through grants, investments or loan guarantees (Schaffer 1983).

These assumptions soon proved mistaken. First, UFCW local 56, the meatcutters, and Super Fresh employees represented by other union locals also opted out. In a May 1983 referendum, local 1357 workers voted to contribute 35 percent of their bonuses to the fund. However, a few months later when the bonuses came due, the retail clerks of local 1357 began to reconsider. Eventually, the contributions to the O&O Investment Fund were made voluntary and limited to 15 percent of any individual's bonus. Almost no one ended up contributing. (Schaffer 1983; Lin 1983).

Without the anticipated revenue, the O&O Investment Fund found itself with a large deficit. The Fund's director had already hired staff and committed money to such projects as an inner-city neighborhood convenience store, also to be called O&O, to be staffed by laid-off former A&P workers and community residents. Some months later, when the Fund's management was taken over by PACE, it was transformed from "a job-security insurance policy" for Super Fresh workers, as local 1357 President Young had termed it, into a conduit for royalties on the O&O logo which were to be paid by any new stores or business operating under employee ownership and connected to the O&O concept. As of mid-1987, three local supermarkets (none previously owned by A&P) had been converted to O&O stores and were paying a sort of franchise fee into the O&O Fund.

How does one interpret the workers' vote of no confidence in the Fund? When Super Fresh opened, the attrition from the original group of 500 interested in O&O suggested that most had seen O&O merely as one possible alternative. This view is even borne out in interviews with O&O workers, where half indicated that they had not initially been committed to O&O, or had seen it as a hedge against no job at all. Those offered positions with Super Fresh faced a choice between a familiar, low-risk option and a novel, high-risk option. Most chose the former. For the same reasons, Super Fresh workers had little incentive to give up the bonus that could help make up for lost income for an O&O Investment Fund set up to give them a buy-out option at a future time. The current success of the Super Fresh stores had reduced their concern about needing such an option in the future.

Furthermore, workers' negative view of the union transferred to the Fund, which was perceived as a creation of the union. Despite the fact that the union was instrumental in saving their jobs, many workers distrusted it and did not see it as concentrating on their best interests.

The Right of First Refusal

One feature of the Super Fresh agreement of which the union and PACE were particularly proud was the right-of-first-refusal clause. The clause gave employees 90 days to purchase a store slated for closing. PACE and the union saw the right-of-first-refusal agreement as a way to afford workers a degree of job security. As Steiner points out, "even if Super Fresh employees decide not to operate a store, they have the right to buy it and immediately re-sell it to the owner of their choice" (Steiner 1982, p. 23).

Expansion of the Super Fresh Corporation

The Super Fresh corporation has opened new stores at a very fast rate—well beyond its original promise to reopen 20 stores. By the end of 1982, Super Fresh had opened 30 markets employing 1500 workers (Kreiner & Lamas 1983). By the beginning of July 1983, there were 51 stores reopened or converted from A&P in the Philadelphia, South Jersey, and Delaware areas. Super Fresh was in fifth place among food retailers in sales and market share in the region. UFCW local 1357 represents the workers in 27 of these stores (Schaffer 1983) with the remainder represented by locals in New Jersey, Southern Pennsylvania, and Delaware. By mid-1985, there were 59 Super Fresh stores open in the three states, and Super Fresh had climbed to third place among the five giants in Philadelphia food retailing in market share and sales.

QWL Training and Implementation

To implement QWL in a particular store, Super Fresh employees were urged to undergo some training. The initial training, under the Busch Center, was done with two stores with an eye to refining the approach there. Then Busch would work with half of the store directors, followed by the workers in their stores, and the upper ranks of management. However, since A&P hurried to open stores in the summer of 1982, most of the stores were opened without staff receiving QWL training.

Training consisted of an orientation to the QWL structure. The Busch Center did not actually conduct training sessions until November 1982, four months after the first stores opened (Steiner 1982). Most stores opened and operated as conventionally-managed supermarkets for some period of time.

The Busch Center's contract expired in January 1983. Several months later, consultants established an in-house training capability. According to Nicholson (1985), "half the employees in a store were brought together for training in among other things, problem solving and team building" (p. 80). They were also encouraged to develop a plan for how QWL would work in their store. Super Fresh's QWL program was designed to adapt to situations in specific stores. Training focused on the process of QWL rather than on the content of meetings or even what, beyond a few basics, constituted a good quality of worklife. After a store underwent training, the trainers (either the consultants or later Super Fresh's in-house staff) encouraged planning boards to meet. Meeting frequency and content were not specified and varied widely across the stores, as we will see in chapter 5. Training in QWL, however, continued to lag behind the store openings. The A&P stores converted later in the region waited the longest time before receiving it.

Implications of the Super Fresh Labor Agreement

As Nicholson (1985) and Blim (1985) have shown, several features of the Super Fresh arrangements have potentially greatest significance for the operation of the stores. These conditions, which are in line with A&P chairman James Wood's goals of reducing labor costs while providing more service include: (1) the wage and benefit reductions, (2) the two-tiered wage structure, (3) the elimination of almost all full-time employment, (only department head or assistant manager positions are full time), (4) the use of high-turnover, low-wage, part-time employees, (5) selectivity in rehiring former A&P employees, and (6) the bonus plan.

The bonus plan, in many ways, can have unintended consequences, in combination with other elements of the cost reduction strategy. For one thing, "the responsibility for the major source of conflict between the corporation and its employees, that is, keeping the labor-rate low, has been transferred to the hourly employees themselves" (Nicholson 1985, p. 177). Similar to a piece-rate pay plan, the bonus could pit worker against worker, although with a different twist. It would seem to be in the interest of workers to reduce the hours of highly-paid workers, in order to keep the labor rate low, insofar as they can influence that. For the union, that may mean that the traditional source of strength, the senior workers, are in disfavor with other workers. For the senior workers, it is a catch-22, in that the more work they do, the lower the bonus to be shared among workers in the store. Nicholson (1985) notes, "some [assistant directors and department managers] recognize that instead of fostering cooperation, as it may have been intended, the [bonus] sets employees against each other" (p. 182). The further discussion in chapter 5 indicates that the workers themselves are well aware of these implications.

Conclusions

The O&O and Super Fresh attempts at job-saving occurred in an extremely turbulent economic environment. The immediate backdrop was the recession, but there were structural changes taking place in Philadelphia's economy and in the grocery industry, and radical changes in A&P corporate strategy. A&P had once been the proud leader, but had fallen behind the other firms in the industry and was trying to revamp itself through downsizing and a tough negotiating stance with labor.

In this setting, UFCW local 1357 had prepared for a fight and developed an unusual strategy promoting ownership and management by workers. A&P returned to the bargaining table with an innovative extension of its developing marketing and labor strategies. A landmark agreement was fashioned through the creation of Super Fresh. Two worker buyouts did take place, while the bulk of the stores and jobs threatened with closure were converted to Super Fresh.

The labor agreement, particularly at Super Fresh, involved significant labor concessions—a wage cut, two-tiered wages, and revised seniority rules—together with management restructuring through QWL and productivity sharing through a bonus plan. It was a bitter pill for workers, but 2,000 jobs were saved, and management practices would be reformed.

Worker/owners at O&O stores seemed to be getting several things in return for their sacrifices that Super Fresh workers were not: capital investments, autonomy on the job, self-determined training, and democratic decisionmaking at all levels. Super Fresh workers, by contrast, received externally-designed and-run training (if they received training at all), and the contradictory implications of the combination of QWL and bonus programs with A&P's part-timer labor strategy.

At least formally, then, the implementation of the store types manifested the advantages and disadvantages of each. Worker/owners had risks to face and had to learn quickly how to succeed in business, but they had complete involvement in the processes and outcomes of work. Super Fresh workers had saved their jobs and received some involvement in decisions and profits, but their involvement was constrained and limited, chiefly owing to formal impediments.

NOTES

1. Around this time, Wendell Young attended a conference at the National Center for Employee Ownership that included Russell Long on ESOPs and Sherman Kreiner giving an orientation about co-ops. According to Kreiner, Young concluded that the cooperative structure was definitely the way he wanted to go.

2. Store managers at Super Fresh are directors; employees are associates.

5
The Implementation Process

Chapter 4 described the setting in which two workplace innovations were conceived and implemented from the top down. The theory of both innovations was that the exchange of wage and benefit cuts—on the one hand for economic incentives (bonus or profit-shares) and more worker influence on how work is done on the other hand—would lead to effective workplaces. Those who designed the changes expected that, through increased participation, the workers would achieve more autonomy over their working conditions, the hierarchy of power would decrease, all levels would be brought closer together, and everyone would be provided with a role in decision-making. The range of issues subject to worker control varied considerably between the two store-types; it was all-inclusive in the worker-owned stores and limited in Super Fresh.

In the initial process of formal change, consultants for the union undertook the training of future O&O workers, while others helped A&P to train workers for QWL. This chapter will look at the major facets of the actual process of implementation of the innovations in each of six intensively studied stores, as described by the workers. First, neither in the O&O stores nor in the individual Super Fresh stores was there random selection of workers. The very ways in which workers were recruited affected store social processes. Second, the implementation of the new forms of participation was affected by variations in the commitment of leaders and consistency of follow-through. Third, our analysis involves the unanticipated and unintended informal social processes which significantly influenced the establishment of worker ownership and QWL. Some of these informal processes can be traced to the continuation of former chain-wide patterns of power relationships. Others can be related to the continuity of specific ties of loyalty to former bosses and co-workers in each store. Still others can be tied to the morale problems in stores, which were affected by contradictions in the contract, by the social composition of the stores and by crisis events that occurred.

In-Person Interviews

The information on which this analysis is based comes from the intensive, face-to-face interviews with workers in the six stores most thoroughly investigated. These included two worker-owned O&O stores and four Super Fresh stores with different degrees of participation. The interview schedule included both open-ended questions and rating scales. The interviews took one to two hours and consisted of five topical areas: (1) career histories; (2) responses to the threatened store closing (perceptions of options and actions); (3) information about families (composition, economic situation, leisure and lifestyle); (4) descriptions and evaluations of participation in the stores; and (5) hopes and expectation for the future.

We tape-recorded the interviews, transcribed them, and prepared a codebook to best reflect differences in responses. Interviews were coded and then analyzed for frequencies and correlations.

We used the material from the personal interviews in three important ways. First, knowledge gleaned from the interviews led to the ultimate grouping of the four Super Fresh stores closely studied as QWL and non-QWL. Our initial assumption that earlier establishment of the program and greater local union support would increase the degree of QWL implementation was not accurate. After we looked directly at the informal process of implementation in the stores, we regrouped the stores as QWL and non-QWL according to the degree of active QWL which had been *actually implemented.* These regroupings agreed with each shop steward's assessment of the strength of QWL in each store.

Second, to develop the self-administered survey, we used the ways in which workers described the innovation and characterized the workplace, their life goals, etc. Our new, in-depth understanding of the way workers thought about their jobs, careers and life goals helped us construct the shorter, more structured instrument used to test the worker outcomes model (chapter 6).

In this chapter, we describe how informal social processes affected the implementation of the innovation. Of particular importance is the role played by the persistence of old roles, expectations and power relationships and their influence on the way each of the new stores was assembled. This provides insight about the way "worker characteristics" (gender, age, skills, and experience) relate to each other. Chainwide patterns of social organization reveal that access to power, knowledge and opportunity is not randomly distributed to all departments and positions.

In addition to chainwide patterns, critical store-specific social processes affected the development of participativeness and, in turn, store and worker outcomes. The process of store formation (the way new store members were recruited) differed between Super Fresh and O&O stores. The degree to which former co-workers were kept together, and the degree to which recruitment brought in workers from key or marginal sectors of former stores, experienced and inexperienced people, and those who were better off or worse off in the new store all affected the store's social process. Managerial experience and style affected each store as well. Finally, each store underwent a unique series of special events and crises which helped to solidify or rupture the experiments with participation. These social patterns help to explain some of the outcomes more formally measured in chapters 6 and 7. One finding relevant to the model-testing in those chapters was that in Super Fresh stores, having a full-time job was almost always identical with department head status. Moreover, these full-time elites were the major "winners" in the innovation, those who did not lose position or hours in the transition.

Chainwide Patterns

Informal Social Organization of Supermarkets: Differential Power and Knowledge

To understand how the former social system has persisted, it is important to look at customary practices developed over the years in the supermarket industry. In spite of formal administrative rules, supermarkets, like all workplaces, have developed informal social structures of roles, opportunities, and power which are shared throughout the industry, and in which supermarket employees have spent their work lives. These real but informal systems were not considered by the innovators, who concentrated on changing the official, formal structures of work. The informal patterns provide crucial insights about what happened.

Supermarkets are, in general, organized into several different social units which vary in opportunities for learning skills, for moving up, for working in teams and for acquiring knowledge about the store as a whole. Formally, the store consists of departments based on the specific product handled, (e.g., meat, produce, etc.). Each department has a "head" or manager who reports to the local chain of command: the assistant managers and the manager.[1] While the formal organization chart treats all departments as equal, there are significant informal differences between them in power and access to information.

The core of the store is the grocery department, whose head is the grocery manager. The grocery manager controls all products but meat, deli and produce. Within groceries, one person—called a manager but with no other employees—is responsible for frozen food and one is responsible for dairy. These two junior managers and the "receiver" who deals with vendors and handles incoming orders are not equal to department heads. However, their guaranteed full-time work and their opportunities for learning business skills (referred to as "paper-work," such as inventory, ordering, etc.) make them important positions in the industry's vertical career ladders. These positions are held by men, who, along with the grocery manager and top store hierarchy, spend time together in the office and are in constant communication about store business. The grocery department is also the administrative home of the night crew, the socially isolated stock clerks who work the night shift when shelves are stocked.

The "back of the store"—the second major component—consists of the meat room and deli, which are physically contiguous and socially intertwined. The job of a meat cutter is skilled, and access is controlled through an apprentice system. Meat cutters—most of whom work full time—tend to belong to a different union local than the retail clerks. The meat wrappers and deli clerks are females, who also belong to this local. Although meat wrapping is a dead-end job, it provides better wages and hours than other "women's" jobs. Consequently, access to meat wrapping positions is also controlled, not by formal apprenticeships, but through informal social connections. Because of their physical separation from the rest of the store, and because meat is a major source of store profit, meat room workers think of themselves as the elites of the store and develop extreme internal solidarity. Joking relationships and close camaraderie— "one big happy family"—prevail. Trust and loyalty are evident in meat room/deli relationships.

The third component, the produce department, is small and similar to the meat department in being physically separate within the store, in requiring very specialized skills, in having a unique set of vendors and specialists, in having problems related to display, freshness and spoilage. However, produce has less "clout" than the meat room. Produce further suffers from being a department with high inventory "shrinkage" due to perishability and customer foraging.

The fourth major component of the store is the "front end" or cashier stations. The front end is a female world of dead-end jobs characterized by part-time hours, competition for favored schedules and fragmented worktime with no opportunity for peer interactions (e.g., cashiers work few hours a week, rarely the same from week to week and take breaks individually). Their interaction is with customers and not with each other.

Women comprise more than half of the store personnel, but because they are primarily part-time workers, they comprise much less than half the payroll. The only routes upward for front-end women are opportunities as front-end manager and in the office (bookkeeping, head cashier, etc.). Like the female meat wrappers, women in the office become loyal and trusted sidekicks to the store management and inner circle of grocery leaders. Women in the office reprimand cashiers about till shortages, which can lead to suspension and other penalties. They are also involved in scheduling cashiers, a task with a lot of pressure due to the competition for "gravy" hours, as good schedules are called. Several women talked with our interviewers about turning down positions in the office. Some said that they would "miss the customers." Others talked about "the pressure" and several said they would have accepted these tasks if office jobs provided opportunity for advancement. However, the most a woman can achieve in the office is the role of loyal assistant to the male workers.

In summary, the store consists of four major parts: groceries, the back (meat/deli), produce, and the front end. One informant talked about his store as "three separate stores." The grocery department contains vertical career opportunities for men, meat is limited in recruitment by an apprentice system, and the front end is a dead-end for women in the workforce. The only positions for women outside the front end are in subordinate positions in the meat room, deli and office.

Worker Characteristics: Type of Workers and Types of Careers

Traditional career patterns in the former A&P supermarkets exhibit a strong internal labor market. Except for meat cutters, almost everyone enters the job at the same level with no skills or experience. Subsequent career trajectories are very different, however. The following patterns are drawn from the 140 career histories collected. All of the workers came from working-class backgrounds, with 60 percent of their parents in blue-collar work, 30 percent in low-level white-collar jobs, 5 percent in farming/mining and 5 percent in small business.

Sixty percent of the current workers were brought into their present jobs by relatives, friends or neighbors who worked in the local store. Of the 40 percent remaining, half got their jobs by walking into their local store. Only 20 percent were hired through a more formal process (application to central office, response to advertisement).

Sixty-seven percent began their supermarket careers at age 14-20 (high school or college years). Almost all of the remaining third are women who entered their jobs upon returning to work after child-bearing or childrearing. Most men had no other work experience except for the military, while women did have experience in other kinds of work. For everyone who entered before the last decade, the supermarket industry was seen as very secure. This was the period of rapid post-war expansion. Over and over, workers stated that groceries was a good industry since "people had to eat," and one worker said "it was steady, like a government job." Sixty-six percent of the workers did not initially plan to make a career in the market.

It is likely that many who entered this workforce to earn money during school years eventually left. Our workers are those who remained because of perceived advantages. Many spoke of the advantages of the hourly wage rate in the industry and the security advantages compared to other comparable jobs; but for men, the opportunities to move through vertical career ladders were also apparent. While women remained part time, men tended to move to full time within one or two years. Women in the front end frequently told of watching 16-year-olds move into the grocery department after several months, when they would have gladly taken the vacancy. One male explanation for this is that grocery clerks need to move large heavy cartons of stock. Young men are quickly put "on the floor" (groceries) where they begin to learn "the business." One woman told of feeling humiliated when a 16-year-old with several months experience was given the keys (the right to open and close the store) when several women with over 10 years experience were present.

Knowledge about vendors and "paperwork" (inventory, ordering, etc.) was available through a variety of both formal and informal positions. Because stores are open more than 40 hours a week, there was an elaborate system of "back-up" personnel needed for times when an incumbent was not there. The managers and assistant managers were backed by a "third man," not formally recognized in title or pay, but able to learn how to run the store and gain the trust of the leadership. The dairy and frozen food managers, the receiver, and the night crew boss were in similar positions for acquiring both knowledge and trust. Moreover, someone has to back-up the dairy and frozen food managers when they are not present.

People used to position themselves in these strategic spots to learn about the business and to develop ties with managers and external chain supervisors (itinerant regional supervisors specialized in groceries, meat, deli, produce, etc.). They used these ties to scout opportunities for moving up in other stores. When the chain was expanding to the suburbs in the 1960s and early 1970s, many positions became available with each new store. More recently, opportunities have only come about as a result of retirement, resignation and sick leave. The strategy has been to engineer a transfer to a store where such a vacancy is expected to open, and then back-up the departing person. Currying favor with managers or external supervisors has been important because such ties could help to locate an opportunity and accomplish the transfer. One way to curry favor has been through working a stint on the night crew, which is hard to staff with reliable people, or to be willing to come in on short notice to fill in for absentees or to work weekends. The careers of successful men used to depend on a vertical series of planned transfers. These led to well-dispersed positive reputations within the corporation and the union. It was important to be identified as an up-and-coming worker. While these patterns based on interstore mobility can help to explain how the new stores recruited their workers (see below), they are no longer relevant in either the O&O or Super Fresh stores.

Movement from store to store did not always mean upward mobility. In recent years, movement was triggered by the frequent closings and the "bumping" rights of more senior workers. Several patterns of rapid demotion developed as senior department heads displaced regular full-time meat wrappers and so on. Those at the bottom were laid off.

In this section, we focus on career patterns before the major chain problems began. Even in better times, there were patterns of downward movement. Male employees who entered the industry at 18 or 20 were rapidly moved up in the first decade. When they became department managers, they could either choose to move to corporate management (product supervisors, warehouse jobs, etc.) or stay in the union and become assistant managers. Another common goal was to use the business knowledge acquired in the chain to buy their own store. This was most frequent among butchers and those with high-level grocery positions.

Store managers were out of the collective bargaining unit and had constrained discretionary power. Product supervisors from the regional office dealt directly with department heads. Decisions on ordering and displays came directly from headquarters. Managers handled predominantly personnel matters: schedules, transfers, etc. As a result, managing was not always desirable as a career choice.

Since there was no room for all male workers at the top, many were stabilized at lower level while others experienced patterns of demotion. While transfers to achieve better positions were voluntary and often initiated by the worker himself, other transfers were chain-initiated. They often involved inconvenient locations, tough managers and were intended to encourage workers to leave.

Transfers were thus used to punish male workers who had "bad reputations." Men who had risen to department head but were strong-willed and often in conflict with managers, were subject to demotions, loss of hours and frequent transfers. Some report being transferred to "punishment" stores with autocratic managers who would "bring them down." Women who ran into trouble were also transferred to inconvenient stores as punishment. Several of our interviewees had protected themselves through the union, however. They had frequently grieved transfers and were soon left alone.

In addition, there were many older workers nearing age 50 and their 30-year retirement option. Those whose careers had leveled off during their prime years when competition was strong were often seen as "dead wood." They were moved around in order to "protect" jobs for the manager's preferred workers.

Except for some office jobs, only female department heads (deli, front end) were full time. Even these jobs were not frequently given to women. Meat wrappers, while given more hours than cashiers, were rarely full time. A very few women with specific skills as bookkeepers or meat wrappers had made some vertical moves as new stores opened with positions available, but most moves for women were horizontal. Their moves were made to accommodate domestic needs, such as residential moves or new hours to fit with children's activities.[2]

Other A&P workers had extremely stable careers, spending years and sometimes decades in the same job and store. This pattern was more common for women, but also characterized the careers of several men. Individuals who had spent over 20 years in the industry but had stayed at the same level in hours and position at one or two stores were common. These steady jobs required a manager's protection, especially during the troubles of the past decade when workers were bumped from store to store on the basis of seniority. A manager could protect a job by transferring less favored workers with more seniority to a reasonably high-level position at an inconvenient store where they were likely to resign, or by securing a bumping for a favored worker to a "good" store with a paternalistic manager. People with this kind of career used family metaphors to describe their workplace. When asked to describe their ambitions in the former store, they overwhelmingly reported that they just wanted to do the best job they could and to make their store the best store. Women were especially likely to state this as their ambition. These workers strongly valued the stability and regularity of their former jobs. They missed their former stores and were less satisfied with their new situation.

In the new setting, they continued to look to their store leaders as patrons, thus ignoring the new potential for active self-determination. They also continued to state a desire to work hard and promote the store welfare as their major ambition. While this view could be interpreted as a result of the new emphasis on teamwork, it is really a continuation of their former goals.

One career pattern we expected to find more frequently than we did involves using the supermarket job as a part-time supplement to a full-time job. This is clearly what the Super Fresh corporation wants most workers to do today. Corporate leaders talk about their jobs as not being intended as primary sources of household incomes.

The first Super Fresh president, Gerry Good, stated several times that, "This is not a welfare system. Workers should not expect to support a family with a supermarket job." However, such a supplemental income strategy only occurred for 12 percent of the male workforce interviewed. In these cases, primary jobs included teaching, firefighting, the construction trades and working in family-owned businesses.

In summary, there are several career patterns, to which gender and age are very significant, which formerly predominated in the industry: (1) The vertical career, which is only available to men and is pursued by those who place themselves in positions to acquire business skills and important patrons as sources of power in order to move up the informal and formal ladders. (2) Horizontal "punishment" transfers, used before the chain's economic decline of the last decade, for "mavericks" who argued with managers or for older workers perceived as "dead wood." (3) Convenience moves, particularly by women, after a change of residence or family schedule. (4) Little movement between stores, a pattern more common for women, who developed strategies of loyalty to assure the protection of a manager, but which applies to men as well. (5) Part-time careers to supplement another full-time job. While today the industry managers see this as the preferred pattern, it rarely occurred in the past.

The union, managers and chain supervisors shared significant information about workers. The chain was and continues to be a relatively closed system. Workers brought spouses and children in. Union staff and current Super Fresh leaders often came up the ranks together. The former A&P workforce of 2,000 was a small community where people knew each other personally, by face or by name. It was easy to get information about most people through one's personal network of contacts in the chain. Reputations outside the store were very important in explaining decisions about participation in the O&O stores. They also help to explain the "call-back" process used by Super Fresh. The order of recall, the quality of store, the position level and the hours for individuals depended on their reputation and clout in the A&P community.

Household Economic Vulnerability: The Importance of
Age Cohorts

The interviews also revealed differences between the experiences of different age and gender cohorts. Not only were gender and age significantly related to career trajectory (skills, knowledge, power), but also to economic vulnerability (the degree to which one's household was dependent on the supermarket income). These factors affected the responses of workers to the A&P shutdown, to recall at Super Fresh, and to new opportunities at O&O.

Most of those entering the supermarket during the difficult past 10 years were 20-30 years old. Most of those younger workers who were successful in keeping jobs were related to old-time supermarket workers. Many were not married, lived at home and considered their income as mostly disposable—for hobbies and recreational activities.

Men aged 30-50 tended to be family men with children at home; they had often achieved vertical careers before the decline. This group had been given the leadership roles in all the new stores. They can be categorized in terms of economic vulnerability: those with working wives and those with homemaker wives. Of those with working wives, a small number had spouses with full-time, middle-level jobs (owning small shops, selling real estate, teaching, nursing); the others had wives with pink-collar, clerical jobs. The most common spouse's job was as a fellow supermarket worker. These secondary sources of income made a difference in the adjustments workers made to the changes in O&O and Super Fresh stores. The men with working spouses were less concerned about the risks of O&O or part-time hours at Super Fresh, since their income was not as vital to the household.

The men over 50 with fewer dependents at home were all thinking of retirement and perhaps second careers. With a pension plan which took effect after 30 years, many were counting the years to this transition. They were less interested in their current work situation than in the future.

Women's age cohorts had different economic needs than men's. While women from 18-22 were, like young men, unmarried and living at home, women in their later 20s were likely to have children. Women aged 23-50 were in the family-rearing stage of the life cycle; many were divorced single mothers. Another large group of women had husbands who were disabled or laid off. Their incomes were also more than supplementary to the household. For both these groups, full-time hours and career mobility were seen as necessary but unattainable. Many of these women wanted full-time jobs and some expressed interest in vertical careers. Thus, while chain policy was based on the assumption that women were willing part-time workers providing supplemental income, this was not true for almost half of the women interviewed.

Women over 50 needed to work to a later age to be eligible for pensions, since they had entered the workforce later or had interrupted their careers. While they had no child dependents, many of these women were widowed, single, or had husbands who were disadvantageously retired, laid off or disabled.

In sum, young entrants to this workforce (women under 22 and men under 30) had experienced hard times but were economically independent. Men from 30-50 had family responsibilities, but many had working wives to supplement income. They were often in a much better position than the large number of women (23-50) whose income was central to their household. Women over 50 were also in less advantageous positions regarding the achievement of timely and adequate retirement income.

Store-Specific Social Processes

For both the O&O and Super Fresh stores, each local workplace underwent a unique process of social formation. The transitions to worker ownership and to QWL were molded and somewhat transformed in each store through differences in recruitment of new workers and in the perpetuation of old relationships, roles and power. These informal social processes greatly affected the degree to which change occurred in each of the six store settings. Important factors included the degree to which former co-workers were recruited to a store, the social composition (in terms of gender, age cohorts, department of origin and career trajectory and economic vulnerability), the manager or leader's style and the critical turning points and events. These in turn seem to have affected the degree to which participative structures were used and the degree to which they were effective.

Choosing Worker Ownership or QWL

As we saw in chapter 4, more than 600 workers signed pledges for worker-owned stores, but less than one-tenth remained after the Super Fresh openings were announced. This group eventually was reduced to 40 as individuals dropped out. How were those who stayed with the O&O different from the rest?

When we asked people to state their reasons for choosing O&O, their responses fell into the following patterns. Most workers chose O&O stores because they did not like or trust A&P. Some waited to be called back to Super Fresh and then examined both concrete options. Others decided right away to avoid A&P. Many voiced the view that they had watched the chain make contradictory and capricious decisions over the years as a result of centralized decisionmaking. They felt they could do a better job.

Job security was the most frequently expressed concern. O&O workers did not trust A&P to stick with the Super Fresh innovation or to succeed. Full-time hours and control over one's schedule and position were also an area of concern. Workers knew their reputations and could evaluate whether their chances for full-time hours or a "living wage" were good at Super Fresh and acted accordingly. This was especially important to women and to the "mavericks" who had lost their influence and position at A&P and had blemished reputations. People who saw the system of patronage as capricious and distasteful wanted to avoid it.

While avoiding A&P was more frequently stated as a reason, a few expressed positive reasons for choosing O&O. The most frequently stated specific reason was a desire to be an entrepreneur, to own one's own business. This is not surprising since it had long been a career goal for many in the industry. Others talked less specifically about a desire for a life change, a "challenge," "something new," indicating the willingness for risk or adventure. Almost no one specifically mentioned worker ownership or democratic worker participation as a motive, but two workers did mention being attracted to the "O&O concept." Changes were mostly discussed in *personal* terms—"I would be working for myself," "I might make more money," etc. Goals emphasized were higher income, the purchase of more stores and fewer owners sharing the profits.

The dominant reason expressed by Super Fresh workers for *not* choosing worker ownership was the social complexity of collective decisionmaking: "getting stuck with people you don't know or like." Several said they had thought about going into business for themselves, "but if I did it I would do it right—buy my own store." Others talked about going in with former co-workers on their own as better than having this change controlled by outsiders.

Turning from what workers said about their reasons to questions of demographic/career differences between the two groups, we see clear patterns which underscore the stated explanations:

(1) People who chose O&O stores formed their stores in such a way as to minimize the risks of "too many bosses" and "getting stuck" with undesirables. In one store, more than half of the workers were experienced males aged 30-50 who had worked with each other before as elites in former stores. This mutually known or vouched-for group became the core of the store. In the other store, several dyads or triads of friends/former co-workers, and even pairs of relatives (parent-child, brothers-in-law, uncle-nephew) opted for the new experiment together. Thus former ties and loyalties mitigated against the concern about collaborating with strangers of unknown capability.

(2) The O&O stores, compared to Super Fresh, contained a significant proportion of "mavericks" with histories of conflict with former managers or union grieving. They also contained the most outspoken women, several of whom were primary breadwinners. Both of these groups needed full-time work and as-

sessed their opportunities at Super Fresh negatively. The women achieved full-time hours at O&O, but the opportunities for new leadership for women have still been limited.

(3) Each O&O store contained a majority of those who had been in dominant grocery and meat positions where they had acquired significant business knowledge. None of the Super Fresh stores contained as large a proportion of such experienced, knowledgeable and confident workers.

(4) Several workers chose O&O to spread the risk in households that had had two A&P pay checks. While the spouse or parent with the greatest opportunity at Super Fresh stayed with the chain, the other family member chose O&O.

Formation of the O&O Stores

The following section will describe similarities and differences between the two O&O stores (A and B) in the process of formation and their resulting social composition. This will be followed by discussion of the formation of Super Fresh stores (C,D,E,F). Discussion of implementation and resulting practice of participation in the stores will also follow.

Store A

One cannot overemphasize the importance of both social ties and the particular store selected in the process of formulation of the O&O store. In the smaller store, Store A, the role played by a closely knit group of nine former co-workers was critical to the workers' decisions to participate. Here, the store involved in the buyout changed over the course of the summer when the desired store was found to have a weak foundation and another store was substituted. The commitment within the group was very strong, however. Although a few people left the group (four left in the summer and one right after the store opened), this turned out to be an advantage since the substitute store did not have the volume to carry as many members as the first one.

In Store A, half of the members (seven) were males ages 32-45. All of them had known each other before, most having worked together in one recent store. All these men had occupied key positions before as department heads, or other positions which provided operational knowledge. They all considered one man as the primary leader. He had taken the lead in recruiting them and keeping them together. While all of these men had families, they also all had wives who worked. None of them was extremely vulnerable economically. They had also all had another option, having been called back to Super Fresh. The core group recruited one woman and one young male from their former store to join them.

The remaining five members were women and older males who were not former co-workers. Four of these five workers chose O&O because it was their only chance for full-time work. Older workers and women were less likely to be given full-time work by Super Fresh. The fifth had been offered full-time work, but was one of the few whose primary motivation was the concept of worker ownership.

The store was thus constructed around a core of former co-workers. As one member of the group said, the leader "wanted a stacked deck." Only one individual in the store was economically vulnerable as the sole support of a family. All of the other workers either had no dependents or had working spouses.

Members of the core group in this store often referred to each other as "my partners." There were several negative remarks made about the idea of a cooperative. One person said, "I don't like the co-op idea. Everyone is not equal. Some are satisfied with less." Other comments were, "I'm not into the concept; I had friends here" and "This is not the wave of the future; there are too many personalities."

Store A workers distanced themselves from the O&O consultants early in the experience. First, they shunned media attention and the talk-show obligations which the other store accepted. They tended to use their supplier, IGA, as the primary source of information about planning (ordering, inventory control, scheduling labor efficiently, etc.) and development. Several people said they would rather be called IGA than O&O. This was in contrast to Store B, which had a major confrontation with IGA over the lack of prominence given to the O&O logo in their newspaper advertisements.

The purchase of a second store by the Store A corporation (accomplished in 1984) was planned from the beginning. The men in the core group often talked about buying more stores to be run by part-time labor (as opposed to the goal of having all workers be owners).

All of this underscores the view that this store was formed by a group of successful, former co-workers who had acquired business skills through their vertical careers. They were more attracted to the entrepreneurial possibilities of the new stores than to the cooperative movement. While three members (including the leader) specifically spoke about the idea of worker ownership at length, this was unusual.

Store B

The larger O&O store has been more committed to the "concept" from the beginning. For this store, location was extremely important for three-fourths of those interviewed. Over and over, people said that this was a first-rate store (potentially) and that they would have dropped out if other stores had been assigned. Social ties also made a difference. Only 3 out of the 25 did not know any new co-workers. There were three pairs of very close friendships, and three pairs of relatives: a mother and son, an uncle and nephew and two brothers-in-law, as well as several people who had worked together or with close friends or relatives of each other in the past. Several workers had been co-workers of as many as five to six others before. Some workers reported being specifically recruited by former co-workers as stores were forming and specific skills were needed. Some reported being close friends of the fathers of two of the younger male owners and of the husband of one of the female owners. There was much testimony to the importance of these ties in terms of continuing attendance at meetings and participation in committees during the summer prior to opening. New friendships were based on mutual acquaintance.

This store contained 13 core males (34-46), with 9 experienced in jobs which provided skills and knowledge, 4 young men (20-30), 6 women and two men in their late 50s. Almost all of these workers had been called back to Super Fresh, but not necessarily for full-time positions. Only two workers had not had the Super Fresh option.

Of the young men, all had parents in the business. None were economically vulnerable. Most were single, one a newlywed with a working wife. Of the women, three were single parents. The other three had income-earning husbands. For all the younger men and the women, positions had improved in the new store because of their full-time hours.

Two owners in this store were part-timers for whom this was a moonlighting job. One had always been an active board member. The other was an older male worker who expected to work at the store full-time when he retired from his other job.

Most of the core males were doing the same job in the new store that they had done before: assistant manager, grocery manager, frozen food manager, night crew boss, receiver, etc. A few had to learn new jobs because of duplication (a former night crew boss became a bookkeeper). We had expected that assignments to positions would have been a major source of conflict in the formation of these stores. In Store B, there had been one problematic placement which was later resolved, but after some initial reorganizations, everyone seemed pleased with his or her role. (In Store A, only a few noncore members expressed dissatisfaction.) They were pleased because jobs were defined flexibly and could be redesigned if necessary. There were possibilities of cross-training and job shifts. Once-coveted department headships were less in demand because of the decrease in hierarchy, the tendency to share work across job categories, and the flattened wage hierarchy.

While all the core males in Store A had working wives, three-quarters of the men in Store B had wives who did not work at all. Adding the three single-parent women, a substantial number of owners in this store were completely dependent on this one income. This group of males had tended to work more than one job before, and many had been forced to give up or cut back on their moonlighting because of the time involved in the new store.

Several owners were concerned about a lack of "chain of command" or lax supervision in the stores. They were concerned that there was too much equality and no clear authority. This theme came out in the discussion of a decision made by the manager to extend store hours on two nights/week. Members were evenly divided between those who felt the manager needed to have authority over such issues and those who thought it should have been brought to the membership for a vote.

Store B was more complex than Store A in size, composition and ideology. It was more tied to the worker ownership movement and the consultants representing the movement. The tie between this store and the movement can be seen in the conflict over IGA advertisement policy. The store "faced down IGA" in a conflict between the O&O and IGA logos in the newspaper ads. This decision was seen by many to be a turning point in the store's independence and ability to control its own situation. It also signified the importance given to the O&O concept. The fight was led by those who identified with the movement. At other times, however, the leaders have been unable to secure sufficient votes to commit store resources to the movement (to help in training for new O&O stores, to open up membership roles, to make the logo accessible to new stores).

Summary

Several common features obtain for both stores. First, as one informant stated, "The stores are a combination of both the most secure [people who were experienced and confident in their ability to do better than A&P] and the most insecure [those not called back]."

The "most secure" were the core-age males who comprised half of each store's membership. They had substantial former experience with key positions in the stores. They also had substantial direct ties of loyalty to each other or indirect ties through relatives and mutual friends.

The least secure were those who, because of age and gender, were less likely to get full-time work or even call-backs to Super Fresh. These included five young men who were only offered part-time work, four older workers (only one of whom was called back) and ten women.

For many of the women, the new structure offered not only a rare opportunity for full-time work, but a chance to break down barriers to leadership roles in the store. Of all the women in O&O stores, 60 percent cited new and expanded roles for women as a major attraction of the innovation. One stated, "I wanted a career, not a job." One of these women left her store shortly after the interviews because of perceived male dominance and inadequate opportunities for women. Two significantly changed roles: one became a major member of the board, and the other broke a gender barrier to become a member of the night crew with a 10 percent increase in pay and hours compatible with parental roles. The old barrier was based on the assumption that women could not manage heavy stock boxes. Three others also experienced cross-training to broaden their skills in other departments and overall store operations.

Forty percent of the women wanted to continue their traditional roles. Several had turned down opportunities for promotion. One woman said, "Let the fellows be department heads. . . . I have other work at home." Most of these women cited full-time hours as their reason for choosing O&O. One was strongly recruited by former co-workers and said that she "couldn't let the guys down."

There was an unusual number of "mavericks" in both stores. These are people who describe themselves as "outspoken," as always knowing they had more ability and ingenuity than the people they worked for. Of the 14 people in one store, 5 described themselves in this way. Of the 25 in the second store 9 described themselves in this way. There was little, if any, such self-description among those who worked in Super Fresh.

When asked about recommending an O&O store to a friend, over and over people stressed the contingent importance of looking at who the co-participants are and the potential of the location. While everyone recognizes that not all people are superworkers, it is important to make sure of the ratio of those who work hard and carry their burden to those who "just bought a job."

Participation in the O&O Stores

The major differences in informal organization between the O&O stores are related to the size of the group, the social processes of formation and the external forces which influenced success (see chapter 4 for a discussion of the differences in experiences with bank loans, store selection, local competition, type of community, etc.).

The stores seemed more concerned about how they were perceived by external institutions—banks, vendors and customers—than about their role in the worker ownership movement. This was true of both stores, but especially of Store A. Many comments made by informants indicated that they wanted to appear like competent, knowledgeable businessmen to the outside groups which exerted so much influence on their success. They talked about behaving appropriately and fitting in with the "business world" as being very important. This led to situations which required minimizing their ties to the consultants and the movement. It is possible that more of the workers will become interested in the worker ownership movement again in the future if a critical mass of worker-owned stores and supporting institutions develop.

For the O&O stores, unlike Super Fresh, there is no question about *whether* a system of worker participation in decisionmaking was developed, because such a system *must* develop if the stores are to operate. Chapter 4 outlines the specifics of governance in the stores contained in the corporate by-laws. Briefly, workers as owners each have equal votes as store members. Monthly store meetings exist to inform members of lower level decisions allowed to managers or board discretion. At these meetings, higher level decisions reserved for maximum participation are also made. A board, elected periodically by the owners, meets bi-weekly and a manager, hired by the owners, oversees day-to-day operations and is responsible to the board and membership.

Formal training occurred only during the summer before the stores opened. There was no formal, follow-up training after the stores opened except that Store B briefly hired a consultant on its own (see below). The summer training described in chapter 4 involved several special task committees which reported to a steering committee. Committees concentrated on both operational start-up issues (work assignment, business skills) and on governance issues (e.g. by-laws, rights, hiring a manager, the role of the board, etc.). Very few worker/owners remembered much about their own committee assignment, the range of committees and the work of other committees. Most stated that they learned almost everything on their own after the stores opened.

Knowing about the former power and authority structures in A&P workplaces, there are several ways of evaluating the degree to which the O&O stores have followed the innovative blueprints. First, regarding the formal structures: To what degree are the formal governance systems in place and operating? To what degree have informal systems of communication replaced them? What is the relationship between the hired manager and his worker bosses?

Second, regarding cooperative management practices: Where does the store fall on a continuum from totally shared decisionmaking to centralized authority? Is power being gradually distributed through rotation of board membership or gradually centralized through a strong leader or a stable board which does not change? Is there an increasing gap between the board and the members? To what degree are all members participating and knowledgeable about issues facing the stores?

Finally, regarding informal social systems: To what degree does the role played by former co-worker ties affect the structure of the decisionmaking in the store? Do former ties of friendship and loyalty lead to cliques and factions and preferential behavior?

The Issues

Both stores have been faced with a considerable number of important issues, many of them externally controlled. Store A was faced with an initially poor profit margin, several crises involving new stores opening within their market area leading to the readjusting of operating hours, a major decision to buy a new store, a decision to terminate the manager's contract, as well as continuous capital investment and personnel decisions. Store B also adjusted its hours to changing local competition, dealt with the illness of its manager and president and eventually the resignation of both. Moreover, this store, the legal owner of the O&O logo, was involved in many votes about the sale of the logo and participation in the training of a workforce for new O&O stores, in addition to on-going capital investment and personnel decisions. While the Super Fresh stores can operate without QWL, the worker-owned stores *require* a structure for participation.

The small size of Store A has led to a tendency for informal processes to operate more than formal structures. In describing the formation of Store A, the presence of a strong leader with a loyal following from a former store was indicated. Conflict with the hired manager resulted in his departure, and the store leader, who was already board president, took over the manager's position as well. He has been described fondly by one colleague as ''an emperor'' who rules with ''tough love.'' In spite of this, he expressed commitment to the concept of a worker-owned cooperative in his interview and subsequent talks.

Regular board meetings occurred, although store meetings were less regular and often replaced by informal one-on-one consultation with every member. The store has maintained an elected board, although its membership has been relatively static from the first and has been almost all male. The manager/board president has struggled to tone down his style and to produce consensus decisions. He has made an effort to restrict the tendency of some of his close friends to by-pass democratic decisionmaking.

The purchase of a second store by the worker/owners of Store B probably contributed to the persistence of shared power. The logistics of staffing and operating two geographically dispersed stores was difficult enough to require cooperation, teamwork and flexibility in the division of labor. There have been many role conflicts among the personnel in the home store and between the two stores, but with every resolution of conflict the team has survived another crisis. The size of this store also makes a difference. With slightly more than half the membership of Store B, and with two stores to run, there are few workers who have not taken a turn at a position of responsibility. The majority of store members are board members or department heads.

Store B has taken great pains to implement the formal structure of worker ownership. The elected board has convened frequently and storewide members (owners) meetings held monthly. Board elections take place at specified intervals and there have also been special elections. (Shortly after the stores opened, special elections were held to reduce the unwieldy size of the board initially designated in the by-laws.) The composition of the board has tended to narrow over time to include the traditional inner circle.

In the beginning, Store B members were disappointed by the way storewide meetings were run. People talked about unimportant issues. Conflicts arose in the meetings. The meetings were seen as endless and without closure on issues. A consultant was hired to train the group in collective decisionmaking. He taught them how to construct an agenda, limit discussion and other procedures to enable them to deal with issues effectively. Most of the workers considered this to be a major turning point in store governance.

The manager in Store B was viewed as having developed a satisfactory relationship in a complex situation. He handled role conflicts with good grace and a sense of humor. He left in the third year to buy a store of his own, however, and was replaced by an experienced grocery department leader.

Store B has also seen power consolidate into the hands of a few. Starting out with a hired manager, an assistant manager (who was president of the board) and a meat manager (who was vice-president of the board), the store went through a period when the manager was hospitalized and the president of the board took over. Then, the president left the corporation in the second year (after the interviewing) and was succeeded as president by the vice-president (meat manager).

To the leaders of the store (the former and current board presidents), the concepts of participation and consensus were *very* important. One said, "it is harder to be ½₂₅ owner than a solo owner because you have to use reason and effort to make a decision—but it's a better decision." Another said, "I think 25 people have more collective knowledge than one person. If I didn't think so, I would quit." (He, like the leader in the other store, sees himself as changing from a self-centered, impatient person to a tolerant, patient leader.)

The potential for a gap between active and less active members exists in Store B because of its larger size in relation to the limited number of headships and board positions. That such a division exists is reflected in comments by both leaders (who complain about nonparticipation) and some members (who complain about board cliquishness). Part of this problem has been addressed by deliberate rotation of board positions. As in Store A, however, there are several people who have been on the board continuously and there is a tendency for department head status and board membership to converge. In this store, women have served on the board, but except for one woman who has been on the board from the beginning, women seem to rotate on and off more frequently.

Summary

The two stores differ in both size and in the significance of former co-worker ties in the store's composition. Size and former friendship ties affected the degree to which formal structures of communication were replaced by informal social processes. Size also affected the degree to which people had access to information and leadership positions. The larger store had the greatest gap between the board and less active members as time went on. In both stores, former ties declined in importance to participation and governance as time elapsed and major problems needed to be solved.

Leaders and workers in both stores continue to be concerned about participation, either in attendance at meetings or in awareness and knowledge of issues. About one-third of the workers are seen as non-participating by their colleagues. They are said to have ''just bought their jobs,'' to ''put time in and walk away'' leaving decisions to the others. Many workers report that they only go to meetings when the issues ''affect my pocketbook.''

Participation and leadership follow an expected pattern if one considers department head status and department membership. The presidents of both boards are meat room managers. In both stores, the meat room and deli workers are supportive and loyal to the leadership. They evoke the ''team'' and ''family'' metaphors so often used in talking about the meat room. The front end and produce departments and the night crew are significantly distanced from the leadership core in both knowledge and attitude.

There has been little role change in the O&O stores, since the leadership has come directly from those who had vertical careers at A&P and who had worked in departments with the greatest access to business skills. With few exceptions women's roles remain quite traditional. Women are underrepresented on the boards and still serve as ''loyal side-kicks'' in the meat room, or on the front end. They have also lost their former office bookkeeping jobs to young males in the new stores, since the bookkeeping functions are seen as more critical in the autonomous store corporation. However, the ability to flexibly redesign jobs and provide a storewide view of issues through meetings and cross-training have allowed women access to new skills and information.

Formation of the Super Fresh Stores

Contradictions in the Contract

The formal features of the Super Fresh contract led to several policies which discouraged active participation in QWL. These features have been described in chapter 4. In the following discussion we describe how each feature acted as an impediment to QWL.

First, tying the bonus to labor costs created an incentive for managers to hire few full-time workers, decrease the hours of part-timers whenever there was a wage rate increase, and replace former A&P workers with newcomers paid at a lower rate. Many workers were well aware of the direct relationship between the bonus and their continuing loss of income and, thus, were hostile to QWL. They saw it as a meaningless feature in comparison to their declining wages.

A schism between part-time and full-time workers developed as a result. Full-time workers felt secure while part-timers worried about further erosion of the number of hours worked. Several workers in one store believed there was a formal policy to reduce everyone to 12 hours per week. Conflicts over hours and schedules prevented the emergence of feelings of equality between department heads (most of the full-timers) and other workers.

Part-time workers have not been kept informed. While meetings were part of clock-time (paid for) in the earliest days of QWL in stores C and E, they are no longer part of compensated work-time at these stores and were never paid for at stores D and F. Part-timers have not been willing to attend meetings scheduled on their time off.

Second, the contract also generated a developing hostility between former A&P workers and new workers. New workers were to be paid less than former A&P workers during the first years of the contract. By the end of the contract this gap would be closed. Thus there was initially an incentive to give more hours to new, lower-wage workers. Where this occurred, it was deeply resented. In addition, former A&P workers felt entitled to some "reparations" for the concessions they made after years of loyalty. They resented the fact that newcomers also received the bonus and that wage-rates were to be equalized. One worker said, "Why should they get the hours when I gave the company 14 good years." Another said, "I thought the bonus was only for us, to make up what we lost."

Third, the contract encouraged high turnover, i.e., replacing former A&P workers with newcomers and replacing experienced newcomers with novice newcomers entering at minimum wage. In one store with an older, more female workforce of former A&P workers, many informants felt that there was a conscious attempt to encourage resignations. The better-off workers sometimes revealed their awareness of their competition with other long-term workers for the bonus and their vested interest in turnover. One worker commented favorably on the resignation of another: "There goes another one-percenter."

Fourth, morale problems developed around the loss of former benefits. The single most resented "give-back" among the workers was the vacation time. Many of them had developed lifestyles (camping, trailers at the beach, etc.) which were based on their former vacations of four-five weeks accumulated after many years. Of all the concessions, this one will probably continue to dampen morale for the longest time.

A fifth feature of the new contract which has led to dissatisfaction and lowered morale was the single-store seniority system. Seniority is now based on the individual stores rather than on service in the chain. Transfers are no longer part of the game. This is good for those who preferred the "store as family" model, but it impedes the upward mobility allowed for by the transfer system. Single-store seniority was based on the assumption that teamwork would best be fostered by stability within the stores. It also enabled Super Fresh to surmount the barriers to profitability engendered by a high-seniority labor force with layoff/transfer protection. Some of the young, ambitious men saw this as a loss of opportunity; women who had wanted more hours or full-time jobs also realized that without transfers they would be limited. However, those who thought the new chain's success would lead to new store openings retained the hope of moving up in the system.

Staffing the QWL Super Fresh Stores

On the surface, there appeared to be a chainwide policy for staffing. While stores were to be staffed by a 3:1 ratio of former A&P workers to new hires, this appears to have been only a chainwide average. In fact, there was considerable latitude in the staffing strategies used in different stores. The four stores in our sample varied considerably.

Variables which made a difference in staffing policy were the knowledge and clout of the manager, the position of the store in the chronological sequencing of openings, and how the process of callbacks was managed. Some callbacks were formal, based on a list of former workers and their positions. Others were informal (managers and union leaders responded to pressure by relatives, workers, patrons and calls by former workers themselves). It was possible for a manager to reconstruct a store largely with former loyal co-workers. While many workers actively worked at being called back, others were totally passive and waited for calls and letters.

The strategy for staffing led to the perpetuation of an already cohesive and mutually-known workforce or to the creation of a new social group. Such differences could affect the social process in developing QWL.

In addition, the following dimensions of store composition are important because of their implications for store functioning and morale:

(1) ratio of former A&P workers to new hires;

(2) inequality among former A&P workers in terms of hours;

(3) inequality between former A&P or new workers in terms of hours;

(4) number of former A&P workers doing better, the same or worse in the new stores in terms of hours and position.

Initially, Stores C & E were grouped together as experiencing early QWL training in an enthusiastic union context while D & F were grouped as experiencing late QWL training in a less supportive union context. However, preliminary qualitative analysis revealed that Stores C & D had more in common in consistent implementation of QWL. C & D had actively practiced QWL while E & F had been less consistent. Thus, in all further analysis, C & D will be treated as QWL stores while E & F will be grouped as non-QWL stores.

Store C

Store C did unusually well in calling back former workers. Seventy percent of the recalled workers had experience in the same store with the same manager. Former workers the manager preferred to exclude or who were unavailable were replaced by workers with good reputations in the chain. Since this was one of the first stores, he had "first pick" and was able to assure most of his former workers of good positions. His workers reported little anxiety over the transition. Not one worker interviewed had considered the O&O option. The store was dominated by 52 former A&P workers who outnumbered the 32 new hires. In each department, oldtimers outnumbered the new.

This manager provided more full-time jobs for former workers than any other. In most stores, only department heads are full time, amounting to about 12 full-time slots. Here, several other jobs in each department were full time so that there were 20 full-time jobs. The manager also made certain that all former workers had more hours than new hires. Under the new system, this kind of staffing was discouraged by the need to keep wage costs down. However, the sales volume and profit in this store permitted the manager to use his formerly successful paternalistic strategy of taking care of "his workers" in return for loyalty and productivity.

Unlike any other store, there were no disgruntled women in the front end at Store C. The manager had called back mostly elite males and staffed the problematic front end largely with new hires. He thus avoided a typical source of disaffection. The women who were called back trusted the manager to take care of them. Only a few people made negative comments or indicated a desire to leave. These included some men, new to the store, who worked in the more socially isolated departments. They simply did not like the neighborhood. The others had common reasons to leave—the need for full-time work or the desire to retire.

Most of the former workers in this store had been called back to positions which were the same (in hours and level) or better than before. Very few had lost anything. Three of the 20-year-old males had achieved rapid advancement to better positions and were very optimistic about the future. Those on the store planning board had a wealth of experience in leadership roles. Store C had the largest number of college degrees in any one store. Moreover, most workers in this store were not economically vulnerable. *All* the leadership males had wives with good jobs and several had one or more business investments on the side. None of the women were primary breadwinners. This was also a young store. The leadership group was 35-45 years old. There were more workers 20-30 years old than in other stores and fewer workers over 45. In many ways, this store resembled the O&O stores in composition. Skilled elite males dominated and there were few unhappy women and older workers. Most workers were "winners," with new positions equal to or better than before. The men were not interested in worker ownership because many of them were already involved in entrepreneurial activities outside of the industry.

Store D

Store D resembled Store C in that the manager was strongly committed to assembling a team when he called back workers. Sixty percent had worked for him before but, in contrast to Store C, many had not worked together or in this particular store. The others were selected by reputation. His "inner circle" or grocery management team consisted of several people for whom this was a significant and rapid promotion. They were enthusiastic and loyal. Many workers, even those in the front end, reported high morale.

Unlike Store C, Store D was opened late in the process and relied on a workforce of mostly new hires (31 former A&P to 86 new). The staff was dominated by newcomers, but newcomers did not have more hours than former A&P workers. The meat department had more former A&P workers and the grocery department was evenly split reflecting the benefits of experience for both departments. Unlike Store C, there were few full-time workers except for department heads. Several men in the 30-45 age group had achieved significant improvement in position, however. There were also a few who lost hours and position (mostly women), but the majority of workers had stayed at the same level in terms of position and hours.

Workers in this store had greater economic vulnerability than those in C, especially the women. Store D was divided into a group of successful men and a group of vulnerable women. Thirty-three percent of the former A&P workers were women supporting families. Half of them had been forced to work second jobs since their Super Fresh callback. Like Store C, there were few older workers (10 percent). All of them had lost position or hours and talked about the chain's age discrimination.

In this store, the idea of QWL and the manager's consistent practice of it created strong feelings of optimism for the future, but, of course, less chance for mobility due to single-store seniority. Four workers (two men and two women) who were already full time wanted management posts. All of them saw their possibilities limited in the new system without transfers. They hoped that the expansion of the chain would lead to new stores and new opportunities.

While there was less actual loss of full-time status and decrease in part-time hours than in stores E and F, the 17 percent who complained about lowered income link the loss of their work hours to the "new system" which they saw encouraging shrinking hours and high turnover.

Both Stores C & D called back workers with an eye to picking those with good reputations and assembling teams of former co-workers. They tended to place people in positions which were better or at least even with their former ones. They maximized callbacks from high-skill departments and former store leaders and minimized callbacks of those likely to be disaffected: front-end women and older workers. Finally, they avoided any appearance of preferential treatment to new workers in regard to the quantity of hours or quality of schedules. These processes of formation in turn led to differences in the informal political and social organization of the store and the morale of the workers which indirectly affected the implementation and success of QWL.

Implementation of QWL in QWL Stores

In looking at the QWL process, there are questions about the degree of implementation which must be investigated. First, regarding the formal structure: have there been QWL meetings? If so, at which levels—store planning board and/or departmental? Second, regarding the centralization or dispersion of decisionmaking: If there have been meetings, how widely disseminated has been the knowledge of them? How broad has been the attendance? How much exposure has there been to QWL meetings outside the store (regional and corporate planning boards)? Third, regarding the substance of QWL: What has been covered at QWL meetings? Have they been viewed as serving all the intended functions or just a few?

Store C

Store C had a strong commitment to QWL on all counts. First, the planning board participants (inner circle) were enthusiastic. Second, everyone in the store knew what QWL was and meetings did take place regularly. Moreover, many of the workers had worked "on this team" before and several stated, that, with this manager, "we always had QWL."

In addition to QWL, this store held formal social events outside the store to maintain solidarity and morale, including holiday parties, softball games and trips.

Store C was open for two months before QWL training began. It was one of the first three stores to be trained by the original consultants. Each department received separate training in a workshop. In addition, the store planning board was also trained together as a group.

All the workers were aware of a functioning QWL program with monthly department meetings. Those not on the store board were vague about the frequency of store meetings, but they knew they occurred. They talked about QWL as promoting teamwork and cooperation, getting along better, allowing input and suggestions, placing job security in their own hands, sharing knowledge and decisions.

In spite of this positive reporting, half the workers reported not going to meetings. One reason for this was that meetings were no longer counted as paid worktime, and many workers chose not to attend on their own time. Overall, 65 percent of the workers in this store viewed QWL positively. Of these, 25 percent thought that QWL made a difference to their jobs, while 40 percent were positive but vague about the contribution of QWL. The other 35 percent were disappointed or hostile. For the most part, QWL was an unimportant feature to those workers who described themselves as ambitious (looking for advancement) or those few who were disgruntled about their hours and position.

Store D

Store D was trained late through a union local which was less supportive of the innovation. This store also has other mechanisms to maintain solidarity, such as an active "sunshine committee" to organize trips and parties and a projected newsletter.

The store planning board met every other week while department heads met every Thursday for a sales meeting. Thus, there are two store-level meetings clearly dividing QWL from operations. There was very little confusion or vagueness among the workers who knew about QWL. (This store had the highest uniformity of knowledge about how QWL operated.) The planning board was also making a strong attempt to involve regular workers in their meetings by inviting four different store members (not regular board members) to each meeting. As a result, more regular clerks and cashiers had actually been involved. On the other hand, there were no individual department meetings.

Forty-five percent of the workers, including the leadership, were quite enthusiastic about QWL, emphasizing teamwork and communication aspects. Several wanted to work harder to involve more workers, however. Twenty percent of the regular workers were not clear or certain about what QWL was or how it worked. Another 35 percent were knowledgeable but disappointed in it, just as in Store C. They saw no increased control, no difference, and complained about "all talk and no action," and the need to pay workers to attend. One worker was very hostile, calling QWL "a joke." This worker had been initially very enthusiastic about workers gaining equality and control. The more satisfied workers were those who had been invited to meetings.

Staffing the Non-QWL Super Fresh Stores

Store E

Like Store C, Store E was also a high volume store staffed early when a large pool of workers was available, but this store was composed of fewer former co-workers who had worked with the manager in the past (only four or 20 percent). More workers were passive callbacks to this store. There was a less desirable ratio of former A&P workers to new hires (36 former to 47 new) than in Store C but a better ratio than in the later-opening Stores D & F. There were also fewer full-time slots than in C. The front end was dominated by new hires, but there was parity in all other departments except meat (which, because of the skill/union factor, was always dominated by former A&P workers).

This less-experienced manager had not been in the position to call back protegés, but had staffed his store predominantly with young workers (20-30 years old) from families with ties to and clout in the chain. His staffing seems to have been influenced by input from workers' relatives and from corporate and union leaders. Half of the workers came from families having parents, siblings or spouses who brought them in and pressured for their recall. Unlike QWL Stores C & D, few workers bettered their position in the new store. Fifty percent reported a loss in hours and position. For some, the new position presented significant demotion from former elite posts. Workers viewed this as age discrimination. The new position represented a promotion for only 25 percent of the former workers. The remaining 25 percent of the workers reported continuity and stability in position and hours. This group included those for whom the supermarket job was a second job or provided supplementary income.

Former A&P workers did receive preference in hours. All of the new cashiers worked 18 hours or less, while all former A&P workers had at least 18 hours and half had more. This favored treatment was true for all other departments as well. Many were still extremely disgruntled, however, by a steady pattern of loss in hours. Most have had their hours cut since they began to work at this store, some by half. Several have seen a pattern of cutbacks with every contractual hourly rate rise, while others believed there was a chain goal of cutting all part-timers to 12 hours.

Even those who were well-connected in the chain or who knew the manager before became disgruntled and fatalistic. The cutbacks had the effect of leading to turnover of one-seventh of our initial group of interviewees in Store E in one year. Although the former A&P component of this store was composed of young workers with few dependents, one young man in his 20s reported the cancellation of his marriage plans. Moreover, for the eight workers over 32 with dependents, the cutbacks have had a severe impact.

Store F

Store F was also managed by a relatively new manager. Most of his recalls were formal (from a list) and passive (workers did not actively seek placement). There were 33 former A&P workers and 50 new hires. Former workers were in the majority in the office, the meat room and the grocery department. Cashiers, deli clerks and produce clerks were predominantly newcomers. Moreover, unlike any of the other stores, all newcomers in the front end had *more* hours of work than former A&P workers, creating a serious morale problem. This store reflected most strongly the results of a system that rewards hiring more new workers at lower rates of pay.

Store F was also skewed in sex and age. We saw that morale problems heavily involve women and older workers. Almost two-thirds of the former A&P workers in Store F were women and almost all of them were 55 or older. Like Store E, 50 percent of the workers in Store F had *lost* significantly in the changeover. Losses included movement from full to part time, loss of part-time hours, moves back to night work and loss of managerial positions. For 35 percent, there was no loss or gain, however many of these individuals had been in one store for over 10 years and reported a sense of loss in terms of the family-like atmosphere of the former store.

All of the 15 percent who gained in the new store moved into managerial positions. This store had more inexperienced department heads than the others and lacked the core of former achievers found in leadership positions in the other stores.

While many of those who lost in Store E were single young persons without dependents, here many of the "losers" depended on the job for most of their income. Thus, many of the problems in this store can be related to its social composition, which was in turn constrained by the nature of the remaining pool of former A&P workers available.

The process of composing stores E & F involved less control over the callback process. This could be related to a lack of managerial experience which led to less knowledge about the pool of former workers, vulnerability to pressure from the chain, a greater dependence on the formal list of names, and in the case of F, a reduced pool of laid off workers from which to choose. Stores were composed of workers with fewer skills and less experience. For the most part, the former A&P workers in these stores experienced lowered status and salaries and were disadvantaged in relation to new workers. These characteristics in turn affected both morale and the ability to implement QWL successfully.

Failure of QWL Implementation in the Non-QWL Stores

Store E, like Store C, was one of the first to receive lengthy training in QWL involving every worker. However, the store planning board went through retraining again a year later under the new consultant team since they were regarded as not having implemented the plan. The store then reported weekly meetings of the planning board, but fewer regular department meetings. The front end and office did meet as a department, however, to air gripes about scheduling and pressure on cashiers. This was the only store to deal with the front-end problem in this way. It was unusual to see the front end participating to this degree. Produce, meat and deli met infrequently and the isolated night crew rarely attended their meetings.

Since the store was beginning to reimplement QWL, members of its planning board were the most enthusiastic workers. They talked of increased involvement and motivation, more departmental autonomy, etc. One, who took the corporate point of view, blamed the failure of QWL on the workers' failure to distinguish between QWL issues and contract issues (hours, wage rates). Others in leadership positions could identify with the workers and noted that QWL would never work until workers were paid to attend meetings or given more hours and better schedules.

Of the workers, 20 percent (mostly those on the store planning board) reported positive results from QWL ("we are equal to management," atmosphere is "open," attitudes are better); 50 percent liked the *idea* but felt it was not operating (no follow-through); 30 percent were disappointed (no change at all, all talk no action, petty beefs dealt with but nothing important).

Store F was least satisfied with QWL. Here, even the department heads recognized that QWL had broken down. There were no planning board meetings in four months prior to our interviews and, as one commented, "the team concept is going under." The leaders saw that one reason for this was the cleavage between former workers with few hours and new hires with more hours. Another reason given was the understaffing resulting from the new system of tying bonuses to labor costs. One department head reported that there were also conflicts between departments and, thus, the store had split into three parts. He wondered why the chain had bothered with all the QWL training.

Thirty-three percent of the regular workers in Store F had never heard of QWL or the meetings. Another third knew that meetings took place, but did not know about QWL or the purpose of meetings. One-third knew what QWL was, but reported it to be broken down. Several said that QWL was for the bosses. Very few could describe the goals of QWL specifically. The clearest statement was that QWL meant "not putting people down."

Summary

It is obvious that QWL has not completely achieved the goals of the formal training in any of the stores. The most that can be said is that members of the planning boards feel they have more "rights" or "say" in how the store works. In one store, (F), few workers have heard of QWL. In Store D, there has been the greatest attempt to implement the formal process of QWL and to reach out to incorporate all the workers. Difficulties with contract issues (hours, schedules, etc.) interfere with a totally positive view of QWL, and workers recognize that these issues are more important to them than the potential rewards of QWL. In Store C, we find both formal implementation of QWL and a long history of "informal QWL" (consultation, discussion, etc.) while in Store E we find less implementation and a real interference due to hour cuts and scheduling difficulties. Whether QWL "works" is clearly a result of two factors: (1) leadership's consistency in running meetings and practicing QWL as they were trained to do; and (2) the degree to which workers' losses of income, position, etc. interfere with their perception of QWL as meaningful. In all these aspects, Stores C & D are similar to each other and unlike Stores E & F.

Understanding QWL in Super Fresh

The most successful aspect of QWL is not its functioning within each store but the automony the stores have gained from centralized chain decisionmaking. No longer do all stocking decisions, display decisions and the like come from the top down. Store leadership has gained latitude to stock for local neighborhood needs, to buy produce from small, individual vendors, and to develop innovations in procedures, which later may be approved as chainwide policy. No longer do specialized product supervisors from the central office control the business operations of each department. Stores are expected to work as teams and their successful work innovations are reported and discussed at regional and corporate planning board meetings. It is at these above-store levels that there has been the most success.

Elite members of store planning boards (department heads and shop stewards) have been able to participate and to see the change most clearly. If they had been to a regional or corporate planning board meeting, they felt the change even more. Even at the top, however, there has been a persistence of old structure. Female department heads were few and they were not always part of the inner circle. For example, in one store, the front-end manager was the only department head not asked to consider promotion when an assistant directorship became vacant. When she approached the director, he seemed surprised at her interest.

In addition to the participative successes at levels above the store, QWL has involved some symbolic changes which are supposed to reinforce the idea of equality, democracy and participation. Status names have been changed so that workers are called "associates" and managers are called "directors," but the new nomenclature has not actually been adopted thoroughly in any store. Workers are still called workers, and in one store all nondepartment heads reported that the term "associate" refers only to members of the store planning board (department heads).

The flattened hierarchy at corporate headquarters is also a manifestation of the notion that there is less distance between the top and bottom and that access to the top is open. Both the first and second corporate presidents have made themselves accessible at training sessions and planning board meetings. They have also been visiting the stores. Many workers commented on the fact that the president is "down at our level," and accessible. They have been impressed by such store visits.

One of the problems is that QWL has overlapped two other broad domains—store operations and contractual issues. Much time and attention have been given to trying to separate QWL from these other domains. "Operations" refers to business details of running a store: keeping records of inventory, payroll costs and, most important, sales volume and profits. In addition, stores must deal with general promotional issues—new products, displays, advertising, etc. Contractual issues include the formal aspects of the contract: how the bonus is calculated, how labor costs are targeted, etc. Even those questions left up to store directors' discretion, such as how to distribute hours among workers, as well as the qualitative issues of who gets good hours, who gets weekends and evenings, are defined as contract issues because there is an awareness that these are management rights, not subject to worker input.

In some stores, store-level meetings have been divided into two parts. The operations part has involved providing information on how the departments have been doing and how the store as a whole has been doing. Innovative suggestions about policies (promotions, customer relations) and work procedures have also been sought. Thus, this has incorporated two aspects of QWL—information sharing and worker input on policy and procedures. Unfortunately, many stores have not defined information sharing and innovation as part of QWL and have excluded these elements from formal meetings.

The QWL part of the meeting largely has involved reducing social conflict and increasing team solidarity. At the very least, QWL has been seen as an opportunity to gripe and be listened to. At best, these sessions have been seen as problemsolving sessions, attempting to deal with such issues as how to train the steady influx of newcomers, how to control absenteeism and turnover, how to decrease the suspensions and grievances related to cash shortages on the front end, etc. Thus, QWL has been focused on increasing morale and team spirit as opposed to increasing worker input to the labor process and control over conditions of work.

What has interferred with morale most are the issues of work assignment, hours and schedules. Since these are management rights, they have been defined as inappropriate for QWL discussions. There is increasing awareness that QWL has been impeded by the inability to deal with the issues which are most important to the workers.

Conclusions

Certain chainwide patterns affected the relationships between workers' characteristics (age, gender) and the workers' experience. Departments varied in their power, opportunity for acquiring knowledge and opportunities for teamwork. The power, knowledge, skills, expectations, success, and career patterns of workers were the result of both their gender and their hiring dates (in the company cycle of rise and decline). Their personal household economic vulnerability was closely related to age (stage in family cycle). The A&P chain had developed patterns of recruiting through families, paternalistic protection of women and the sponsorship of mobility for males identified as worthy, all patterns which are difficult to change. Moreover, assumptions made by A&P that women were less interested in careers and were mostly supplementing income are contradicted by the large number of self-supporting single women, single parents and women with husbands who were laid off, disabled and unemployed.

When A&P shut down and the stores reopened as Super Fresh or as O&O, the traditional patterns of employment and careers did not go back to what they had been. Many jobs were saved, but many workers had hard adjustments to make in the new settings. Not only did the workers take wage and benefit cuts, they also lost many of the sources of security and mobility they had had. First, while we did not focus on them in this study, a number of former A&P workers did not find jobs in the new setting and went elsewhere. Second, only a small, select group were able and willing to risk becoming worker/owners. Third, while some full-time elites retained status in Super Fresh, many more former A&P workers had their hours reduced, as the chain adopted more flexible schedulings and staffing. Rapidly, four of the major career patterns we identified became almost extinct, while a previously uncommon pattern—the part-time supplement to a different full-time job—became preferred by managers. A strong internal labor market was broken up in favor of a more external, unstable labor market.

The old patterns left a legacy that influences the innovations in the O&O and Super Fresh stores. In both the O&O and the Super Fresh stores, the traditional social organization of the store (the status, power and potential for knowledge of different departments and positions) still underlies social process in the new stores and interferes with the implementation of change. Moreover, traditional views of age and gender still create stereotypes.

The process of recruiting differed for all stores, influencing the number of people with pre-existing ties and experience working together. This is true not only among the four Super Fresh stores, but also between the two worker-owned stores. The proportion of experienced, knowledgeable core workers (former department heads, assistant managers, and the like from the grocery or meat department) to less knowledgeable, less integrated workers (front end, night crew, produce) also varied from store to store. Finally, stores differed according to their manager's style and the unique events and crises they experienced.

It is important to note that both O&O stores are formed around a core of self-selected, experienced, and knowledgeable supermarket workers and had very small numbers of former part-timers or front-end women. It is questionable whether the stores could have succeeded without the experience of former meat and grocery managers. This is of great interest to the future of worker ownership in this industry.

In both types of stores, the innovators' goals of involving workers in decisionmaking of extending equality of influence and of changing workers' views of their rights and roles has not been fully realized. In the Super Fresh stores, this can be directly traced to dissatisfaction with hours as well as positions, and to perceived possibilities of advancement. Although formal mobility was limited in the O&O stores too, there was greater flexibility in the design of jobs. In the worker-owned stores in contrast to Super Fresh, hours were not a problem, but department status remained an obstacle to some extent. For all stores, the relative status and social centrality of one's department played a big role in predicting involvement and knowledge. However, in contrast to the Super Fresh stores, there was no problem of perpetual part-time status or hour cutbacks among owners in the worker-owned stores, since any owner who wished full-time work could have it. Moreover, those outside the leadership circle learned much more about storewide operations and diverse departments and functions than their counterparts in Super Fresh.

One major consequence of worker ownership has been the development of a storewide perspective and the dissemination of cross-training, skills and knowledge across department lines. This level of understanding of "the business' in Super Fresh existed only among the store leaders, who are the rare full-time department heads or shop stewards who serve on the store planning boards.

The two innovations are extremely different in their organizational functioning and labor strategy, and this difference affects participativeness. In Super Fresh, the primary problems in implementing QWL stem from the elimination of decisions about labor strategy and deployment of resources from the QWL process. In the worker-owned stores, these decisions are made by the worker/owners. The differences between the QWL and non-QWL stores are clearly the result of differences in previous social ties, leadership styles, worker characteristics and whether workers were winners or losers in the new store. These differences affect the degree to which worker participation is successful. Success can be viewed in terms of whether meetings are held at all, the degree to which workers know about and attend them, and whether they are limited to store elites. Other issues include whether meetings are limited to airing complaints and resolving disputes or whether they provide workers with information about store operations and encourage innovations from below.

In the months following our interviews, we continued to maintain communication with the stores. While the four Super Fresh stores continued to be very different from each other, the two O&O stores seemed to be becoming more alike. In spite of their differences in size, process of formation, patterns of board and store meetings, leadership styles, experiences with hired managers and other crises and events, they have developed similarities in functioning. Both have been led by former meat managers and have centralized power in their boards of directors.

Compared to the Super Fresh stores, the dispersion of knowledge and the frequency of participation is much greater in both O&O stores, and the range of issues continues to be broad. Even the non-owners (mostly part-timers) in the O&O stores who have previously worked in chains report that these are improved workplaces. They see a flattened hierarchy, a less sharply defined division of labor, and feel that they are trusted and given more responsibility.[3]

We must remember that the O&O owners were not drawn by the ideology of worker ownership. They were would-be entrepreneurs, people who needed full-time jobs, and those strongly disaffected by A&P. In cooperating to make the stores work, they have established the necessary mechanisms for collective decisionmaking.

As a result of their experiences, they are now poised between being a group which is clearly committed to the ideology of worker ownership and democratic workplaces and a group of dominant store elites who are partners in small business. The important factors in their transition are not limited to previous experience with formal decisionmaking. The ability to cross-train those in low status positions, to impart a store-wide perspective on operations, and to make the division of labor more flexible and the hierarchy flatter has probably played a major role. The diversification of day-to-day work has, in turn, had a major impact on participation. This process has been absent in the Super Fresh stores, where daily work, access to knowledge, and autonomy have improved for the elite but deteriorated for the rest of the former A&P workforce.

NOTES

1. In the Super Fresh stores, these are called assistant director and director while workers are referred to as associates. The new nomenclature is intended to reduce the perception of hierarchy.

2. Recently A&P lost an EEOC suit regarding discrimination of women and is obligated to pay significant compensation. We note that in all new Super Fresh stores (56 as of 1986) there is only one woman store director.

3. Preliminary reports from interviews with non-owners conducted by Simon and Granrose (unpublished document).

6

Outcomes for Workers in Worker-Owned, QWL, and Non-QWL Supermarkets

In the previous chapter, the social processes involved in changing from A&P to new types of organizations were discussed. This chapter will answer questions such as: "How did the workers themselves make out in the job-saving efforts at the O&O and Super Fresh stores?" "What happened to the former A&P workers who became worker/owners through a buyout and those who became Super Fresh employees?" "How were they doing financially?" "What degree of sacrifice was imposed on them by the shutdown and subsequent events?" "Did their job security and working conditions improve?" "Was power redistributed to them in meaningful ways through worker ownership and the effective implementation of QWL?" "Which was better for workers: getting some influence in decision-making through QWL or accepting the responsibility of ownership?" "What happened to their satisfaction with their jobs, lives, and economic status?" While these are not easy questions to answer, they are among the most important questions of all for present and future worker/owners.

To identify what happened to the workers, we surveyed former A&P workers at the six stores described in chapter 5: the two worker-owned stores (O&Os), the two Super Fresh stores that effectively implemented QWL, and the two Super Fresh stores that had not fully implemented QWL. The distinction between QWL and non-QWL stores was based on shop stewards' responses, as well as the in-person interviews discussed in chapter 5.

This survey information differs in method of data collection from that of chapter 5, which used open-ended interviews to examine the

161

actual social processes in each store. The worker outcomes in this chapter are drawn from outcome measures derived from a precoded instrument. The information elicited independently by each method strongly corroborates the other.

To clarify the dynamics which can answer the questions posed for this chapter, we use the framework developed in chapter 2. First, we describe mean differences in characteristics, attitudes, perceptions, and results between workers in the three work settings. Then we use statistical modeling to identify the relative importance of factors that played a role in bringing about workers' outcomes.

The Worker Model

Figure 6.1 illustrates the parts of the larger model examined in this chapter. The primary difference between this model and the one presented in chapter 2 is that we omitted some factors—the role of unions, the business environment, and store characteristics—because theoretically these factors have their primary impact on store outcomes, not on individuals. Since the performance of the organization should directly influence worker outcomes, however, we included store economic outcomes.

We hypothesized that store participativeness would be a function of the skills, characteristics, and resources of its workers, of the formal structure of the store (QWL or worker ownership) and of consultant advice and help. We also proposed that participativeness would influence store functioning, including the labor strategy the store adopts, the extent to which it trains workers, the informal ways that workers interact, and worker motivation and effort. Finally, we expected that store functioning, store economic success, and worker characteristics would determine workers' financial outcomes. In addition, we expected these factors plus participativeness to influence workers' satisfaction with their jobs and lives.

The next sections describe the sample, how we measured and operationalized these theoretical constructs, and the similarities and mean differences among the three groups. Tests of statistically sig-

Figure 6.1. Research Model

Inputs   Organizational Processes   Outcomes

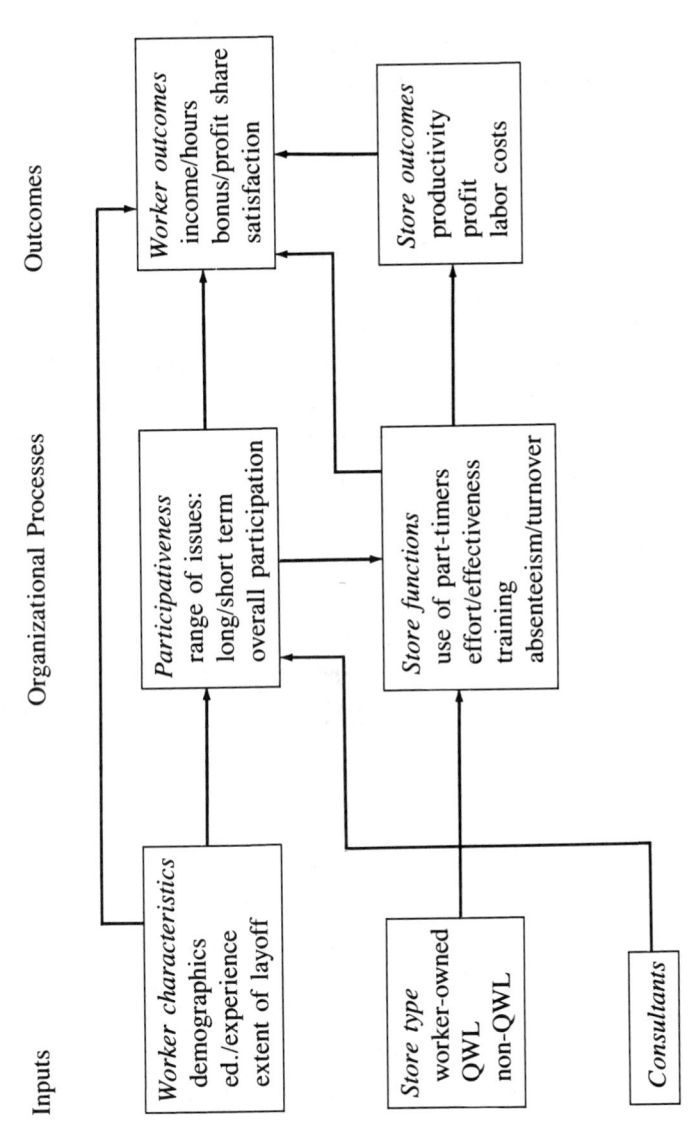

nificant differences involved analyses of variance (ANOVA) and least significant difference (LSD) multiple range tests for comparing mean scores of groups of unequal size, $p = .05$. These mean differences may be due to many factors, not just store type, however, so caution should be used in interpreting the results. A clear explanation of *causal* relationships will appear in the subsequent section on model testing.

The Sample

As indicated in chapter 3, two years after the A&P shutdown, we asked former A&P workers in six stores—two O&Os, two QWL Super Fresh, and two non-QWL Super Fresh—to fill out questionnaires about their experience, training, perceptions, attitudes, satisfaction, household situations, and economic outcomes. Workers sampled were those interviewed for chapter 5. Table 6.1 shows the distribution of responses.

Table 6.1
Questionnaire Survey Responses by Store Type

Store type	N sampled	N responded
O&O	25	22
QWL Super Fresh	48	46
Non-QWL Super Fresh	49	43
TOTALS	122	111

Because our focus was on job-saving strategies in response to the Philadelphia A&P shutdown, our sample was representative of former A&P workers now employed in O&O and Super Fresh stores. The sample does not represent all workers in these stores. In particular, it does not include the following: (1) part-time workers at the worker-owned stores who were not owners, though very few of these were former A&P workers; (2) those Super Fresh workers who had never worked for A&P—about half of the workers in these stores—working mostly part time. Because part-time workers played a big part in Super Fresh and *responded* in different ways, we report the results of full-time and part-time workers, separately.

Mean Differences Among the Groups

Worker Characteristics

We expected that the simultaneous establishment of the O&O and Super Fresh stores in the wake of the A&P shutdown would result in little variation in worker characteristics, because all of the workers in our sample were long-term A&P employees. Even so, self-selection was operating in O&O stores and selective recruitment occurred in Super Fresh. As we have already seen in chapter 5, there is reason to believe that the worker/owners were a special group, and that recruitment differed between QWL stores and non-QWL stores. To explore variations in motivations, resources, and expectations that might occur because of these selection processes, we looked at demographic characteristics, job experience, and personal values.

Demographic Characteristics and Job Experience

O&O and Super Fresh workers were fairly similar in cultural background, family situation, and job experience (see table 6.2). They were primarily high school-educated, married, white, middle-aged and mid-career, with many years of supermarket experience behind them. In Super Fresh stores, however, part-time workers said they knew how to do fewer jobs and generally had fewer years of experience than full-timers.

One apparent difference was that fewer women were worker/owners. Previous research indicates that while women whose pay provided a substantial part of family income were very interested in becoming worker/owners, they sometimes did not have the financial resources to do so. Women contributing less than one-third of household support were less likely to choose worker ownership in the A&P shutdown and were more likely to be part-time workers (Granrose and Hochner 1985). But, among *full-time* workers, O&Os had a higher proportion of women than did Super Fresh stores. Many

Table 6.2
Mean Differences in Worker Characteristics

Worker characteristics	Store type		
	O&O	QWL	Non-QWL
Full time	(N = 20)	(N = 24)	(N = 14)
Part time	(N = 2)	(N = 22)	(N = 29)
Age	41.52	41.84	43.36
% Female	27.3[b,c]	47.8[a]	60.5[a]
FT	30.0	20.8	21.4
PT	00.0	77.3	79.3
%Married	77.3	64.4	76.2
%Catholic	57.1[c]	45.5[c]	71.4[a,b]
%White	100.0[b]	91.1[a,c]	100.0[b]
# of dependents	2.48	1.98	1.76
FT	2.35[d]	2.37[d]	2.46[d]
PT	5.00[b,c,d]	1.50[a,d]	1.43[a,d]
Years of education	12.86	12.98	12.28
FT	12.55[d]	12.96[d]	12.28
PT	16.00[b,c,d]	11.95[a,d]	11.96[a]
Yrs. seniority in markets	18.59	17.30	18.67
FT	18.75	20.92[d]	24.07[d]
PT	17.00	13.36[d]	16.07[d]
# Jobs know how to do	8.73[c]	7.24[c]	5.39[a,b]
FT	8.55	9.29[d]	9.28[d]
PT	10.50[c]	5.00[d]	3.52[a,d]
Months of layoff	5.68	3.89	5.90
FT	5.83[d]	2.44	2.54[d]
PT	3.00[b,c,d]	5.75[a]	7.46[a,d]
Values[1]			
Accomplishment	4.82	4.65	4.63
Growth	4.59	4.39	4.52
Co-worker relations	4.45	4.67	4.61
Pay and fringe benefits	4.04[c]	4.50	4.56[a]
Worker ownership or QWL	4.14	3.89	3.62
Job security	4.82	4.74	4.78
Independence	4.50	4.15	4.22
Promotions	3.14	3.87	3.57
Relations with boss	4.00[b,c]	4.76[a]	4.51[a]

1. 5 = Extremely Important, 1 = Moderately Important.
a. Sig. dif. from O&O;
b. Sig. dif. from QWL;
c. Sig. dif. from non-QWL;
d. Sig. dif. between PT/FT in same store type;
p = .05.

Super Fresh employees were part-time cashiers, a heavily female-dominated job. As discussed in chapter 5, this gender-based internal labor market kept women in dead-end jobs and resulted in a larger overall proportion of females in Super Fresh stores.

The most striking difference among the three types of stores was that 90 percent of the O&O worker/owners had full-time jobs compared to half of the QWL workers and less than a third of the non-QWL workers. This is not surprising, since the desire for full-time work was one of the primary reasons for choosing O&O reported in the interviews.

Personal Values

Values may be important in determining worker results because of their role in forming expectations. Several significant differences emerged among the groups in their evaluation of their relationship to the bosses and of their economic rewards.

Worker/owners placed lower importance on good relations with their bosses than did Super Fresh workers. As predicted by many theorists (e.g., Webb and Webb 1920), worker/owners were sometimes unclear about how to resolve the relationship duality of being owners who hire the store manager and workers subordinate to the manager. The new roles in a hierarchy subject to democratic decisionmaking may have reduced the usual emphasis on getting along with the supervisor. Eliminating the need for protection from bumping and for sponsorship by supervisors, which used to occur in A&P, also has changed this relationship.

Workers in non-QWL stores were more likely to value economic rewards than worker/owners. Participativeness, or the lack of it, may affect workers' evaluation of tradeoffs between job satisfaction and economic outcomes. Or part-time workers with low incomes could now be placing a particularly high value on economic rewards. All workers in both stores took a $2/hour cut in wages compared to their former A&P jobs, so some concern about financial welfare was expected for all workers. Because many part-time workers formerly worked full time, this double loss created financial difficulties for many of these workers.

Store Participativeness

In accordance with our multidimensional definition of participativeness, we looked at a number of measures of this construct: (1) the perceived degree of overall worker control in the store; (2) the perceived distribution of influence within the store hierarchy; (3) the perceived involvement of workers in decisionmaking on a range of issues; and (4) the perceived extent of participation, that is, how many workers frequently participate.

Perceived Degree of Overall Worker Control
We asked two general questions, "How much are workers' opinions taken into account in the store?" "How much say or influence do workers have on what goes on in the store?" Worker/owners' average responses were equal to the average responses of QWL Super Fresh workers. However, part-time Super Fresh workers, particularly in non-QWL stores, perceived less overall worker control compared to full-timers. (See table 6.3)

Perceived Hierarchical Influence Distribution
We asked workers a set of questions derived from those Tannenbaum (1968) made popular: "How much say or influence 'did' and 'should' each level of the store hierarchy have in what goes on in the store?" (See figure 6.2.) There was no difference between QWL and O&O workers' perceptions of the actual influence hierarchy, but non-QWL workers, especially part-timers again, reported less influence for every level except for managers.

With respect to the *desired* distribution of influence, it appeared that QWL was especially effective in raising workers' desires for control of work at all levels of the supermarket hierarchy. These aspirations may have colored their perceptions of what was actually happening in these stores and how satisfied it made them feel.

Perceived Worker Involvement in a Variety of Issues
We asked workers about the degree of worker involvement in nine decision areas. Three were decisions regularly made on a daily basis: task assignments, work schedule, and working conditions. Four were

Table 6.3
Mean Differences in Participativeness

Participativeness	Store type		
	O&O	QWL	Non-QWL
Full time	(N = 20)	(N = 24)	(N = 14)
Part time	(N = 2)	(N = 22)	(N = 29)
Degree of worker control[1]	7.14	7.44[c]	6.37[b]
FT	7.05	7.96[d]	7.23[d]
PT	8.00	6.86[c,d]	5.96[b,d]
Range of issues			
In daily decisions[2]	14.09[b,c]	10.73[a,c]	8.07[a,b]
FT	14.10	13.30[d]	13.00[d]
PT	14.00[b,c]	8.04[a,c,d]	5.69[a,b,d]
In intermediate decisions			
Hiring workers	3.77[b,c]	2.04[a]	1.84[a]
FT	3.85	3.50[d]	3.00[d]
PT	4.00	2.04[d]	2.11[d]
Selecting department heads	3.91[b,c]	2.02[a]	1.58[a]
FT	4.45[b,c]	3.42[a]	3.36[a,d]
PT	5.00	2.86	2.25[d]
Beginning training	3.86[b,c]	2.59[a,c]	1.67[a,b]
FT	4.25[c]	4.17[c,d]	3.14[a,b]
PT	4.00	3.14[d]	2.78
Changing vendors	3.59[c]	2.85	2.09[a]
FT	3.50	3.54[d]	3.71[d]
PT	4.50	2.09[d]	1.131[d]
In long-term decisions[3]	8.27[b,c]	2.91[a]	2.67[a]
FT	8.40[b,c]	3.21[a]	3.64[a,d]
PT	7.00[b,c]	2.59[c]	2.21[a,d]
Extent of participation			
% who often participate	55.00[c]	35.00[c]	5.00[a,b]

a. Sig. different from O&O;
b. Sig. different from QWL;
c. Sig. different from non-QWL;
d. Sig. difference between FT/PT workers in same store type:
p = .05.
Multi item scales were:
1. Sum of 2 items, How much worker's opinions are taken into account when decisions are made in the store, 1 = none, 5 = a great deal; How much say workers have in what goes on in the store, 1 = very little say, 5 = very much say.
2. Sum of 3 six point items for influence in tasks, choice of hours, and working conditions, 1 = I am not involved, 6 = I can decide on my own.
3. Sum of 2 six point items (as in 2 above) for influence in capital investments and shutting the store.

Figure 6.2

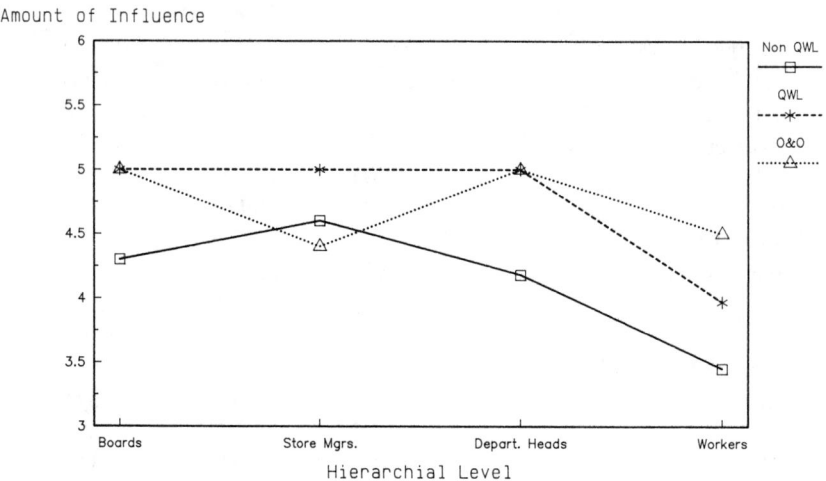

**Perceived Influence Gradients
for Non-QWL, QWL amd O&O Stores
Manager Survey**

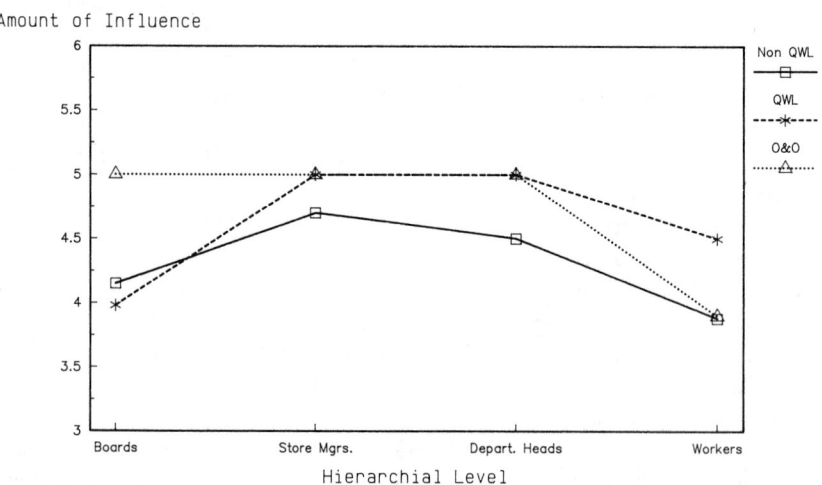

**Ideal Influence Gradients
for Non-QWL,QWL and O&O Stores
Manager Survey**

Figure 6.2 (continued)

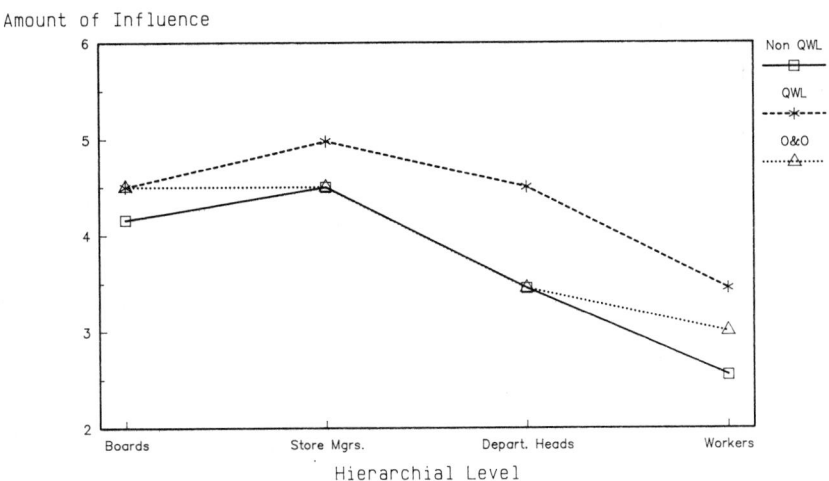

**Perceived Influence Gradients
for Non-QWL, QWL amd O&O Stores
Steward Survey**

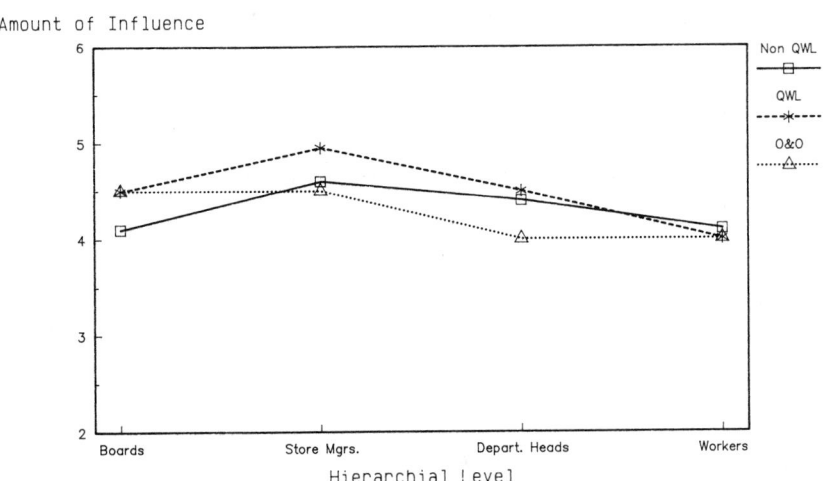

**Ideal Influence Gradients
for Non-QWL,QWL and O&O Stores
Steward Survey**

Figure 6.2 (continued)

Amount of Influence

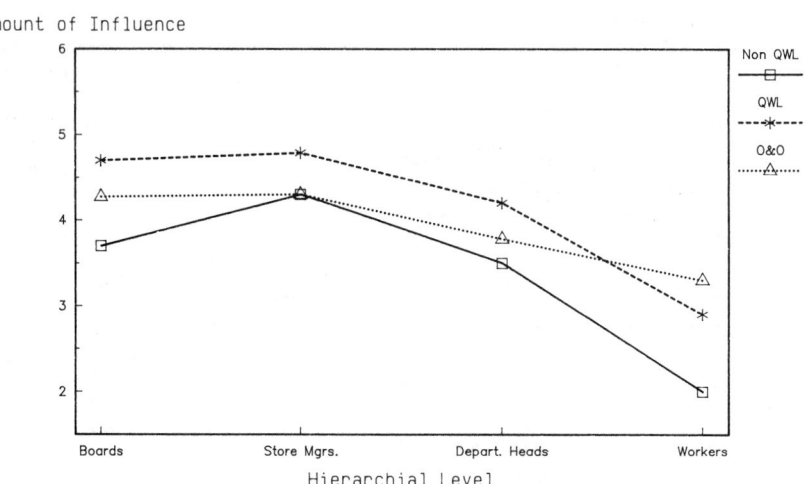

Perceived Influence Gradients
for Non-QWL, QWL amd O&O Stores
Worker Survey

Amount of Influence

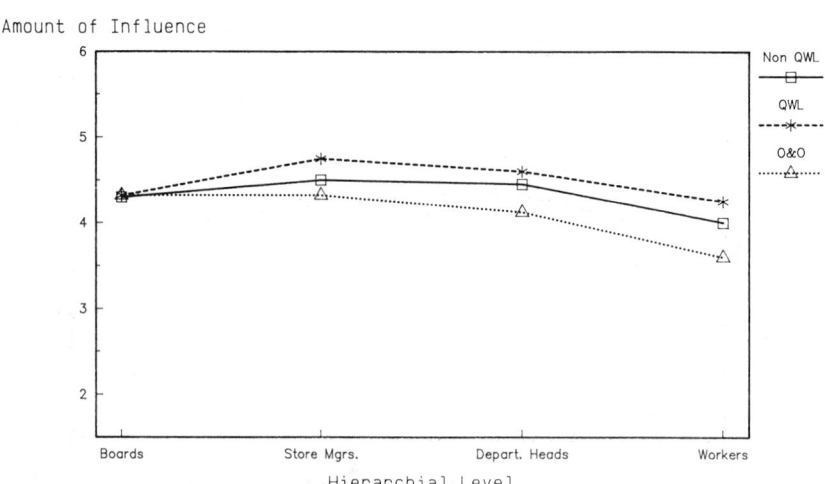

Ideal Influence Gradients
for Non-QWL,QWL and O&O Stores
Worker Survey

decisions with an intermediate time focus: hiring and firing workers, selecting department heads, initiating training programs, and changing vendors. Two were strategic or long-term decisions: making capital investments and shutting down the store.

One of the biggest differences one would expect, based on formal store type, was the range of issues in which workers could be involved. As anticipated, worker/owners experienced the most involvement and non-QWL workers, especially part-timers, experienced the least involvement in every kind of decision. Super Fresh part-time workers felt disenfranchised from all decisions, whether they worked in a QWL store or not. In fact, the longer the time period covered by the implications of the decision, the more involvement O&O worker owners reported, compared to others.

In issues surrounding daily work, among full-timers, Super Fresh workers' perceptions equaled the worker/owners'. In long-term decisions, however, worker/owners reported and desired considerably more influence. This occurred because long-term decisions, particularly important for workers who had experienced a series of retail shutdowns in their city, were outside the jurisdiction of labor-management committees in the Super Fresh QWL program.

Percent Participating Often

According to the shop stewards, the O&Os had the largest percentage of workers who often participated in decisionmaking in their stores, QWL stores had slightly fewer, with a third participating often, and non-QWL stores trailed far behind, with about 5 percent participating often. The assessment agrees with the picture of participation developed in chapter 5.

In summary, while many people participated in the worker-owned stores, full-time Super Fresh and full-time O&O workers perceived equal levels of worker control over daily store life. The major difference was that worker/owners also controlled long-term decisionmaking.

Store Functioning

Our theoretical framework implies that participativeness should affect how stores function and, in turn, influence worker outcomes.

We examined several aspects of store operational practices, including the labor strategy adopted (full time vs. part time), the number of innovations in work methods, how many new skills workers learned formally or informally, and perceived worker motivation and effectiveness, as well as perceived results of the new forms of decisionmaking. We took the assessments of labor strategy and innovations from the store manager survey; all other measures came from the worker survey.

Labor Strategy, Training, and Motivation

We expected that worker-owned and worker-controlled stores would deploy human resources in ways more favorable to workers and would make more effective use of those resources. This point will be further elaborated in chapter 7. The O&O stores adopted the labor strategy of providing full-time jobs for owners who desire them and for some nonowners as well. This strategy, in contrast to the Super Fresh part-time strategy, was accompanied by low turnover and absenteeism rates (see table 6.4).

For our measure of training, we combined workers' responses about how many training programs they had attended, and how many new jobs and new skills they had learned in the new setting. Not only did the O&O worker/owners make greater use of consultants for training workers in business practices, but they learned more jobs and skills than Super Fresh workers. This confirms the interview data about cross-training and job flexibility discussed in chapter 5. Specifically, they reported having learned significantly more interpersonal and group skills, more willingness to speak up at meetings, greater confidence, more knowledge about teamwork, and a greater ability to listen to others' opinions. They also reported feeling significantly more responsible for their work. Ironically, despite greater opportunities for full-time jobs and for learning new skills, worker/owners did not feel more motivated, effective, or innovative.

QWL Super Fresh workers reported greater gains than O&O worker/owners in confidence and in learning about supervising and influencing others. One interpretation of this may be that while QWL store planning board members, who had limited responsibility and authority over store survival, had time to think about and discuss

Table 6.4
Mean Differences in Store Functioning

Store Functioning	Store type		
	O&O	QWL	Non-QWL
Labor strategies			
Av. hrs./week part time	20.00[b,c]	23.00[a,c]	16.50[a,b]
Absenteeism (Weekly)	2.00[b]	6.50[a,c]	2.50[b]
Turnover (Annual)	8.00[b]	176.50[a,c]	25.50[b]
Operations			
Innovations[1]	10.00[c]	10.50[c]	11.50[a,b]
Training[2]	9.50[b,c]	6.07[a]	4.12[a]
FT	9.68[b,c,d]	6.09[a]	5.00[a]
PT	6.00[b,c,d]	6.05[a]	3.68[a]
Individual effort & effectiveness[3]	7.27	6.43	6.02
FT	7.50	7.39[d]	8.08[d]
PT	5.00	5.38[d]	5.10[d]
Perceived consequences of decisionmaking			
New effort & effectiveness[4]	7.24	6.49	6.12
FT	7.47	7.36[d]	7.86[d]
PT	5.00	5.40[d]	5.24[d]
Improved interactions[5]	16.73	17.36[c]	13.88[b]
FT	17.20[b]	21.26[a,c,d]	15.33[b]
PT	12.00	12.39[d]	13.09
Slower decisionmaking[6]	3.36	2.76	2.97
FT	3.40	3.09	3.17
PT	3.00	2.33	2.86

a. Sig. dif. from O&O;
b. Sig. dif. from QWL;
c. Sig. dif. from non-QWL;
d. Sig. dif. between FT/PT in same store type;
p = .05.

1. Sum of 3 items; innovations in jobs, procedures and equipment.

2. Sum of 3 items; How much job-related training received since began working there, 1 = none, 5 = a great deal; plus count of # new jobs and # new skills learned since shutdown.

3. Sum of 2 items; How often it is true that working hard leads to high productivity and doing the job well, 1 = never, 5 = almost always.

4. Sum of 2 items; Extent opportunity to contribute to decisionmaking influences extra effort and effectiveness on the job, 1 = none at all, 5 = a great deal.

5. Sum of 5 items; Consequences which occurred because of system of DM: greater acceptance and quality of decisions, higher trust of manager, more open disagreement, disagreement more easily resolved; 1 = definitely not, 5 = definitely yes.

6. Takes longer to make decisions because of system of decisionmaking. 1 = definitely not, 5 = definitely yes.

store process, the daily pressures at the O&O stores led to a situation where events required decisions so rapidly, the same level of consideration could not be given.

Perceived Influence of Participation on Store Functions

We asked workers whether worker ownership or QWL (1) improved aspects of informal interactions in their stores, such as the acceptance or quality of decisionmaking, trust between manager and workers, open communication of differences, and conflict resolution; (2) slowed down decisionmaking; and (3) improved overall motivation and effectiveness. Surprisingly, there were almost no differences among worker/owners, QWL, and, non-QWL workers in these perceptions. However, full-time QWL Super Fresh workers reported more improvement in interactions than any other group of full- or part-timers. And compared to full-timers in their stores, part-time Super Fresh workers perceived the least improvement in motivation and effectiveness as a result of the new decisionmaking systems.

In summary, O&O worker/owners got more training, while QWL Super Fresh workers got less training, and had higher turnover and absenteeism. Full-time Super Fresh workers believed interpersonal interactions had improved as a consequence of QWL, but most other worker perceptions of store functioning did not differ among the store types.

Store Outcomes

Both theoretically and practically, one would expect that workers' welfare would be influenced by the success or failure of the stores in which they worked (see table 6.5). The Super Fresh stores in which we interviewed and surveyed former A&P workers were slightly larger and had been more profitable in 1981 than the O&O stores. Even so, 1983 O&O labor costs were lower and profits higher than these Super Fresh stores.

Table 6.5
Mean Differences in Store Characteristics and Store Outcomes

	Store type		
	O&O (N = 2)	**QWL** (N = 2)	**Non-QWL** (N = 2)
Store characteristics			
# Square feet	18500[b,c]	28000[a,c]	5000[a,b]
# Employees	42[b,c]	115[a,c]	117[a,b]
% Full-time workers	44.6[b,c]	16.9[a]	14.1[a]
Union and consultants[1]	7.50[b,c]	2.50[a]	1.00[a]
Store economic outcomes			
Profit 1981[2]	.05[b,c]	.09[a]	.08[a]
Profit 1983	.10[b,c]	.08[a]	.08[a]
Unit labor costs 1981[2]	.16	.14	.14
Unit labor costs 1983	.09[b,c]	.11[a]	.11[a]

a. Sig. dif. from O&O;
b. Sig. dif. from QWL;
c. Sig. dif. from non QWL;
p = .05.
1. Sum of number of times 6 possible kinds of help were received from 7 possible sources.
2. Per $ of sales.

These store outcomes will be more completely considered in the following chapter.

Worker Outcomes

What were the effects of the job-saving efforts through worker ownership and participation in decisions? We focused on four areas of impact on individuals: (1) financial benefits from job income and bonuses; (2) perceived economic well-being, including comparisons with their pre-shutdown situations; (3) job satisfaction; and (4) life satisfaction.

Financial Outcomes

Although the worker-owned stores reported greater profitability, success or failure of an individual store does not insure the same result for workers. Because union contracts fix wage rates for each position, differences in job income correspond either to differences in position or to differences in number of hours worked.

As can be seen in table 6.6, O&O worker/owners clearly came out ahead of non-QWL Super Fresh workers in average job income, primarily because all but two worker/owners were full-time, compared to less than a third of the non-QWL workers. But compared to full-time Super Fresh workers, full-time worker/owners received slightly lower job incomes, even though they worked more hours. Why this discrepancy? First, the worker/owners contributed "sweat equity"— several unpaid hours of work per week. Second, at the O&Os, there were more full-time women working in lower paid positions and there were fewer highly paid meatcutters. While meatcutter wages were the highest of any position in the O&O stores, Super Fresh meatcutter wages were higher still. Third, our sample may not adequately represent the true average job income of O&O worker/owners because fewer of them responded to questions about their income.

Though wages might be the total job income in conventional supermarket jobs, the innovations at O&O and Super Fresh added a bonus form of gainsharing to the pay package. With respect to bonuses, however, comparing O&O worker/owners and Super Fresh workers was difficult because different distribution rules existed and because worker/owners were more reluctant to report incomes and bonuses.

At Super Fresh, bonuses represented a portion of store revenues, but they were tied to store labor costs. As labor costs went down, bonuses went up; the exact formula was determined by the union contract. Full-time workers in QWL stores obtained higher bonuses than their counterparts in non-QWL stores, and of course part-timers got smaller bonuses than full-time workers in both types of stores.

Not only was the O&O bonus formula different, tied to profits rather than to costs, but according to their loan agreements, O&O worker/owners were not supposed to vote themselves a dividend until

Table 6.6

Mean Differences in Outcomes for Workers

Worker outcomes	Store type		
	O&O	QWL	Non-QWL
Full time	(N = 20)	(N = 24)	(N = 14)
Part time	(N = 2)	(N = 22)	(N = 29)
Financial			
Job income	$19,183[a]	17,039	14,413[c]
FT	$19,513[b,c,d]	22,687[a,d]	24,560[a,d]
PT	$13,572[b,c,d]	9,822[a,d]	9,514[a,d]
Hours/Week	44.86[b,c]	30.78[a]	26.81[a]
FT	46.65[b,c,d]	40.46[a,d]	42.28[a,d]
PT	27.00[c,d]	20.23[a,d]	19.34[a,d]
Bonus	$309.37[b,c]	2,010.05[a,c]	1,144.90[a,b]
FT	$309.37[b,c]	2,599.14[a,d]	1,514.61[a,d]
PT	——	1,247.71[d]	966.89[d]
Economic well-being			
Satisfaction with pay[1]	3.32	3.13	3.19
Satisfaction with economic[1] situation	3.59	3.40	3.62
Postshutdown changes in budget[2]	18.95[c]	17.74	14.95[a]
FT	18.84	20.13[d]	16.14
PT	21.00[b,c]	14.84[a,d]	14.28[a]
Satisfaction			
Job satisfaction, overall[1]	4.27	4.22	3.95
with supervision	3.28[b,c]	4.32[a]	3.95[a]
with co-workers	3.14[b,c]	4.17[a]	3.90[a]
with job security	3.91[c]	3.26	3.00[a]
with system of decisionmaking	3.73[c]	3.39[c]	2.68[a,b]
with promotions	2.91	3.49[c]	2.72[b]
with growth	3.50	3.58	3.25
with accomplishment	3.82	4.19	3.83
with independence	3.45	3.75	3.52
Life satisfaction, overall[1]	4.04	4.44	4.40
with leisure	3.04[b,c]	4.27[a]	4.47[a]
with family	4.14[c]	4.53	4.80[a]
with health	4.04[b,c]	4.53[a]	4.50[a]
with career	4.09	3.81	3.93
with self	4.36	4.44	4.48

1. 1 = Very dissatisfied, 5 = very satisfied.
2. Sum of 7 items, how savings compare with preshutdown. 1 = much worse, 5 = much better; how much owed compared to preshutdown,
a. Sig. dif. from 0 & 0;
b. Sig. dif. from QWL;
c. Sig. dif. from non-QWL;
d. Sig. dif. between PT/FT in same store type; p = .05.

1 = much more, 5 = much less; how food, clothing, transportation, leisure, and housing budget were affected, 1 = less in budget, 5 = more in budget.

after their start-up debt was retired. However, both O&Os apparently voted year-end bonuses anyway, since a few workers from each store reported receiving one. The reported bonuses were within the range of Super Fresh bonuses, but many workers simply reported a zero or left this question blank. The figures for mean bonuses among worker/owners thus do not accurately reflect the actual bonuses received, since some workers reporting "0" or a blank probably received a bonus but were aware of the legal prohibitions so did not answer the question accurately.

The O&O worker/owners did have another economic benefit, not captured by these data, in the growth of equity accumulating through the $5,000 share each contributed to become an owner. A percent of profits was distributed to each shareholder's account, based on the number of hours worked, but the owner was not free to withdraw this money until he or she left the store or until the debt was retired. With the information we had available, we could not calculate the dollar value of this equity growth. Nevertheless, in future studies of other organizations, the equity growth value ought not be ignored when considering the comprehensive financial benefits to worker/owners.

Perceived Economic Welfare

Although we were unable to capture the dollar total of pay, bonus, and equity for worker/owners, we could compare perceptions of economic well-being. First, we asked workers how satisfied they were with their pay and fringe benefits, and with their overall economic situation. On both measures, all three groups of workers were equally satisfied. This satisfaction was associated with higher personal cost, however, since many Super Fresh workers were managing to maintain their standard of living only by holding down second jobs or by relying on other family members' incomes. Household incomes ranged from $2,000 to $90,000, but the average annual *household* incomes did not differ between full-time and part-time workers.

Second, we used a series of questions asking workers to compare their current situation to their situation before the A&P shutdown. When we asked workers whether they had more or less savings, debt, or money in their budget for food, clothing, transportation, leisure, or housing since the shutdown, O&O workers believed they were significantly better off compared to before the shutdown than did the non-QWL workers. Part-time Super Fresh workers reported the greatest loss. Worker/owners also reported a greater ability to engage in discretionary purchases, such as buying a car, paying for a wedding, going on vacation, retiring, and paying for leisure activities. Though Super Fresh workers generally felt able to get by overall, they recognized that they pinched more pennies now than before the shutdown.

Job Satisfaction

We asked workers to rate how satisfied they were with their jobs overall and with each of eight aspects of their jobs, in addition to their pay satisfaction mentioned above. Overall job satisfaction and a sum of the nine separate satisfaction questions (overall job satisfaction plus the other eight aspects) showed no significant differences.

Considering each nonfinancial aspect of satisfaction separately, however, differences did emerge. Worker/owners were much more satisfied with their job security and worker ownership system than non-QWL Super Fresh workers were with their job security and with QWL. On no aspect, however, were worker/owners more satisfied than QWL workers. In fact, worker/owners were much less satisfied with supervision and co-workers than Super Fresh workers. Comments made during the interviews suggested that the dissatisfaction with supervision arose from unclear expectations of the boss's power and identity resulting from role conflict between the manager, board members, and members at large and from perceiving supervision as too lax. Some worker/owners reported wanting a clearer chain of command. Dissatisfaction with co-workers came from unresolved differences of opinion over store decisions and also from some workers feeling excluded from decisionmaking cliques in the stores.

Full-time QWL workers were more satisfied than other workers with promotions and job opportunities. This is curious because these workers actually lost their long-held, interstore transfer right, which was the primary route for promotion to the top in the old A&P. However, particular store managers singled out many of the older, male elite workers and called them back to work at Super Fresh, frequently as department heads. In our interviews, Super Fresh workers expressed the hope that the retail chain would succeed, and that new stores would be opened to which they would be transferred because they were known as good workers. In Spring 1986, Super Fresh did announce openings of several new Philadelphia-area stores. Perhaps a few workers will achieve their dream, but some later disillusionment among workers not chosen for new stores would not be surprising.

Part-time QWL workers were not as satisfied with their promotion opportunities as other workers. They were also less satisfied with their pay, with QWL, and with their job security. In sum, they had a fairly realistic assessment of their situation. Why then did they report a high level of overall satisfaction? It may be due to the high proportion of part-time workers who were females and to the familiar finding that women report higher job satisfaction than men, even under poorer working conditions. Also, as the interviews show, some of these women were satisfied to simply provide supplementary household income and *wanted* to have part-time jobs to fit their homemaking schedules.

Life Satisfaction

We also asked workers several questions about satisfaction with their lives. In addition to general life satisfaction, they rated satisfaction with their families, leisure, career, health, and self-esteem. They responded as they had when we asked about their jobs: in overall life satisfaction there were no differences, but in particular aspects of their lives, differences appeared. Worker/owners expressed the heavy toll of working extra hours, learning how to run a supermarket, and being responsible for the business through lower ratings of satisfaction with leisure, family, and health.

Both innovations had affected workers' lives away from the workplace. There is much worker testimony from the interview data about the time demands of worker-ownership. One older worker said, "The store owns me." He had hoped for a more relaxed preretirement period. For workers with dependent children or sick family members, the time demands were most difficult. Several casual remarks were made about spousal pressure to become less involved with the store. Those worker/owners who had second jobs, serious hobbies or were active in voluntary organizations found these activities incompatible with the demands of worker-ownership.

Some might believe that those who became worker/owners were more critical, less satisfied people in general—less satisfied with A&P and with most aspects of their lives. Worker/owners were *not* dissatisfied with everything, however. Their economic situations and their careers pleased them, but their concern was the heavy price paid in other parts of their lives—a complaint expressed by many entrepreneurs in the early years after opening a new business.

The new work structure affected Super Fresh workers very differently. Formerly, elite A&P workers tended to work overtime; those same workers, now in new Super Fresh, full-time leadership positions, were not working any more than in the past. Since few part-time workers participated in QWL, they felt no excessive time demands. Many spoke of the extra time they had with nothing to do as a result of cutbacks in hours. The major noneconomic effect of working in Super Fresh was clearly the loss of vacation time. The reduction to a single week vacation was severely felt by workers who had had up to a month's vacation in the past and who owned homes and businesses in vacation areas.

Theoretical Model Testing

The previous sections of this chapter described mean differences in worker characteristics, perceived organizational processes, and worker outcomes among the three groups—O&O worker/owners, QWL, and non-QWL Super Fresh workers. Such descriptive results cannot tell us much about which factors were most important or influential in contributing to these differences, however, and they do not tell us whether these differences arose from working in a particular store type or from some other factor.

To determine how much support we had for our hypotheses, we tested them through simultaneous equation modeling, using a Three-Stage Least Squares (3SLS) technique. Our theoretical model posited one-way causal relationships, i.e., it was recursive. However, to allow for the possibility of unspecified interactions among the dependent variables or feedback loops, we chose the 3SLS technique. The remaining statistical tables of this chapter report, for each set of dependent variables in the model, the unstandardized model coefficients for each independent variable. The magnitude or absolute value of these coefficients is not meaningful because of the arbitrary scale values they represent. The direction of effect (positive or negative) and the significance of the coefficient are of key importance. They express the direction and existence of a relationship between independent and dependent variables as specified in the model. Unlike single equation regression models, summary statistics such as R^2 are not relevant in simultaneous equation models. The simultaneous equations for the model are as follows:

(Eq. 6.1) store participativeness = f(Worker Characteristics, Store Type, Consultants).
In (Eq. 6.1a), store participativeness is measured by the degree of worker control.
In (Eq. 6.1b), store participativeness is measured by the degree of worker participation in daily decisions.
In (Eq. 6.1c), store participativeness is measured by the degree of worker participation in long-term decisions.

(Eq. 6.2) worker outcomes = f(Worker Characteristics, Store Participativeness, Store Functioning, Store Economic Outcomes).

For each worker outcome, we estimated a model comprising four simultaneous equations.[1] The first three equations, of the form of equations (6.1a), (6.1b), and (6.1c) estimated three measures of perceived participativeness. The fourth equation, of the form of equation (6.2), included the three estimations of perceived participativeness derived from equations 6.1, as well as nonestimated variables which measured aspects of worker characteristics, store functioning, and store outcomes.

Analysis of each worker outcome included essentially the same set of model variables:

A. Worker Characteristics. We used education, total supermarket seniority, number of jobs known, department head status and months of layoff in all equations of the form (6.1). Education, sex, number of dependents and years of seniority were included in equations of the form (6.2).
Worker Attitudes and Beliefs. For all analyses except the two concerning job income and weekly hours, we also included in equation (6.2) three worker attitudes and perceptions characteristics: satisfaction with supervision, satisfaction with co-workers, and a measure of perceived economic gain since the A&P shutdown.[2] We included the satisfaction measures to represent some aspects of manager selection and self-selection processes in recruitment to particular stores, which loomed as so important in the worker interviews (see chapter 5). In addition, we expected that worker attitudes about their outcomes would be affected by the degree of sacrifice endured or gains accrued since the A&P shutdown.

B. Store Type.[3] Two dummy variables, ownership and QWL, were used in all forms of equation (6.1).

C. Consultants. The sum of the number of times several kinds of consulting was received was included in all equations of the form (6.1).

D. Participativeness. We used the three measures: the degree of worker involvement in daily decisions, the degree of worker involvement in long-term decisions, and the perceived degree of overall worker control.[4]

E. Store Functioning. We used average weekly part-timer hours in the store,[5] weekly store absenteeism,[6] and measures of training, motivation, and informal processes in all forms of equations (6.2).[7] We could not use another apparently important measure of labor strategy, namely, the percentage of full-time workers in the store, because it was too highly correlated with store type, as well as with worker involvement in long-term decisions.

We estimated the model with and without two additional measures of informal store functioning included in equation 6.2. The first was a sum of five perceived interpersonal consequences of the system of store decisionmaking (worker ownership or QWL). These consequences included greater acceptance and better quality of decisions, higher trust of managers, more open disagreement, and disagreements more easily resolved. The second, a single-item measure from the same set of questions which did not load on the same factor as the others, is the perceived slowness of decisionmaking. Using these variables reduced the sample size by about six or seven people, and reduced the degrees of freedom. In a few cases these variables had a significant effect.

F. Store Economic Outcomes. Though both unit labor costs and profits for the current year were considered, the small sample size dictated that only one store financial measure be used. Profit was our choice. We expected that workers in more profitable stores might benefit, financially or otherwise.

The worker outcomes examined included the economic outcomes of job income, hours worked per week, satisfaction with pay and fringe benefits, and satisfaction with overall economic situation. Job satisfaction measures included satisfaction with job overall, with job security, and with the system of decisionmaking. Life satisfaction aspects examined were satisfaction with life overall, and with family, leisure, and health. We decided to use the two satisfaction items as separate dependent measures rather than summing them into multi-item scales for two reasons. First, mean differences were found between worker/owners, QWL, and non-QWL workers for individual satisfaction items. Second, variables in which we were interested might have had opposite effects on different aspects of satisfaction and cancel each other out, resulting in no significant effect on overall measures, if a summed scale was used.

Participativeness

We used three multiple-item measures of participativeness as dependent variables for equation (6.1): degree of worker involvement in daily decisions, degree of worker involvement in long-term decisions, and perceived degree of overall worker control. This means that every time the model was calculated, four equations were included, three estimating participativeness and one for a worker outcome. Because we earlier noted differences within the stores between full- and part-time workers, we tested our model separately for the sample as a whole and for full-time workers.

Worker Characteristics
Our theoretical model and our interview data (see chapter 5) suggested that individual workers with different backgrounds and previous experience might have different perceptions of store participativeness. Therefore, we examined the effect on perceived participativeness of a series of background variables. Differences that arose from selection processes or self-selection, are captured by including these demographic data. Differences due to experience on the planning boards or boards of directors are also captured by the inclusion of seniority and department head status, since board membership in all store types tended to reflect these leadership characteristics.

Being male, married, and older predicted perceptions of greater participativeness in preliminary regression analyses, but all of these characteristics were highly correlated with the number of jobs known, which we chose for inclusion in the simultaneous equation model.

Worker values also were related to perceptions of participativeness. While the small sample size precluded use of all of these variables in the final model, initial single equation regression analyses found that those who valued good relations with their co-workers and boss, who liked job security, and who valued independence were likely to perceive more participativeness, regardless of where they were working.

Several worker characteristics had a significant effect on participativeness. Tables 6.7 and 6.8 only illustrate results for equations of the form (6.1) for the model run which had the largest N. They are representative of the effects found regardless of the worker outcome used in equation (6.2). The first table presents results for all workers, the second for full-time workers only.

Table 6.7
Representative Three-Stage Least Squares Model Parameters for Predictors of Perceived Participativeness Among All Workers (Equation 6.1)

	Perceived participativeness		
	Daily decisions (N=89)	Long-term decisions (N=89)	Degree of worker control (N=89)
Input	Coefficients	Coefficients	Coefficients
Worker characteristics:			
Yrs. of education	0.606***	0.156***	1.408***
Yrs. seniority	0.016	0.006	0.047**
# of jobs known	0.276***	0.052	0.114***
Department head[1]	3.813***	0.926**	0.165
Mo. of layoff	−0.155**	0.037	0.045
Store type			
Worker-owned[2]	3.269**	4.655***	0.261
QWL[2]	−0.595	−0.321	0.548
Unions & consultants			
Consulting[3]	0.045	0.040	−0.043

*p<.1; **p<.05; ***p<.01; two-tailed t-test.
1. Dummy coded, 1 = dept. head, 0 = nondepartment head.
2. Dummy coded against non-QWL.
3. Sum of the # of times 6 kinds of assistance were received from 7 sources.

Generally, workers' perceptions of power in the store reflect their experience, skills, and status. Within each store type, those with more education perceived more participativeness. In addition, those with more seniority and knowledge of more jobs perceived more overall worker control. In daily decisions, those workers who knew more jobs or were department heads perceived more participativeness while those with longer layoffs perceived less. Department heads also had stronger perceptions of involvement in long-term decisions.

Table 6.8

Representative Three-Stage Least Squares Model Parameters for Predictors of Perceived Participativeness Among Full-Time Workers (Equation 6.1)

	Perceived participativeness		
	Daily decisions (N = 46)	Long-term decisions (N = 46)	Degree of worker control (N = 46)
Input	Coefficients	Coefficients	Coefficients
Worker characteristics:			
Yrs. of education	0.760***	−0.027	0.438***
Yrs. seniority	−0.002	0.063	0.057
# of jobs known	0.239***	0.090	0.065
Department head[1]	2.356***	1.499**	0.266
Mo. of layoff	0.171	0.255***	0.083
Store type			
Worker-owned[2]	0.467	3.261***	−0.131
QWL[2]	−1.101	−0.296	0.336
Unions & consultants			
Consulting[3]	−0.003	0.112	−0.057

*p<.1; **p<.05; ***p<.01; two-tailed t-test.
1. Dummy coded, 1 = dept. head, 0 = nondepartment head.
2. Dummy coded against non-QWL.
3. Sum of the # of times 6 kinds of assistance were received from 7 sources.

Store Type

As we expected, the formal worker ownership structure did influence participativeness (see tables 6.7 and 6.8). Controlling for worker characteristics and consulting received, worker/owners perceived greater participativeness in daily and long-term decisions (for full-time workers, worker ownership increased perceptions of involvement in long-term decisions only).

Surprisingly, perceived overall worker control was not higher among worker/owners, other things being equal. Comments made in the interviews suggested that before the shutdown, A&P corporate activities had limited what workers could do in the stores. After workers became owners, however, they still saw their choices as constrained, but the constraints were more general: "That's how things are in business."

Compared to working in a non-QWL store, working in a QWL store had no influence on perceptions of any dimension of participativeness. Since worker characteristics did have an influence, this suggests that store staffing patterns, not QWL, truly differentiated QWL and non-QWL stores from each other.

Consultants

Consultant help, which was measured by store managers' reports of the number of different kinds of help received from each of a variety of sources, did not predict worker perceptions of participativeness.

In summary, our model found incomplete confirmation of the effect of input factors on participativeness. The formal structure of worker ownership, as set up in the O&Os, has been translated into organizational participative processes, particularly on long-term issues. Super Fresh's QWL program seems not to have such an effect, though it may *seem* effective (i.e., when one only looks at mean differences) because staffing and self-selection processes recruited senior workers into the stores we studied, and having more experience and education consistently had a positive effect on workers' perceptions of participativeness.

Worker Outcomes

According to our model, worker characteristics, participativeness, store functioning, and store outcomes should either directly or indirectly influence worker outcomes. In the following sections we re-

port the results for each group of outcome variables [equation 6.2]—
economic outcomes, job satisfaction and life satisfaction. When
these results were computed, three equations of the form (6.1) were
included in the system of simultaneous equations, but a description
of these parameters will not be repeated for every outcome reported
here.

Economic Outcomes

We looked at four measures of individual economic outcomes: supermarket job income for the year preceding the survey; usual
weekly hours of work; satisfaction with pay and benefits; and satisfaction with one's overall economic situation. The results of equation 6.2 model analyses for economic outcomes are shown in tables
6.9 and 6.10.

Few of the variables significantly predicted workers' 1984 job income and hours. Worker involvement in daily decisions had a positive effect on income and hours worked, whereas involvement in
long-term decisions increased only hours worked. Among full-time
workers, perceptions of more overall worker control were related to
higher individual income. Seniority, as one would expect, led to increased weekly hours. For full-time workers, however, women
earned less than men, presumably because of the sex-based internal
labor market which usually gave men the higher paying positions.

Surprisingly, store functioning variables tended to be poor predictors of income and hours. Store profit similarly had no significant
impact. The only effect of store functioning on worker job income
was that workers believing themselves harder working and more effective were among the lowest paid. Although conventional wisdom
suggests that effective workers should be reaping the benefits of their
work, the opposite was true in this case if the workers' perceptions
are accurate. Our worker interviews suggested that women, particularly deli clerks and meat wrappers, were highly motivated and believed they were effective in their jobs, yet were in relatively low-
paying positions.

We found a number of unexpected relationships for workers' satisfaction with economic outcomes. Those who were satisfied with

Table 6.9
Three-Stage Least Squares Model Parameters for Predictors of Economic Outcomes Among All Workers
(Equation 6.2)

Worker characteristics	1984 personal income from supermarket job (N = 85) Coefficients	Weekly hours (N = 89) Coefficients	Satisfaction with pay & benefits (N = 82) Coefficients	Satisfaction with overall economic situation (N = 82) Coefficients
Demographics				
Yrs. of education	384.70	0.825	0.121	−0.014
Sex	−896.45	−1.440	0.703	1.007***
# of dependents	132.12	0.575	0.045	−0.136
Yrs. of seniority	138.21	0.282***	0.022	0.011
Attitudes and beliefs				
Satisfaction with supervision	——	——	0.219	0.283*
Satisfaction with co-workers	——	——	0.339**	−0.244**
Comparative economic gains since shutdown	——	——	0.023	0.040*

Participativeness				
Daily decisions	1065.89***	1.374***	−0.021	0.120
Long-term decisions	−264.69	1.565***	0.087	−0.196
Degree of worker control	1279.66	0.259	0.119	0.195
Store functioning				
Avg. weekly hours of part-timers	10.55	——	0.105	−0.008
Absenteeism (weekly)	−134.29	−0.103	−0.220***	−0.054
Perceived effort and effectiveness	−825.55*	−0.641	−0.150	0.065
Training	−22.14	0.271	0.034	0.034
Increased effort	169.98	−0.013	−0.021	−0.103
Store economic outcomes				
1983 Profit	−33.387	−10.503	−29.969*	8.843

NOTE: Variables are defined in footnotes on tables 6.1 to 6.6 and in the text.

*p<.1; **p<.05; ***p<.01; two-tailed t-test.

Table 6.10
Three-Stage Least Squares Model Parameters for Predictors of
Economic Outcomes Among Full-Time Workers
(Equation 6.2)

	1984 personal income from supermarket job (N=46) Coefficients	Satisfaction with pay and benefits (N=45) Coefficients	Satisfaction with overall economic situation (N=45) Coefficients
Worker characteristics			
Demographics			
Yrs. of education	698.06	0.181	−0.091
Sex	−2554.12*	0.690	0.580
# of dependents	167.30	0.206	−0.144
Yrs. of seniority	25.81	0.022	0.028
Attitudes and beliefs			
Satisfaction with supervision	———	−0.115	−0.073
Satisfaction with co-workers	———	0.518**	0.047
Comparative economic gains since shutdown	———	0.003	0.042
Participativeness			
Daily decisions	186.92	0.243	0.224
Long-term decisions	−520.34	0.081	−0.205*
Degree of worker control	2999.55***	−0.229	0.147
Store functioning			
Avg. weekly hours of part-timers	−457.24	0.129	−0.035
Absenteeism (weekly)	269.40	−0.078	0.071
Perceived effort and effectiveness	−513.29	−0.376**	−0.004
Training	26.72	0.000	0.017
Increased effort	267.43	0.124	−0.132*
Store economic outcomes			
1983 Profit	65.859	−38.122	19.854

NOTE: Variables are defined in footnotes to tables 6.1 to 6.6.
*p<.1; **p<.05; ***p<.01; two-tailed t-test.

their co-workers were satisfied with their pay and benefits; those who worked in stores with lower profitability and higher absenteeism, and those full-timers who perceived they were less effective, were also more satisfied with their pay. Not surprisingly, since pay and benefits were regulated by the union contract and not affected by either form of participation, participativeness had no effect.

Workers' satisfaction with overall economic situation is somewhat different. Women, those satisfied with their supervisor, and those who made postshutdown gains were more satisfied; those who perceived more participation in long-term decisionmaking, who were less satisfied with their co-workers, and who were working harder—that is, primarily the O&O workers—were less satisfied with their overall economic situation.

With respect to the low impact of participativeness and store functioning on economic outcomes, these findings are surprising. First, we expected any effect of participativeness, especially in long-term decisionmaking which is highest for worker/owners, to be positive. Second, we expected participativeness to positively influence workers' satisfaction with economic outcomes, but to influence worker financial outcomes only indirectly through store functioning and store profits. However, participativeness seems to affect worker outcomes directly in our tests, and we shall see more of this effect below when we discuss other worker outcome measures.

How can we explain these apparent anomalies? First, perhaps worker/owners had very high expectations of prosperity; they may have wanted to be in an even better position than they found themselves. Second, the actual causality may run opposite to that pictured in our model; that is, those with higher incomes and more hours perceive higher worker participativeness, perhaps because they generalize from their own power in the stores. After all, full-time workers had higher mean levels of perceived participativeness and, because of their schedules if nothing else, were more available to participate. Also meatcutters, who were very powerful, received higher wages.

Third, some stores with high levels of participativeness may have maintained a labor strategy of high wages and high average weekly hours for former A&P workers. While this would be expected to show up in store functioning, we could not use percent of full-time workers as a measure of this strategy in the worker model because it was too highly correlated with store type. The measure of labor strategy we used, average weekly part-timer hours in the store, neither affirms nor rules out this third alternative. Our interview findings (see chapter 5), support this third explanation by showing that some very participative Super Fresh managers hand picked former employees and made certain they received good positions. Thus, labor strategy is probably quite important even if measures included in the worker model had few significant effects. The high correlation of store type with percent of full-timers indicates store type may indeed be identical to labor strategy.

Job Satisfaction

We looked at overall job satisfaction and two other specific aspects of job satisfaction, job security, and decisionmaking. A comprehensive set of predictors of job satisfaction was not included in this analysis because, unlike many other studies, our purpose was not to predict as much of the variance in job satisfaction as possible. Rather, we were trying to find out whether the specific innovations in formal structure—worker ownership or QWL—led to store processes which affected job satisfaction. Predictors of job satisfaction not differing by store type were assumed to be distributed similarly in each store and assumed not to have significant interaction effects with store type that would necessitate their inclusion in this system of equations. This assumption remains to be tested in future studies. Results of the analyses for equation (6.2) for these outcomes are shown in tables 6.11 and 6.12.

It is often claimed that if people participate in decisions which affect them, they will be more satisfied with the results. This expectation was modestly confirmed. The degree of worker control had a barely significant effect on overall job satisfaction among full-timers, but not when their results were combined with those of the part-timers. Worker involvement in long-term decisions also positively affected individual satisfaction with decisionmaking and job security.

Table 6.11
Three-Stage Least Squares Model Parameters for Predictors of
Job Satisfaction Among All Workers (Equation 6.2)

	Satisfaction with job overall (N = 82) Coefficients	Satisfaction with job security (N = 82) Coefficients	Satisfaction with system of decisionmaking (N = 74) Coefficients
Worker characteristics			
Demographics			
Yrs. of education	0.090	0.019	0.041
Sex	0.423	0.053	−0.480
# of dependents	−0.127	0.057	0.015
Yrs. of seniority	0.014	0.042**	0.014
Attitudes and beliefs			
Satisfaction with supervision	0.109	0.260	0.275
Satisfaction with co-workers	0.227**	0.415***	0.480***
Comparative economic gains since shutdown	0.033*	0.026	0.013
Participativeness			
Daily decisions	0.011	−0.010	−0.019
Long-term decisions	0.047	0.266**	0.272**
Degree of worker control	0.151	0.011	−0.104
Store functioning			
Avg. weekly hours of part-timers	0.022	0.061	0.217*
Absenteeism (weekly)	−0.032	−0.045	−0.087
Perceived effort and effectiveness	−0.063	−0.041	−0.049
Training	0.013	0.038	0.014
Increased effort	0.067	−0.108	−0.027
Store economic outcomes			
1983 Profit	3.410	−24.294*	−25.151*

NOTE: Variables are defined in footnotes of tables 6.1 to 6.6.
*$p<.1$; **$p<.05$; ***$p<.01$; two-tailed t-test.

Table 6.12
Three-Stage Least Squares Model Parameters for Predictors of Job
Satisfaction Among Full-Time Workers (Equation 6.2)

	Satisfaction with job overall (N = 45) Coefficients	Satisfaction with job security (N = 45) Coefficients	Satisfaction with system of decisionmaking (N = 43) Coefficients
Worker characteristics			
Demographics			
Yrs. of education	0.067	0.160	0.262**
Sex	0.381	−0.027	−0.471
# of dependents	−0.049	−0.019	0.038
Yrs. of seniority	0.012	0.010	−0.055**
Attitudes and beliefs			
Satisfaction with supervision	0.013	0.422	0.294
Satisfaction with co-workers	0.023	0.304	0.445*
Comparative economic gains since shutdown	0.026	−0.005	−0.005
Participativeness			
Daily decisions	0.113	−0.023	−0.158
Long-term decisions	0.008	0.404***	0.433***
Degree of worker control	0.297*	−0.006	0.121
Store functioning			
Avg. weekly hours of part-timers	−0.002	0.153*	0.201**
Absenteeism (weekly)	−0.062	−0.079	−0.145
Perceived effort and effectiveness	−0.143	−0.264	−0.139
Training	0.004	−0.015	−0.040
Increased effort	0.027	0.043	0.059
Store economic outcomes			
1983 Profit	−6.949	−38.627	−50.017**

NOTE: Variables are defined in footnotes of table 6.1 to 6.6.
*p<.1; **p<.05; ***p<.01; two-tailed t-test.

Contrary to our hypotheses, few store functioning variables had any effect on overall job satisfaction. Those who reported themselves to be more hard-working and more effective full-time workers were less satisfied with their job security. These same workers were also less satisfied with their pay and fringe benefits. This may indicate some complacency on the part of more senior workers, or some particularly motivated workers may be in positions of low pay and low job security.

When differences in worker characteristics and levels of participativeness and store functioning are controlled, the most profitable stores had workers least satisfied with decisionmaking and job security. Were workers unaware of how well or how poorly their stores were doing in comparison with others and thus using some unrealistic standard for comparison? Or were the most profitable stores somehow dissatisfying to work in? We do not have the data to choose between these alternative explanations.

Participativeness had some interesting effects on life satisfaction (see tables 6.13 and 6.14). In contrast to the negative effects worker control had on some aspects of job satisfaction, we found that the degree of overall worker control had a positive effect on overall life satisfaction and on satisfaction with family and health. For full-time workers, worker involvement in daily decisions positively affected their overall life satisfaction and satisfaction with health. More worker involvement in long-term decisions meant less satisfaction with leisure, however. Most likely, worker/owners have been too busy to enjoy themselves outside of work.

Store functioning variables affected life satisfaction in some odd ways. Those believing themselves more effective and seeing improved interpersonal interactions in the new work setting were *less* likely to be satisfied with their lives overall, and with their family life. Perhaps these were also the people who invested more of their time trying to make their stores successful, and they suffered from it. Also, those working in stores with higher absenteeism were more satisfied with their lives. When coupled with the negative impact of worker involvement in long-term decisions, these findings indicate that work interfered with nonwork aspects of worker/owners' lives.

Table 6.13

Three-Stage Least Squares Model Parameters for Predictors of Life Satisfaction Among All Workers (Equation 6.2)

	Satisfaction with life overall (N=82) Coefficients	Satisfaction with family (N=82) Coefficients	Satisfaction with leisure (N=81) Coefficients	Satisfaction with health (N=82) Coefficients
Worker characteristics				
Demographics				
Yrs. of education	−0.141**	−0.047	0.046	−0.179**
Sex	0.573*	0.573*	0.534	0.615*
# of dependents	−0.227***	−0.060	−0.082	−0.170*
Yrs. of seniority	−0.024	−0.032	−0.007	−0.030*
Attitudes and beliefs				
Satisfaction with supervision	0.070	0.028	−0.033	0.107
Satisfaction with co-workers	0.124	0.135	0.214*	0.195*
Comparative economic gains since shutdown	0.011	−0.005	0.008	0.023

Participativeness				
Daily decisions	0.049	0.009	0.040	−0.001
Long-term decisions	−0.154	−0.172	−0.348**	−0.104
Degree of worker control	0.699***	0.748***	0.331	0.701***
Store functioning				
Avg. weekly hours of part-timers	−0.057	−0.093*	−0.059	−0.060
Absenteeism (weekly)	0.027	0.000	0.055	0.048
Perceived effort and effectiveness	0.046	0.068*	0.124	−0.002
Training	0.011	0.012	−0.032	0.002
Increased effort	−0.106*	−0.117*	−0.060	−0.058
Store economic outcomes				
1983 Profit	23.953**	24.269*	18.499	27.478**

NOTE: Variables are defined in footnotes of table 6.1 to 6.6.

*p<.1; **p<.05; ***p<.01; two-tailed t-test.

Table 6.14
Three-Stage Least Squares Model Parameters of Life Satisfaction Among Full-Time Workers (Equation 6.2)

	Satisfaction with life overall (N=45) Coefficients	Satisfaction with family (N=45) Coefficients	Satisfaction with leisure (N=45) Coefficients	Satisfaction with health (N=45) Coefficients
Worker characteristics				
Demographics				
Yrs. of education	−0.157	−0.114	−0.079	−0.235*
Sex	0.009	0.223	−0.127	0.201
# of dependents	−0.182*	0.005	−0.059	−0.095
Yrs. of seniority	−0.006	0.006	0.020	0.008
Attitudes and beliefs				
Satisfaction with supervision	0.098	0.243	−0.070	0.165
Satisfaction with co-workers	0.074	−0.016	0.251	0.101
Comparative economic gains since shutdown	−0.016	−0.016	−0.017	−0.000

Participativeness				
Daily decisions	0.275**	0.213	0.234	0.321*
Long-term decisions	-0.064	-0.109	-0.318**	-0.034
Degree of worker control	0.429**	0.432*	0.158	0.263
Store functioning				
Avg. weekly hours of part-timers	-0.064	-0.123	-0.114	-0.051
Absenteeism (weekly)	0.154*	0.070	0.177	0.164
Perceived effort and effectiveness	0.068	0.084	0.164	-0.101
Training	-0.019	0.002	-0.052	-0.034
Increased effort	-0.075	-0.153	-0.104	-0.018
Store economic outcomes				
1983 Profit	19.495	20.152	27.096	18.075

NOTE: Variables are defined in footnotes of table 6.1 to 6.6.

*p<.1; **p<.05; ***p<.01; two-tailed t-test
.

Conclusion

Contrary to extreme claims that worker ownership is a failure or that it is a panacea, the findings of our analyses suggest that the men and women who bought out their stores managed to devise a well-run decisionmaking system that pleased them and managed to be satisfied with their job security. They also paid a substantial price, however: they reported more conflict with co-workers and supervisors, longer work hours, less leisure time, and poorer health.

As we expected, the formal structure of worker ownership worked to increase worker involvement in long-term decisions. Worker/owners have used this power to adopt store labor strategies preserving full-time jobs for all owners, including cashiers and others in low-paying jobs. They also used cross-training of workers to increase their flexibility and provide growth and career opportunities.

Worker ownership, through the cooperative system of decision-making, has had a more modest impact on other aspects of store functioning. While some worker/owners claimed to be working harder and more effectively, others did not. The worker/owners' average estimates of motivation did not differ from workers in Super Fresh. We found a similar lack of difference in levels of trust, conflict, and acceptance of decisions.

The Super Fresh alternative, which also saved many workers' jobs, promised increased worker involvement in decisions, though these were limited to daily matters, and a bonus share of profits if workers helped keep labor costs low. Super Fresh adopted a dual labor force strategy with a small core of full-time workers and a larger group of lower-paid part-time workers, however; thus most of the jobs saved were part time.

This strategy had a different impact on full-time and part-time Super Fresh workers. Full-time Super Fresh workers felt workers had as much control overall and in daily matters as did worker/owners, they earned larger job incomes than worker/owners, and they were as satisfied as worker/owners with their economic situations, jobs, and lives outside of the job. They did not have a say in intermediate and long-term decisions in their stores, however. The QWL program it-self was not crucial in obtaining benefits for Super Fresh workers. The full-time workers got their influence in store decisions through their own human capital attributes—seniority, education, job knowl-edge, and department head status.

The large group of part-timers (85 percent) at Super Fresh bore the primary costs of the Super Fresh method of job-saving. Com-pared to full-time Super Fresh workers and all worker/owners, these part-timers made less than half the income and reported a postshut-down loss of economic welfare and lower satisfaction with QWL, pay, promotions, and job security. A small number of women gained family satisfaction from their part-time schedules, but they were not so many or so satisfied that they could raise the average satisfaction levels of their stores.

In theoretical terms, the results supported many of our hypothe-ses, but a few results were surprising. Worker ownership and worker experience did increase perceived participation, but QWL had few effects on worker outcomes. Differences in store functioning had a limited impact on worker outcomes. The full-time labor strategy adopted by the O&Os positively affected workers' hours and income, but other changes in informal interactions in the stores were modest and had little impact on worker outcomes.

Participativeness, which we expected to have an indirect effect through store functioning, had instead repeated substantial direct ef-fects on worker outcomes. While limitations of our measurement of store functioning may be a partial explanation, this is unlikely to account for every effect. We did expect participativeness to affect worker satisfaction. More worker participation increased some per-ceptions of job quality and earning power, but was costly to workers in diminishing some aspects of job and life satisfaction.

Curiously, these results give some indication that the supermarkets did not always reward workers for their efforts and effectiveness. Workers who perceived themselves to be hard-working and effective were less satisfied with their pay, benefits, and job security. Workers in more profitable stores had less satisfaction with their job security, and their form of decisionmaking. Either there are inequalities, in which effective workers are not well-rewarded, or else high expectations of effective workers have led to dissatisfaction with rewards given.

Chapters 5 & 6 have presented outcomes from the workers' point of view. The next chapter will look at the differential economic outcomes for the stores themselves among the three types of organizations.

NOTES

1. We had many possible measures for each of the constructs in these equations. Therefore, we had to reduce the data considerably through preliminary analyses before we could precisely define the actual equation model to test. We used two primary techniques for this task. First, we factor analyzed all attitudinal and perceptual measures of each construct. If we could identify clear, meaningful factors, we used summary scales of the measures comprising the factors. Our general rule was to look for measures which had loadings on one factor over .4 and less than .2 on all other factors. Items to be summed had to have a similar factor structure for workers, managers, and shop stewards before we would consider them as summed scales. These factor analyses are available from the authors.

Second, we used correlation and multiple regression techniques to identify suitable measures of the constructs. (a) We eliminated from further analyses variables reported in the descriptive results above which neither significantly related to other model variables nor were clearly important in theory. (b) We selected variables representing our theoretical constructs but which were not highly correlated with each other. However, even potential multicollinearity problems did not eliminate some variables, because we used them in separate alternative versions of the model.

2. Because these variables were measured in the same way and were physically located near the other satisfaction questions in the questionnaire, any significant effects on satisfaction outcomes may be the result of measurement bias. In spite of this, it seemed important to include them so that the influence of other variables in the model could be determined, net of these worker characteristics.

3. Store type is represented by two dummy-coded variables, O&O and QWL. Non-QWL is the omitted category with which comparisons are made.

4. The simultaneous equation model estimates each of the three participativeness measures described earlier (equation 6.1) and then enters these estimated values variables in the worker outcomes equation (equation 6.2).

5. This measure came from the store managers' survey.

6. Employee turnover in the store was too highly correlated with average weekly part-timer hours in the store to be used in the same equation. However, absenteeism could be included. The measure of absenteeism also came from the store managers' survey.

7. Training was a sum of the number of new jobs and new skills learned since the shutdown, plus a five-point rating of how much training workers said they received in their new stores. Perceived worker effort and effectiveness (motivation) was measured through a sum of two items asking for workers' estimates on a five-point scale of the degree to which they believed that working hard leads to high productivity and to doing one's job well.

7

Economic Performance of Worker-Owned, QWL and Non-QWL Supermarkets

The O&O buyout of two A&P stores, and the conversion of most of the Philadelphia-region A&P stores to Super Fresh stores with varying degrees of worker participation, presented a unique opportunity to examine and compare the economic performance of worker-owned firms with that of conventionally-owned firms with and without QWL. The common history of these stores as part of the failing A&P chain, their common location within the Philadelphia metropolitan area, the common experiences of most of the full-time and many of the part-time workers as former A&P employees, and the coverage of workers in all of the stores by similar union contracts means that the major dimensions along which these stores vary are type of ownership and extent of worker participation. Differences in industry, geographic location, general economic climate, experience of workers and unionization, which ordinarily confound the interpretation of the effects of worker ownership and worker participation on economic performance, are absent in this case study. Thus, this study of the O&O and Super Fresh stores two years after the A&P shutdown is an exceptional opportunity to test the model, developed in chapter 2, of the way economic outcomes for individual stores are affected by the type of store (worker-owned, Super Fresh with QWL or Super Fresh without QWL), the extent of store participativeness, and the effect of participativeness on store functioning.

This chapter analyzes the economic performance, measured in terms of profitability, productivity, and unit labor costs, of each of the three types of stores in our sample. In the next section we analyze the theoretical issues involved in comparing the economic performance of worker-owned and traditional firms. This is followed by a descriptive section detailing important differences and similarities among the three store types. This section also compares the perceptions of shop stewards and store directors or managers regarding how the store is functioning and how participative it is. Finally, the model described in chapter 2 is tested. The empirical work reported here provides considerable support for that model.

Theoretical Issues

One of the persistent questions concerning such workplace innovations as worker participation is their effect on the economic performance of the enterprises in which they are introduced. Proponents of worker participation in managerial decisionmaking through worker ownership or quality of worklife programs argue that these practices increase productivity and profit. Giving workers scope to utilize the knowledge they have acquired about the firm's production process, customer requirements, regulatory environment or business climate, according to this view, increases sales, reduces waste and inefficiency and increases the flexibility with which workers can be assigned to jobs. The resulting productivity gains support increases in wages as well as profits while holding unit labor costs down (Levin 1984). In contrast, critics of worker participation support the traditional hierarchical organization of the firm in which decisionmaking and authority are centralized at higher levels of the bureaucracy. They argue that close supervision and control of the work process as well as the ability to lay off workers or reduce their hours of work are essential to achieving productivity targets and to holding down costs.

Differences in Objectives

Discussion of the contribution of worker participation to the financial success of an enterprise is further complicated when firms owned by their workforce are considered. The objective of a traditional firm is to maximize profit, so profitability is an appropriate measure of its financial success. Worker-owned firms, however, have multiple goals. Like their more traditionally-managed competitors, they must operate successfully in the market if they are to continue to exist. Whether profit maximizing or not, they must nevertheless be profitable if they are to generate internal funds for investment and expansion. Moreover, profit is the standard which suppliers and banks, themselves organized as traditional firms, apply in determining the credit-worthiness of worker-owned firms. Profitability, therefore, remains an important goal even in cooperative enterprises.

At the same time, worker-owned firms do not single-mindedly pursue the objective of maximum profits. Such firms also have a strong commitment to providing employment security, full-time wages and the hours of work desired (usually full time) to worker/owners. High and steady worker income ranks with profits as a goal of such enterprises (Berman 1967).

Furthermore, the distinction made in traditional firms between "variable labor"—ordinary workers whose numbers and/or hours are increased during periods of high demand and reduced during periods of slack—and "overhead labor"—managerial and professional employees who are viewed by the firm as a quasi-fixed cost of doing business—is not a meaningful distinction in the case of worker-owned firms. Here, the entire worker/owner labor force must be viewed as a quasi-fixed cost to the firm, to be spread over as large a sales volume as possible. Thus, sales volume looms as a much more important variable for worker-owned firms, than for comparable traditional enterprises.

While worker-owned firms may be less likely, except under extreme circumstances, to reduce the hours of work of worker/owners, they do have greater control over employee compensation than is the case for conventional firms. Even where wage rates are bargained uniformly by a union representing both worker/owners and employees in traditional firms, worker-owned firms have some flexibility with respect to compensation. Worker/owners can vote themselves small or zero bonuses, and they can vote to provide "sweat equity" in the form of unpaid hours of work above their scheduled full-time paid hours. In contrast to traditional firms, worker-owned firms are more likely to vary compensation rather than hours of work to achieve higher profits and productivity, should this prove necessary. They are reluctant to do this, however, since full-time wages and high income for worker/owners is an important objective of these firms.

Both conventional firms and worker-owned firms have strong incentives to increase productivity and reduce unit labor costs. Rising productivity leads, in general, to higher profits. It also makes possible wage increases without increases in unit labor costs. Of course, the distribution between wages and profits of the gains from making the enterprise more productive are likely to differ in traditional and in worker-owned firms. Traditional firms are responsible to shareholders, and have an incentive to hold down wages while capturing increases in productivity in the form of higher profits. In contrast, worker-owned firms, whose shareholders are also their workforce, desire to raise worker incomes, subject to the need to sustain a satisfactory level of profits.

These differences have important implications for the kinds of strategies which worker-owned and conventional firms adopt to hold down unit labor costs. The concept of unit labor costs refers to payroll costs per unit of output. It can easily be shown that payroll costs per unit of output are equivalent to the average wage paid to workers divided by the average product (or output per employee hour) of labor.[1] Traditional firms may find reducing the average wage an attractive strategy for holding down unit labor costs. They can pursue this strategy by hiring large numbers of part-time workers for dead-end jobs at lower wages, saving on training and fringe benefit costs as well. Or they can encourage high turnover so that a large proportion of the labor force is employed at entry level wages. Reducing average wages may appear less costly or less risky than pursuing the alternative strategy of making workers more productive. This alternative strategy might include instituting training programs to increase skill levels and allow greater flexibility in the assignment of tasks, providing opportunities to increase product knowledge and better meet customer desires, or encouraging and rewarding effort and hard work. Other productivity-enhancing alternatives might include valuing the knowledge of experienced workers and providing ways in which this knowledge can be heard and acted upon, undertaking investment in modern technology and implementing technology and work processes so as to enhance rather than reduce worker skills. In general, productivity can be increased by encouraging continuous on-the-job learning experiences for the firm's workforce.

Worker-owned firms, with their commitment to full-time hours and wages for worker/owners, have little leeway for reducing average wages. Like those Japanese firms with a commitment to lifetime employment, they must concentrate on raising productivity if they are to remain competitive. With a high wage, high seniority, mostly full-time labor force, the impetus for achieving productivity gains is especially high in worker-owned businesses.

Important differences in the behavior of worker-owned and traditional firms are suggested by this analysis. They can be expected to differ in their use of full-time employees, in the hours of work of part-time employees, in the amount of turnover, in the number of training programs and the opportunities for learning new jobs and new skills that they provide, in the rewards they provide for hard work and effort, and in the extent to which they encourage worker participation in a wide range of decisions. These differences, which may be quite acute in comparisons between worker-owned and conventionally managed firms, may be ameliorated when traditional firms adopt quality of worklife (QWL) programs which provide workers with training and with some opportunities to participate in decisions. Traditionally-managed firms that implement QWL do so in order to achieve the productivity gains made possible by increasing the knowledge and skills of workers and by utilizing the knowledge of workers through worker participation in decisions. In this respect, they resemble worker-owned firms. QWL firms differ from worker-owned firms, however, in that they continue to be owned by shareholders and to pursue the objective of profit maximization.

In light of the emphasis on productivity growth through skill development and participation in worker-owned stores, it is possible that such firms have increased productivity and achieved lower costs despite higher worker hours and wages. As a result, the "high" profits of worker-owned firms need not fall below the "maximum" profits of traditional firms.

Similarities and Differences Among Worker-Owned, QWL and Non-QWL Stores

Unlike the previous two chapters, this one is not limited to six intensively studied stores. It is based on a sample of 25 stores—2 O&O stores and 23 Super Fresh stores. Questionnaires were distributed to each store manager as well as to the UFCW local 1357 (clerks) shop steward and the UFCW local 56 (meatcutters) shop steward at each Philadelphia store and the UFCW local 27 shop stewards (clerks) in the two stores outside of Philadelphia. The analysis in this chapter is based on data obtained from these questionnaires. In addition, 1981 financial data for all of the stores prior to the A&P shutdown, and for the Super Fresh stores in 1982 and 1983, were obtained from A&P corporate headquarters. Financial data for the O&O stores came from the manager's questionnaire and from published sources.

We characterized the 23 Super Fresh stores as QWL or non-QWL on the basis of the assessment by the shop steward of the extent to which a formal QWL program was in place in his or her store.

For the four Super Fresh stores studied in depth, the judgment of the researchers coincided squarely with the evaluation of the shop stewards regarding implementation of QWL (see chapter 5). This increases our confidence in the shop stewards' evaluation of QWL in the larger sample of stores. Shop stewards were asked to rate, on a scale of 1 to 5, both the extent to which a formal QWL program had been implemented in their stores and the extent to which workers were encouraged to attend store QWL meetings. Stores which scored 3 or better on *both* of these scales were classified as having a QWL program in operation; all others were classified as non-QWL stores. Based on this classification scheme, our sample consists of 13 QWL stores and 10 non-QWL stores, in addition to the two O&O stores.

Note that this refers only to whether a formal QWL program was implemented and not to the effectiveness of the program in involving workers in decisionmaking.

Table 7.1 reports mean values by store type for the variables which the model (see chapter 2) hypothesizes will affect the economic performance of the stores—worker characteristics, use of consultants, union support, store participativeness, store functioning and store characteristics. Questions about participativeness, as well as those concerned with such aspects of store functioning as interpersonal processes, slowness of decisionmaking, number of training programs and amount of peer training, were asked of both store managers and shop stewards. Many of these same questions were also asked of the workers in the six stores where workers were interviewed. In all, the shop steward and manager questionnaires had 57 questions in common while the manager, shop steward and worker questionnaires had 54 questions in common.

The UFCW local 1357 and 27 shop stewards, who represent everyone in the store except the meatcutters, are generally more knowledgeable about store conditions and returned more complete questionnaires than the UFCW local 56 shop stewards. We have, therefore, used the responses of the UFCW local 1357 or 27 shop stewards in this analysis except for the four stores where only the UFCW local 56 shop steward responded. An analysis of the responses of the shop stewards by union local indicates that there are no significant differences between them in their assessments of participativeness and store functioning.

Analysis of the responses of the shop stewards and workers to questions about participation and store functioning in the six stores in which workers were interviewed indicates that the shop stewards' views are largely representative of those of the workers in their stores. Their views of participation are slightly less enthusiastic than those of other full-time workers, but more positive than those of part-time workers who had less opportunity to participate.

Moreover, in the 13 QWL stores, analysis of the responses of managers and shop stewards indicates that the two groups share very similar perceptions of participation and its effects. Only in the

Table 7.1
Comparison of Mean Values By Store Type

Variable	O&O	QWL	Non-QWL
	(N = 2)	(N = 13)	(N = 10)
Worker characteristics			
Percent female	42.41	39.03	38.95
Percent nonwhite	5.47	21.19	5.50
Percent high school graduate	94.12	77.12	82.88
Consultants and union			
Consultants[1]	13.00[b,c]	2.75[a]	2.71[a]
Union support	2.50[b]	4.77[a]	4.00
Store participativeness			
Manager's perceptions			
Decisions about daily tasks[2]	7.00[b,c]	8.15[a]	9.40[a]
Long-term decisions[3]	2.00[b,c]	3.23[a]	2.30[a]
Perceived overall degree			
of worker control[4]	8.50	6.69	8.40
Frequency of participation	65.00[b,c]	23.00[a]	23.33[a]
Amount of say mangers have	—	4.61	4.60
Amount of say dept. heads have	5.00	4.15	4.60
Shop steward's perceptions			
Decisions about daily tasks	9.50	8.15[c]	5.30[b]
Long-term decisions	10.00[b,c]	3.00[a]	2.60[a]
Perceived overall degree			
of worker control	7.00	6.69	4.67
Frequency of participation	30.00	22.78	12.86
Amount of say managers have	4.50	4.69	4.30
Amount of say dept. heads have	3.50	4.00[c]	2.89[b]
Store functioning			
Number of employees	42.00[b,c]	96.61[a]	93.00[a]
Pct. full time	44.59[b,c]	16.45[a]	17.17[a]
Turnover (per year)	8.00	58.38	22.56
Absenteeism (per week)	2.00	6.31	4.40
Avg. weekly hours part time	20.00	18.46	17.30
Pct. at top pay	44.00	32.62	40.25
Pct. at bottom pay	13.00	20.77	25.11
Pct. can do more than 1 job	49.71	45.06	61.20
Innovations[5]	10.00	8.00[c]	11.10[b]
Manager's perceptions			
Interpersonal interactions[6]	22.00[b,c]	19.31[a]	21.67[a]
Slowness of decisionmaking[7]	2.00[b,c]	3.08[a]	3.10[a]

Table 7.1 (con't)

Variable	O&O	QWL	Non-QWL
# of training programs since reopening	0.00	5.85	6.22
Amt. of peer training	5.00[b]	3.62[a]	4.30[a]
Manager's say over hiring	6.00	5.54	5.80
Shop steward's perceptions			
Interpersonal interactions	18.00[b,c]	19.92[a,c]	11.44[a,b]
Slowness of decisionmaking	4.50[c]	3.15[c]	1.75[a,b]
# of training programs since reopening	1.50	3.00	2.20
Amt. of peer training	1.50[b,c]	3.33[a]	2.90[a]
Increased effort[8]	6.50	6.77	6.00
Perceived effort and effectiveness[9]	8.00	7.46	6.89
Implementation of participation	4.50[c]	3.58[c]	1.40[a,b]
Workers encouraged to attend meetings	4.50[c]	4.54[c]	2.60[a,b]
Worker satisfaction with participation	3.00[b,c]	2.66[a]	3.50[a]
Store characteristics			
Size in square feet (000)	18.50	22.08	23.67
Number of competitors	6.00	3.46	3.90
1981 sales volume (000)	4337.80[b]	8293.60[a]	7556.18
1981 profit (cents per $ of sales)	5.31	5.88	6.44
1981 labor productivity	1.45	1.64	1.55
1981 unit labor costs (cents per $ of sales)	15.67	14.51	14.96
Ease of obtaining credit	5.00	4.09	4.75
Store economic outcomes			
1983 sales volume (000)	6731.40	9687.20	9050.60
Pct. sales growth 1981–83	53.18[b,c]	17.65[a]	19.41[a]
1983 value added (cents per $ of sales)	21.18	19.61	18.42
1983 profit (cents per $ of sales)	10.39	6.92	5.11
1983 labor productivity	2.32[c]	1.78	1.59
1983 unit labor costs (cents per $ of sales)	9.15[b,c]	11.16[a]	11.67[a]

a. Significantly different from O&O;
b. Significantly different from QWL;

c. Significantly different from non-QWL;
p = .05.

Multi-item scales:

1. Sum of the number of times 6 kinds of assistance were received from 7 sources.
2. Sum of 3 six-point items for influence in tasks, choice of hours, working conditions (1 = I am not involved, 6 = I can decide on my own).
3. Sum of 2 six-point items for influence in capital investment and shutting the store (1 = I am not involved, 6 = I can decide on my own).
4. Sum of 2 items, How much worker's opinions are taken into account when decisions are made in the store (1 = none, 5 = a great deal) and How much say workers have in what goes on in the store (1 = very little say, 5 = very much say).
5. Sum of 3 items, innovations in jobs, procedures and equipment.
6. Sum of 5 items, consequences which occurred because of new system of decisionmaking: greater acceptance and better quality of decisions, higher trust of manager, more open disagreement, disagreements more easily resolved (1 = definitely not, 5 = definitely yes).
7. Takes longer to make decisions because of the new system of decisionmaking (1 = definitely not, 5 = definitely yes).
8. Sum of 2 items, How often it is true that working hard leads to high productivity, to doing the job well (1 = never, 5 = almost always).
9. Sum of 2 items, Extent to which the opportunity to contribute to decisionmaking influences extra effort, extra effectiveness on the job (1 = none at all, 5 = a great deal).

non-QWL stores did we find that managers and shop stewards differed widely in their perceptions of virtually every aspect of participation and store functioning about which both were asked. Compared to the shop stewards, managers of the non-QWL stores reported extremely optimistic views of the percentage of workers who participate often in store QWL meetings, of the participation of workers in decisions about daily tasks, of the overall degree of worker control, of the number of training programs in the store and the amount of peer training, and of improvements in interpersonal processes within the store as a result of the QWL program.

In non-QWL stores, managers, but not shop stewards, reported values for these measures as high as, or even higher than, values reported by managers in the QWL stores. Our interpretation of this discrepancy is that managers in non-QWL stores exaggerated when answering questions concerning participation and the effects of QWL on store functioning in order to impress Super Fresh corporate management which favors QWL and has encouraged store managers to implement it. For this reason, and in light of the close correspondence between the views of shop stewards and managers in the QWL stores as well as between the responses of shop stewards and workers in the six stores where both were interviewed, we have elected to use the shop stewards' perceptions rather than store managers' responses regarding store participativeness and its effects on store functioning in testing our model. Factual data from the managers' survey has been utilized in the analysis.

Store Economic Outcomes

Average values, by store type, for the measures of economic performance are reported in table 7.1. Significant differences (p = .05) were identified using ANOVAs and LSD multiple range tests for comparison of means of groups of different size. As predicted by our theoretical analysis, the O&O stores with their much larger proportion of full-time workers and with more workers at the top of the pay scale appear to have pursued sales growth more aggressively than the Super Fresh stores in order to spread these high, quasi-fixed labor costs over a larger volume of sales. Our results show that sales growth at the O&O stores was significantly higher than at either type of Super Fresh store. Sales revenues at the O&O stores increased on average by 53 percent between 1981 and 1983, while sales at the Super Fresh stores increased by 18 percent for the QWL and 19 percent for the non-QWL stores.

All three types of stores actively attempted to increase productivity, reduce unit labor costs and increase profit in order to reverse the poor performance of the former A&P stores, become economically viable and protect the jobs of workers. Productivity, in this analysis, is defined as value added per dollar of payroll, where value added is the gross margin or difference between sales revenue and the cost of goods sold. The productivity measure preferred by economists is value added per employee hour, but 7 store managers failed to report total employee hours for their stores. A comparison of value added per dollar of payroll with value added per employee hour for the 18 stores for which both measures of productivity are available shows that the two measures are highly correlated, with a correlation coefficient of .824. Thus value added per dollar of payroll, which is available for all 25 stores, is a good alternative measure of productivity.

Unit labor costs are, conceptually, very closely related to productivity, especially as we have defined it above. Unit labor costs are defined in the usual manner as payroll costs per dollar of sales, and are inversely correlated with profit. For this sample, the correlation between profit and unit labor costs is $-.752$.

A comparison of 1983 average values for labor productivity and unit labor costs with 1981 average values indicates improvement for the O&O stores as well as for both QWL and non-QWL Super Fresh stores in comparison with the performance of the former A&P stores at these locations. However, the improvements were most marked for the O&O stores. These worker-owned stores, which had been among the poorest performing A&P stores, had significantly lower unit labor costs in 1983 than either the QWL or non-QWL Super Fresh stores, despite the fact that they employ a larger proportion of full-time, highly paid workers. In 1983, unit labor costs in the worker-owned stores averaged a little more than 9 cents per dollar of sales, which compared favorably with the Super Fresh stores, whose unit labor costs averaged between 11 and 12 cents per dollar of sales. This was achieved despite the fact that more than 44 percent of O&O workers were full-time employees, compared with only 16 to 17 percent full-time employees at Super Fresh. Moreover, the O&O stores had 44 percent of workers at the top of the pay scale, compared with 33 percent at the QWL stores and 40 percent at the non-QWL stores—and fewer workers at the bottom of the pay scale—13 percent compared with 21 percent at the QWL stores and 25 percent at the non-QWL stores. Part of the explanation for this may lie in the improvement in labor productivity achieved by the O&O stores, increasing from 1.45 to 2.32 between 1981 and 1983. Smaller improvements were achieved by the Super Fresh stores, from 1.64 to 1.78 for the QWL stores and from 1.55 to 1.59 for the non-QWL stores.

Value added per dollar of sales is another interesting indicator of economic performance. It shows the gross margin, or difference, between sales revenue and cost of goods sold as a percent of sales. Higher values on this measure indicate either a higher profit margin, perhaps as a result of improvements in dealing with wholesalers, or a reduction in wastage due to spoilage, stocking inappropriate merchandise, shoplifting or employee pilfering. Higher value added is generally associated with higher profit independent of the effect of unit labor costs on profit. In this sample, the correlation between value added per dollar of sales and the rate of profit is .973. Value added averaged 21 cents per dollar of sales for the O&O stores, 20 cents per dollar of sales for the QWL stores and 18 cents per dollar of sales for the non-QWL stores. These differences, however, are not statistically significant.

The rate of profit in the retail food industry is reported per dollar of sales rather than as a return on assets. We were unable to obtain data on either the assets or fixed costs of the stores in our sample. Accordingly, the rate of profit in this analysis was computed by taking sales revenue less cost of goods less operating expenses less payroll and then dividing by sales revenue. Multiplying by 100, we obtained a rate of profit expressed in cents per dollar of sales. It should be understood that this is a gross profit measure which includes some fixed costs such as rent that would have to be subtracted in order to obtain a purer measure of net profit. The rate of profit for the O&O stores averaged over 10 cents per dollar of sales in 1983. This was double the rate of profit in the non-QWL stores, which averaged just over 5 cents per dollar of sales, and was above the average profit rate of 7 cents per dollar of sales for the QWL stores. Despite these large differences by store type in the *average* rate of profit, however, the differences were not statistically significant. This was due to the very large variation in the rate of profit among individual Super Fresh stores, both QWL and non-QWL. Differences in store functioning that contributed to these variations in the profit rate are examined below as part of the model testing.

Thus, the multiple objectives pursued by the O&O stores—providing full-time employment at high wages to a large proportion of the labor force as well as earning an acceptable rate of profit—did not cause profitability to suffer in comparison to Super Fresh stores, where the emphasis was on profit maximization.

The model developed in chapter 2 hypothesizes that worker characteristics, store type, help from consultants, formal organization of the store and union support will influence a store's participativeness. Store participativeness, in turn, is expected to affect store functioning—both the kind of labor strategy the firm adopts and the informal processes that go on within the store. Finally, store functioning and store characteristics are expected to influence the store's economic performance—its profit, productivity and unit labor costs. Mean values for variables in each of these categories are also reported in table 7.1.

Mean values are reported by store type, however the role of store type in affecting store economic outcomes cannot be inferred from the mean values. Caution must be exercised in interpreting these mean values. They are merely descriptive and neither confirm nor disconfirm hypothesized causal relationships. Those are tested below, in a later section of this chapter.

Worker Characteristics

The O&O stores employed a higher proportion of female workers and a higher proportion of high school graduates while the QWL stores had the highest proportion of nonwhite employees. None of these differences is significant, however, because of the wide variation among individual stores in each category.

Consultants and Union

The O&O stores received significantly more different kinds of consultant help from a variety of sources than either QWL or non-

QWL Super Fresh stores. Help from consultants is measured by a variable that reports the number of different types and sources of consulting the store received. Union support for participation was measured by a single five-point item on the shop steward's questionnaire that asked how much the union supported worker ownership (for the O&O stores) or QWL (for the Super Fresh stores). The O&O stores reported significantly lower union support. This surprising outcome results from the reduced role of the union in the O&O stores, where grievances and other differences are more likely to be resolved through informal processes established through participation in decisionmaking by worker/owners. In contrast, the union has an important, formally designated, and time-consuming role to play in the QWL program.

Store Participativeness

Shop stewards and store managers were asked to evaluate worker participation in their stores. The extent to which workers participate in decisionmaking within the stores can be measured along several dimensions, including the overall extent of worker control, the range of decisions in which workers participate, and the intensity of the participation. The overall influence of workers on decisionmaking, which we have termed "degree of overall worker control," combines the responses to the questions, "How much are workers' opinions taken into account?" and "How much 'say' or influence do workers have on what goes on in the store?" It is measured on a scale of 2 to 10. Both managers and shop stewards rated the degree of overall worker control higher on average at the O&O stores, but the difference was not statistically significant.

The range of decisions over which workers have control is another important aspect of participation. Shop stewards at the O&O and QWL stores rated workers as having significantly more control over decisions relating to daily work—schedule, working conditions and tasks—in comparison with the rating by shop stewards at non-QWL stores. Shop stewards rated workers at O&O stores as having significantly more control over such long-term decisions as capital investments or shutdowns than workers at either QWL or non-QWL Super Fresh stores. Managers at the non-QWL stores, however, rated their workers significantly higher than other workers were rated in control over decisions about daily work; and managers at O&O stores rated their workers significantly lower than managers at Super Fresh stores in control over long-term decisions. The shop stewards' perceptions of the range of issues over which workers have control in each type of store closely parallel those of the workers themselves (compare table 7.1 and table 6.2 in chapter 6).

Workers at O&O stores were more likely than other workers to participate often in decisionmaking. When asked to give the percent distribution of workers who participate often, sometimes, rarely or never, managers at O&O stores reported that 65 percent of workers participate "often," compared with 23 percent at both QWL and non-QWL Super Fresh stores. Shop stewards estimate the proportion who participate "often" more conservatively. According to the shop stewards, 30 percent of O&O workers, 23 percent of QWL workers and 13 percent of non-QWL workers participate "often."

The distribution of power in the hierarchy, measured by how much "say" or influence managers (also called store directors) and department heads have, is another indicator of store participativeness (see figures 6.1 and 6.2). O&O managers did not answer this question about themselves; they rated the influence of department heads as very high (a score of 5 on a scale of 1 to 5). Managers at both QWL and non-QWL stores rated both themselves and department heads as influential in decisionmaking (scores of approximately 4.6 out of 5). Shop stewards at the O&O stores rated the amount of influence managers have as high (4.5) and that of department heads as somewhat lower (3.5). These ratings probably reflect the fact that the managers at both of the O&O stores are also owners and have a very influential position as a result. Shop stewards at the Super Fresh stores gave high ratings to the amount of influence managers have at both QWL and non-QWL stores. As would be expected if QWL were effective, department heads at QWL stores were rated as significantly more influential than department heads at non-QWL stores. This is because QWL gives a large, formal role to department heads, as part of the store planning board, in influencing decisions.

Store Functioning

Under store functioning, we examined the strategies stores adopt in training and deploying workers, as well as the nature of informal store processes. Our hypothesis, tested later in this chapter, is that store participativeness influences both of these aspects of store functioning. More participative stores are expected to do better in meeting worker requirements for hours of work, to provide more training and to be more innovative. They are also expected to encourage peer training. In addition, participation is expected to have a positive effect on what we have termed interpersonal processes—the quality of decisionmaking and the willingness of people to accept decisions, the degree of trust between manager and workers, the discussion and resolution of disagreements or conflicts, as well as how much people know about what is going on. More worker participation may, however, slow down the decisionmaking process. It is via these changes in store functioning that greater store participativeness is expected to translate into higher productivity and profit.

Labor Strategies

The effects of participation and the QWL program at Super Fresh have been distorted by a labor contract that works at cross purposes to some of the goals of participation as discussed in chapters 4 and 5. The contract established a two-tier wage system paying new employees substantially less than former A&P workers, and it developed a bonus plan in which workers in stores that hold down unit labor costs receive a share of the store's profits, distributed among workers according to the number of hours worked.

The result is that managers at some of the QWL stores, with the participation and support of the department heads who make up most of the full-time workers, have adopted a labor strategy that penalizes the rest of the store's labor force. They have attempted to keep unit labor costs low by holding down the number of full-time workers and by encouraging turnover so that more workers will be at the bottom of the pay scale. The large number of part-time employees in these stores are disenfranchised from effective participation in the QWL program and in decisionmaking. This labor strategy is even harsher in its treatment of new employees than the strategy adopted at many of the non-QWL stores, though former A&P workers, who are prominent among full-time workers in these stores, may have benefited from QWL.

These approaches to labor strategy show up clearly in table 7.1. The O&O stores, as noted above, have a higher percentage of full-time workers and a higher percentage at the top of the pay scale. Non-QWL stores have, on average, a slightly larger percentage of full-time workers and a larger percentage of workers at the top of the pay scale than QWL stores. Part-time workers at the O&O stores average more weekly hours (20 compared with 18 and 17 at QWL and non-QWL stores), and a smaller percentage of O&O workers are at the bottom of the pay scale (13 percent compared with 21 and 25 percent respectively). Turnover and absenteeism are also highest, on average, for the QWL stores and lowest for the O&Os. Averages can be misleading, however. There was wide variation in the performance of QWL stores on all aspects of labor strategy, and mean differences by store type, while large, were usually not significant.

Non-QWL stores had more workers who could be assigned to more than one job and had introduced more innovations in job design and ways of doing things, according to the managers, than other stores. These questions were not asked of the shop stewards. Again, the very positive responses of managers at non-QWL stores to these and other questions appear to reflect their overly optimistic view of events in their stores.

Informal Store Processes

Managers at non-QWL stores rated the positive effects of participation on the quality of decisionmaking, trust, conflict resolution and other interpersonal processes nearly twice as high as did shop stewards at those same stores. They also gave higher ratings to the amount of peer training than did shop stewards and reported significantly more slowing down of the speed of decisionmaking as a result of QWL. Managers at O&O stores gave significantly higher ratings to the positive effects of participation on interpersonal interactions and reported that participation slowed down decisionmaking to a lesser extent than Super Fresh managers at either QWL or non-QWL stores. The O&O shop stewards' rating of the effect on interpersonal interactions, while not significantly different from the managers' perceptions, were somewhat lower. This may account for the fact that the QWL stores scored significantly higher than the other two store types, and the non-QWL stores scored significantly lower in the shop stewards' ratings of effect of participation on interpersonal interactions. O&O shop stewards also reported the greatest slow down of decisionmaking, and non-QWL shop stewards the least, as a result of participation.

Both managers and shop stewards reported fewer training programs at the O&O stores since reopening. This is because these stores (and some of the QWL stores as well) had many training programs prior to reopening and, unfortunately, we did not ask questions on the survey that allowed this training to be captured. We do know from the personal interviews that workers remember little from the programs and claim to have learned most of what they know about operations and governance after the stores opened.

The shop stewards were also asked about the effects of participation on worker motivation. There were no significant differences among the stores in perceptions that extra effort makes a difference, or in the perception that participation in decisionmaking makes extra effort and hard work effective in increasing productivity. Our measure of extra effort is based on two items: how often it is true that working hard leads to high productivity or to doing the job well. Our measure of perceived effectiveness comes from the two items: extent to which the opportunity to contribute to decisionmaking influences extra effort or extra effectiveness on the job.

Store Characteristics

The O&O stores, on average, are somewhat smaller, have more competitors, and obtain credit more easily than the Super Fresh stores, though none of these differences are significant. As A&P stores in 1981, the O&O stores had had the poorest economic performance while the QWL stores had, on average, the best.

Testing the Model

The model developed in chapter 2 hypothesizes that worker participation in decisionmaking within stores depends on worker characteristics, type of formal store structure (i.e., worker-owned, conventional ownership with QWL, conventional ownership without full implementation of QWL) and union and consultant support in implementing participation. Store functioning—both the informal processes that go on within stores and the strategies which stores adopt with respect to the training and deployment of workers—is hypothesized to depend on store participativeness and the business environment. Finally, the model hypothesizes that store economic outcomes are affected by store functioning and store characteristics.

The model to be tested is described by the following system of equations:

(Eq. 7.1) participativeness = f(Worker Characteristics, Store Type, Union Support, Consultant Help).

(Eq. 7.2) store functioning = f(Participativeness, Business Environment).

(Eq. 7.3) store economic outcomes = f(Store Functioning, Store Characteristics).

Participation is measured by overall extent of worker control or, alternatively, by degree of involvement in a range of decisions. In the latter case, two participation equations are estimated, one for participation in daily decisions and one for participation in long-term decisions.

A large number of store functioning variables are available in our data set. They include labor strategy variables such as percent offull-time workers, average weekly hours of part-time workers, percent at the bottom of the pay scale and amount of peer training. They also include variables that measure informal store processes—whether workers are making a greater effort, whether they believe that working harder gets results, whether interpersonal interactions have improved, whether participation has slowed decisionmaking, whether workers are satisfied with participation.

Store economic outcomes are measured by profit, productivity, and unit labor costs. A separate version of the model is estimated for each of these outcomes.

Methodological Issues

The theoretical model underlying this study is essentially recursive, however we have estimated the system of equations using Three-Stage Least Squares (3SLS) to allow for the possibility of unspecified interactions among the dependent variables.

The small size of our sample—data for 25 stores—affected the way we tested the model. As table 7.1 shows, there are many possible measures in our data set for each of the variables in the model. The small sample size precludes use of more than a few of these in any particular test of the model. We have, therefore, tested alternative versions of the theoretical model using different measures of participation and of store functioning. One version used involvement in a range of decisions—decisions about daily tasks and long-term decisions—as the measure of participation. A second version of the model used the overall degree of worker control as the measure of participation.

In the case of store functioning, fidelity to the theoretical model led us to include one measure of informal store processes and one measure of labor strategy in each variant of the model. The results for 10 such pairs of store functioning variables are reported in tables 7.3 through 7.12. These variants of the model are tested first using degree of involvement in a range of decisions in which workers participate as the measure of participation and then using overall degree of worker control. We report results, in all, for 20 variants of the model, each run three times with profit, productivity and unit labor costs entered separately as the dependent variable in the store economic outcome equation.

Each of the structural equations in the model is identified. Thus, using Three-Stage Least Squares to estimate the coefficients yields estimates that are both consistent and asymptotically efficient. That is, we have used the available data as efficiently as possible and have obtained consistent estimates of the coefficients. The signs of the coefficients are, in general, as hypothesized in the theoretical model. The small size of the sample suggests the importance of exercising caution in interpreting tests of hypotheses, however. While the test statistics are distributed asymptotically normal (0,1), very little is known about their actual distribution when the sample size is small and the number of observations, as in this study, is in the range of 10 to 25. We think that the large t-statistics on many of the key model variables, frequently greater than 3 and sometimes even greater than 4, create a strong presumption that the true coefficients of these variables are not zero and that these variables do have the effects hypothesized in the model.

Even recognizing the limitations of the small sample size, it seems reasonable to conclude, as we do in the next section of this chapter, that the data provide support for the hypotheses regarding the influence of ownership and participation on the economic performance of stores. Certainly, the model warrants further and more conclusive testing with a larger number of firms.

Results of the Model Testing

The participation equations were estimated as part of the system of equations in each of the 20 versions of the model reported here. Half of the model variants employ two equations for range of decisionmaking—participation in decisions about daily tasks, participation in long-term decisions—as the participation variables; half employ a single equation for overall degree of worker control. On the basis of a preliminary regression analysis that included such variables as race, sex and seniority, we selected the percentage of high school graduates in a store as the most appropriate measure of worker characteristics for inclusion in the participation equations. Store type is measured in these equations by two dummy variables, one for QWL and one for worker-owned, with non-QWL as the omitted category. Consultant help counts the number of different kinds and different sources of consulting the store received. Union support had to be omitted from the analysis because several shop stewards did not answer this question.

Participation Equations

As described above, we estimated many variations of the basic model and each of the participation equations appears in 20 model runs. The results of the model testing for the version using involvement in a range of decisions (daily and long-term decisions) as the measures of participativeness are reported in the two left-hand columns of each table (7.2 to 7.12); results for the alternative version, which uses degree of overall worker control, are reported in the two right-hand columns of each table.

Table 7.2 reports typical coefficient estimators and t-statistics for the variables in the participation equations (Eq. 7.1). They are reported for the version of the model in which store functioning is measured by percent full time and increased effort (N of stores = 23), and in which profit is the dependent variable in the economic outcome equation. Estimates of the coefficients may vary in other model specifications, but variables with large t-statistics had such t-values in all model runs. The small number of observations makes us cautious about drawing inferences.

The high t-value for the education variable in each of the participation equations suggests that the proportion of high school graduates in a store increases worker participation in decisions about daily tasks and in decisions with long-term implications and also increases the perceived overall degree of worker control. That is, the worker characteristic variable of education has a positive effect on all measures of participation.

Worker ownership appears to increase worker involvement in long-term decisions compared with traditionally-owned and managed-stores, but, surprisingly, it does not increase participation in decisions about daily tasks nor does it increase the degree of overall worker control. Workers in stores with formal QWL programs may participate more in decisions about daily tasks and may have a greater degree of overall worker control than those in stores without such QWL programs, but the evidence is inconclusive. This finding is probably an artifact of the small number of O&O stores and the wide variation in participativeness for the QWL stores.

Another explanation for the unexpected finding about the effect of worker ownership is that the structures of formal decisionmaking in the worker-owned stores tend to be reserved for long-term decisions. Worker/owners may be very autonomous in their daily tasks, as the discussion in chapter 5 indicates. They may not report high degrees of worker control because they make their decisions informally and not in structured meetings.

Store Functioning Equations

Tables 7.3 through 7.12 report the effects of participation in decisionmaking on store functioning (top half of each table) and the effects of store functioning on each of the store economic outcomes (bottom half of each table). The hypothesis that worker participation in decisionmaking affects store functioning receives some support in this analysis.

With respect to measures of labor strategy, greater participation in long-term decisionmaking increases the percentage of full-time workers in a store (tables 7.3 to 7.9), but it does not affect the average number of hours worked by part-time employees (tables 7.10 to 7.12) or the percent of workers at the bottom of the pay scale (table 7.12). Regardless of store type, greater involvement in daily-decisions does lead to higher average work hours for part-time workers (tables 7.10 to 7.12), but does not affect the proportion of full-time workers (tables 7.3 to 7.9). Contrary to our hypothesis, however, greater worker participation in daily decisions is associated with a higher percentage of workers at the bottom of the pay scale (table 7.12). This apparent paradox may result from the fact that in those Super Fresh stores where former A&P workers are favored in their hours, managers have attempted to hold down costs by hiring a larger number of low-paid new workers in part-time jobs. The older workers, with longer or full-time hours, who participate in daily decisions may not object to this management strategy.

The third measure of participativeness, perceived degree of overall worker control, affects store labor strategy as well, regardless of store type. Greater perceived overall worker control in a store leads to a larger proportion of full-time workers (tables 7.3 to 7.9) and leads to a higher average number of hours worked by part-timers (tables 7.10 to 7.12). It also appears to increase the proportion of employees at the bottom of the pay scale (table 7.12).

While many of these results tend to confirm the model, one cannot rule out reverse causation. In other words, the presence of former A&P workers who have more full-time positions or part-time positions with more hours may itself lead to greater perceived overall worker control.

With respect to other aspects of store functioning, those having to do with internal store processes, the hypothesis that greater participation in long-term decisions would be a positive influence was not confirmed in the analyses (tables 7.3 to 7.12). Other measures of participativeness did act in accordance with our hypotheses, however. Both involvement in daily decisions and perceived overall worker control appear to improve the quality of interpersonal interactions (tables 7.3 and 7.11), to lead to greater effort (tables 7.4 and 7.10), to strengthen the perception that participation makes working hard more effective (table 7.5), to lead to more innovation (table 7.8), and to increase the amount of peer training (table 7.9). Participativeness also appears to slow decisionmaking (table 7.6). In addition, greater perceived overall worker control increases satisfaction with participation (table 7.7).

Measures of the business environment, such as the availability of credit, did not appear from our preliminary statistical work to affect store functioning. Thus, these measures are not included in the final analysis.

Store Economic Outcomes

There appears to be support for the hypothesis that participativeness—particularly as measured by involvement in decisions about daily tasks and by overall worker control—improves store functioning, which in turn improves the economic performance of stores.

Each of the store economic outcomes is estimated in each variant of the model as a function of two store functioning variables and the number of competitors (Eq. 7.3). Other measures of store characteristics and the business environment, including availability of credit, floor area of store in square feet, and 1981 sales volume, were included in other analyses of the model. None had high t-values in any of the versions of the model, however, and the analyses are not reported here. The results from (Eq. 7.3) are found in the bottom halves of tables 7.3 to 7.12.

Unit labor costs are measured in the usual way as payroll per dollar of sales, but productivity is measured in this analysis by value added per dollar of payroll rather than per hour of work. As a result, increases in productivity as measured here need not reduce unit labor costs. It is still true for our measures of profit, productivity, and unit labor costs that an increase in productivity, other things equal, increases profit while an increase in unit labor costs reduces profit. Thus developments within supermarkets that have the effect of increasing unit labor costs may nevertheless increase profit if they have a sufficiently positive effect on productivity. Conversely, store policies designed to reduce unit labor costs may actually reduce profit if they have a sufficiently negative effect on productivity.

The effects of store functioning—labor strategies and informal store processes—on productivity, labor costs and profit are possibly the most important of our results. Table 7.3 examines the joint effects of the proportion of full-time workers and interpersonal interactions. We find that a larger proportion of full-time workers neither increases unit labor costs nor raises productivity, and hence it has no effect on profit. Improved interpersonal interactions raises unit labor costs, but it also increases productivity. The net effect on profit, if any, is probably positive.

Table 7.4 examines the joint effects of the proportion of full-time workers and productivity-enhancing effort. Again, the percent of full-time workers does not affect labor costs, productivity or profit. An environment in which increased effort pays off does appear to increase costs, but it also increases productivity. As a result, profit is neither increased nor reduced.

Table 7.5 examines the joint effects of the proportion of full-time workers and of effective effort through worker participation in decisionmaking. Again, percent full time has no effect on labor costs, productivity and profit, while increased effort and effectiveness raised both labor costs and productivity. The joint effect leaves profit unaffected.

Table 7.6 examines the joint effects of the proportion of full-time workers and any slowdown in decisionmaking that occurs. The effects of full-time work are the same as before. Slower decisionmaking raises labor costs, but the decisions are apparently better decisions. Productivity is higher where decisionmaking is slower and the net effect on profit, if any, is positive.

Table 7.7 examines the joint effects of the proportion of full-time workers and satisfaction with participation. Again, proportion full time has no effect. Unit labor costs are higher in stores in which workers are perceived as more satisfied with participation. Productivity in such stores is, if anything, higher and profit is not affected.

Proportion full time is combined with innovativeness of the store in table 7.8. Again proportion full time has no effect while greater innovativeness increases both labor costs and productivity and has no effect on profit.

Table 7.9 examines the joint effect of the proportion of full-time workers and the amount of peer training. As with the other store process variables, peer training increases both labor costs and productivity but has no effect on profit. Proportion full time, as usual, has no effect on labor costs and profit though it may have a positive effect on productivity. This suggests the possibility of an interaction between the proportion of full-time workers and the amount of peer training, which affects productivity.

Table 7.10 examines the joint effect of average hours for part-time workers and of productivity-enhancing effort. Consistent with the results reported in table 7.4, increasing the hours of part-time workers does not increase labor costs or productivity and has no effect on profit. It is surprising that increased effort in this analysis also has no effect on labor costs, productivity or profit.

Table 7.11 examines the joint effect of average hours of part-time workers and interpersonal interactions. Consistent with table 7.3, the result of improved interpersonal interactions is to raise productivity and profit. However, the result of increasing the hours of part-time workers obtained here is somewhat anomalous in light of the findings in model runs reported in earlier tables. Unit labor costs are increased, productivity is unaffected and profit, if anything, may be reduced.

Discussion

Though small sample size requires that caution be exercised in drawing conclusions, we interpret these results as providing strong support for several of our central hypotheses. We cannot confirm an independent role for the influence of worker ownership on store functioning, however. This may well be a statistical artifact due to the fact that only two of the stores are worker-owned.

The unique effect of worker ownership on the operation of supermarkets occurs mainly through its effects on the goals of worker-owned firms. In addition to high profits, these include full-time hours at high wages for worker/owners. Our analysis indicates that these latter goals have been accomplished without increasing unit labor costs or reducing profit in comparison with firms with a higher proportion of part-time workers or a higher proportion of workers at the bottom of the pay scale.

Greater participation in decisions about daily tasks and a higher overall degree of worker control, whether as a result of worker ownership or a QWL program, improves the effectiveness of informal store processes. More effective store processes—improved interpersonal interactions, increased effort, increased effectiveness, more peer training, more innovativeness, greater satisfaction with participation and even the slowing down of decisionmaking as workers participate—all appear to contribute to greater productivity. Thus, despite the higher labor costs associated with more effective store processes, profit does not appear to be reduced. If anything, improved interpersonal interactions and slower decisionmaking as a result of participation may increase profit.

Findings with respect to labor strategies are somewhat surprising. A higher percentage of full-time workers and, with the possible exception of one of the model runs, increasing the hours of part-time workers do not appear to increase labor costs. A higher proportion at the bottom of the pay scale does not appear to reduce them. Further, having more full-time workers or fewer workers at the bottom of the pay scale does not appear to raise productivity, while the productivity effect of more hours for part-time workers is ambiguous. The effects of these variables on profit are weaker but in the same direction as their effects on productivity. That is, increasing the hours of work of part-timers does not reduce, and may even increase, profit; while having many low-paid workers does not increase, and may reduce, profit.

An important implication of this finding is that if Super Fresh bonuses were tied to increases in productivity or profit, rather than to reductions in unit labor costs, their impacts might be very different. Stores have been rewarded for reducing labor costs without taking into consideration the strategies employed to achieve this end and the effect of such strategies on productivity. It is likely that bonuses have gone to some stores which would not have received them if profit, rather than unit labor costs, had been the criterion of economic performance. The bonus provision of the contract distorted the incentives for both managers and full-time workers, and resulted in incorrect decisions in some stores regarding how the store should function.

Nevertheless, punitive labor strategies engaged in by some managers—reducing the percentage of full-time workers, reducing the hours of part-timers, encouraging high turnover so that many workers earn entry level wages—are not particularly successful strategies for reducing unit labor costs. They are even less effective in raising profit. Yet these are the usual justifications for such strategies.

The profit of firms that provide a greater proportion of full-time jobs, more hours for part-timers, fewer jobs at the bottom of the pay scale, greater participation for workers in decisions about daily tasks, and higher overall worker control does not suffer in comparison with the profit of firms that adopt more punitive labor strategies and more authoritarian management techniques.

In general, improvements in the quality of jobs do appear to raise unit labor costs. However, these improvements in the quality of work also make it possible for workers to do their jobs better and have a positive effect on productivity. As a result, profit is not jeopardized when better jobs and working conditions are provided, despite the increase in unit labor costs. Profit does not appear to be lower in stores in which the quality of jobs is better. Improving interpersonal interactions and slowing down decisions through participation in decisionmaking may actually increase profit.

These conclusions challenge the conventional wisdom among managers about strategies for increasing profit. In our sample of stores, so-called cost-cutting labor strategies did not reduce unit labor costs or raise profit. And participative management and more effective store processes raised unit labor costs but, because of their positive effect on productivity, did not reduce profit. These results of our analysis, which must be viewed as tentative until they are replicated in other studies in which the sample of firms is larger, raise serious questions about the wisdom of managerial decisions adopted by many service sector firms today as they attempt to become more competitive and to increase profitability.

To see these store outcomes in a broader perspective, we need to integrate them with the results reported in previous chapters. The following final chapter presents this integration and the policy implications which we draw from this experience.

NOTE

1. Payroll, or the wage bill, is the product of the average wage (w) and total employee hours (N). It can be written wN while output can be written Q. Then unit labor costs can be expressed as ULC = wN/Q. Q/N is output per employee hour or average product. It follows that unit labor costs equal the average wage divided by the average product of labor.

Table 7.2
Participation in Decisionmaking

Equation	Involvement (N = 23)		Overall control (N = 24)	
	Coefficient	t-value	Coefficient	t-value
Participation[1] (Eq. 7.1)				
Involvement in decisions— daily tasks*				
% high school graduates	7.226	6.799		
QWL store type[2]	2.810	2.583		
O&O store type[2]	2.360	1.043		
Consultants	−0.033	−0.193		
Involvement in decisions— long term				
% high school graduates	3.024	7.203		
QWL store type	0.227	0.536		
O&O store type	6.682	7.258		
Consultants	0.043	0.655		
Degree of overall worker control				
% high school graduates			6.028	7.658
QWL store type[2]			1.728	2.314
O&O store type[2]			1.486	0.958
Consultants			0.051	0.407

*In reading this and subsequent tables, note that the dependent variable in a particular model equation is printed flush with the left hand margin while the independent variables for the equation are indented under it. Thus, in the first equation reported here, "Involvement in decisions, daily tasks" is the dependent variable and the "percent of high school graduates" employed in the store has a positive effect on this measure of participativeness.

1. All measures of participation reported in this and subsequent tables were derived from shop stewards' responses.
2. Both measures of store type are dummy coded against the omitted type, non-QWL.

Table 7.3
**System of Equations* that Includes Percent Full Time and
Interpersonal Interactions as Measures of Store Functioning**

Equation	Including degree of involvement (N = 21)		Including overall worker control (N = 22)	
	Coefficient	t-value	Coefficient	t-value
Store functioning (Eq. 7.2)				
Percent full time				
Daily decisions	0.009	1.363		
Long-term decisions	0.041	3.046		
Overall worker control			0.030	8.374
Interpersonal interactions				
Daily decisions	2.090	5.175		
Long-term decisions	0.594	0.701		
Overall worker control			2.839	16.154
Economic outcome (Eq. 7.3)				
Productivity				
Percent full time	1.730	0.800	0.473	0.210
Interpersonal interactions	0.076	3.519	0.081	4.264
# of competitors	0.026	0.363	0.051	0.664
Unit labor costs				
Percent full time	0.109	0.789	−0.001	−0.009
Interpersonal interactions	0.005	3.125	0.005	4.391
# of competitors	0.003	0.671	0.004	1.283
Profit				
Percent full time	−0.000	−0.001	−0.062	−0.376
Interpersonal interactions	0.003	2.358	0.004	2.828
# of competitors	0.001	0.146	0.002	0.304

*System also includes participation equations as reported in table 7.2.

Table 7.4
System of Equations* that Includes Percent Full Time
and Increased Effort as Measures of Store Functioning

Equation	Including degree of involvement (N = 22)		Including overall worker control (N = 24)	
	Coefficient	t-value	Coefficient	t-value
Store functioning (Eq. 7.2)				
Percent full time				
Daily decisions	0.008	1.301		
Long-term decisions	0.041	3.620		
Overall worker control			0.032	9.217
Increased effort				
Daily decisions	0.880	5.724		
Long-term decisions	−0.053	−0.179		
Overall worker control			1.061	13.972
Economic outcome (Eq. 7.3)				
Productivity				
Percent full time	1.754	0.924	0.514	0.292
Increased effort	0.207	3.084	0.232	3.904
# of competitors	0.009	0.108	0.027	0.339
Unit labor costs				
Percent full time	−0.045	−0.390	−0.199	−1.872
Increased effort	0.018	4.481	0.021	5.881
# of competitors	−0.001	−0.127	0.003	0.639
Profit				
Percent full time	0.098	0.772	0.068	0.563
Increased effort	0.006	1.417	0.007	1.762
# of competitors	0.001	0.159	0.001	0.165

*System also includes participation equations as reported in table 7.2.

Table 7.5
System of Equations* that Includes Percent Full Time and
Perceived Effort and Effectiveness as Measures of Store Functioning

Equation	Including degree of involvement (N = 22)		Including overall worker control (N = 23)	
	Coefficient	t-value	Coefficient	t-value
Store functioning (Eq. 7.2)				
Percent full time				
Daily decisions	0.008	1.412		
Long-term decisions	0.040	3.560		
Overall worker control			0.032	8.960
Perceived effort and effectiveness				
Daily decisions	1.024	5.204		
Long-term decisions	−0.061	−0.162		
Overall worker control			1.190	17.455
Economic outcome (Eq. 7.3)				
Productivity				
Percent full time	1.851	1.177	0.843	0.531
Effort and effectiveness	0.180	4.037	0.215	4.763
# of competitors	0.001	0.021	−0.006	−0.090
Unit labor costs				
Percent full time	−0.052	−0.520	−0.213	−2.116
Effort and effectiveness	0.016	5.458	0.019	6.705
# of competitors	−0.000	0.095	0.002	0.638
Profit				
Percent full time	0.108	0.896	0.106	0.873
Effort and effectiveness	0.006	1.696	0.007	1.993
# of competitors	−0.000	−0.051	−0.002	−0.341

*System also includes participation equations as reported in table 7.2.

Table 7.6
System of Equations* that Includes Percent Full Time and Slowness
of Decisionmaking as Measures of Store Functioning

Equation	Including degree of involvement (N = 21)		Including overall worker control (N = 22)	
	Coefficient	t-value	Coefficient	t-value
Store functioning (Eq. 7.2)				
Percent full time				
Daily decisions	0.008	1.280		
Long-term decisions	0.040	3.424		
Overall worker control			0.032	8.628
Slowness of decisionmaking				
Daily decisions	1.299	3.747		
Long-term decisions	0.195	1.298		
Overall worker control			0.478	13.946
Economic outcome (Eq. 7.3)				
Productivity				
Percent full time	−1.110	−0.407	−2.518	−1.163
Slow decisionmaking	0.608	3.592	0.653	4.773
# of competitors	0.042	0.579	0.074	1.025
Unit labor costs				
Percent full time	−0.041	−0.232	−0.256	−1.898
Slow decisionmaking	0.036	3.235	0.044	5.091
# of competitors	0.002	0.553	0.006	1.688
Profit				
Percent full time	−0.104	−0.596	−0.144	−0.943
Slow decisionmaking	0.027	2.527	0.029	3.060
# of competitors	0.002	0.301	0.002	0.418

*System also includes participation equations as reported in table 7.2.

Table 7.7
System of Equations* that Includes Percent Full Time and
Satisfaction With Participation as Measures of Store Functioning

Equation	Including degree of involvement (N = 18)		Including overall worker control (N = 20)	
	Coefficient	t-value	Coefficient	t-value
Store functioning (Eq. 7.2)				
Percent full time				
Daily decisions	0.006	1.263		
Long-term decisions	0.040	4.608		
Overall worker control			0.030	8.002
Satisfaction with participation				
Daily decisions	0.324	2.403		
Long-term decisions	−0.202	0.738		
Overall worker control			0.512	7.003
Economic outcome (Eq. 7.3)				
Productivity				
Percent full time	2.091	0.831	3.202	1.574
Satisfaction with participation	0.397	2.175	0.329	2.277
# of competitors	0.020	0.201	0.034	0.380
Unit labor costs				
Percent full time	−0.162	−1.114	−0.160	−1.536
Satisfaction with participation	0.051	4.914	0.049	6.290
# of competitors	−0.003	−0.584	− 0.001	−0.221
Profit				
Percent full time	0.153	0.853	0.272	1.660
Satisfaction with participation	0.007	0.534	−0.001	−0.099
# of competitors	0.002	0.319	0.004	0.506

*System also includes participation equations as reported in table 7.2.

Table 7.8
System of Equations* that Includes Percent Full Time and
Innovations as Measures of Store Functioning

Equation	Including degree of involvement (N = 23)		Including overall worker control (N = 24)	
	Coefficient	t-value	Coefficient	t-value
Store functioning (Eq. 7.2)				
Percent full time				
Daily decisions	0.009	1.527		
Long-term decisions	0.039	3.484		
Overall worker control			0.033	9.359
Innovations				
Daily decisions	1.171	3.458		
Long-term decisions	0.152	0.234		
Overall worker control			1.480	1.001
Economic outcome (Eq. 7.3)				
Productivity				
Percent full time	1.908	1.204	3.451	2.321
Innovations	0.118	3.492	0.090	2.766
# of competitors	0.046	0.712	0.041	0.633
Unit labor costs				
Percent full time	−0.150	−1.549	−0.169	−1.991
Innovations	0.014	6.904	0.014	7.451
# of competitors	0.002	0.572	0.004	1.312
Profit				
Percent full time	0.161	1.271	0.297	2.442
Innovations	0.002	0.631	−0.000	−0.181
# of competitors	0.003	0.548	0.002	0.279

*System also includes participation equations as reported in table 7.2.

Table 7.9
System of Equations* that Includes Percent Full Time and
Amount of Peer Training as Measures of Store Functioning

Equation	Including degree of involvement (N = 23)		Including overall worker control (N = 23)	
	Coefficient	t-value	Coefficient	t-value
Store functioning (Eq. 7.2)				
Percent full time				
Daily decisions	0.008	1.359		
Long-term decisions	0.041	3.618		
Overall worker control			0.032	8.854
Peer training				
Daily decisions	0.543	7.246		
Long-term decisions	−0.304	−2.121		
Overall worker control			0.500	13.111
Economic outcome (Eq. 7.3)				
Productivity				
Percent full time	3.623	2.497	3.558	2.458
Peer training	0.302	3.864	0.285	3.769
# of competitors	0.019	0.278	0.033	0.468
Unit labor costs				
Percent full time	0.090	1.169	0.058	0.781
Peer training	0.028	6.421	0.027	6.744
# of competitors	0.002	0.502	0.003	1.164
Profit				
Percent full time	0.170	1.555	0.175	1.560
Peer training	0.009	1.496	0.008	1.398
# of competitors	0.001	0.150	0.001	0.172

*System also includes participation equations as reported in table 7.2.

Table 7.10
System of Equations* that Includes Average Hours Worked
Part Time and Increased Effort as Measures of Store Functioning

Equation	Including degree of involvement (N = 22)		Including overall worker control (N = 22)	
	Coefficient	t-value	Coefficient	t-value
Store functioning (Eq. 7.2)				
Avg. hours PT				
Daily decisions	2.331	6.349		
Long-term decisions	0.124	0.177		
Overall worker control			2.954	13.336
Increased effort				
Daily decisions	0.891	5.813		
Long-term decisions	−0.086	−0.292		
Overall worker control			1.059	13.943
Economic outcome (Eq. 7.3)				
Productivity				
Avg. hours PT	0.153	1.611	0.146	1.809
Increased effort	−0.189	−0.643	−0.193	−0.762
# of competitors	0.045	0.514	0.083	1.063
Unit labor costs				
Avg. hours PT	0.004	1.099	0.001	0.167
Increased effort	0.002	0.149	0.015	0.808
# of competitors	0.001	0.236	−0.002	−0.398
Profit				
Avg. hours PT	−0.006	−0.818	0.007	1.052
Increased effort	−0.009	−0.395	−0.013	−0.602
# of competitors	0.003	0.437	0.005	0.731

*System also includes participation equations as reported in table 7.2.

Table 7.11
System of Equations* that Includes Average Hours Worked Part
Time and Interpersonal Interactions as Measures of Store Functioning

Equation	Including degree of involvement (N = 21)		Including overall worker control (N = 22)	
	Coefficient	t-value	Coefficient	t-value
Store functioning (Eq. 7.2)				
Avg. hours PT				
Daily decisions	2.310	6.097		
Long-term decisions	0.443	0.565		
Overall worker control			2.983	12.230
Interpersonal interactions				
Daily decisions	2.069	5.220		
Long-term decisions	0.638	0.770		
Overall worker control			2.837	16.149
Economic outcome (Eq. 7.3)				
Productivity				
Avg. hours PT	−0.010	−0.298	−0.023	−0.637
Interpersonal interactions	0.102	2.841	0.106	2.949
# of competitors	0.037	0.661	0.074	1.362
Unit labor costs				
Avg. hours PT	0.007	4.745	0.006	3.625
Interpersonal interactions	−0.001	−0.913	−0.000	−0.101
# of competitors	0.001	0.606	0.003	1.544
Profit				
Avg. hours PT	−0.006	−2.125	−0.006	−2.100
Interpersonal interactions	0.010	3.292	0.009	3.196
# of competitors	0.002	0.329	0.003	0.730

*System also includes participation equations as reported in table 7.2.

Table 7.12
System of Equations* that Includes Average Hours Worked
Part Time and Percent at the Bottom of the Pay Scale as Measures
of Store Functioning

Equation	Including degree of involvement (N = 22)		Including overall worker control (N = 23)	
	Coefficient	t-value	Coefficient	t-value
Store functioning (Eq. 7.2)				
Avg. hours PT				
Daily decisions	2.299	6.592		
Long-term decisions	0.115	0.172		
Overall worker control			2.885	13.496
Percent at bottom pay				
Daily decisions	3.039	3.652		
Long-term decisions	−0.742	−0.478		
Overall worker control			3.133	5.809
Economic outcome (Eq. 7.3)				
Productivity				
Avg. hours PT	1.153	3.712	0.152	4.972
Percent at bottom pay	−0.054	−1.779	−0.063	−2.795
# of competitors	0.026	0.513	0.059	1.185
Unit labor costs				
Avg. hours PT	0.004	1.682	0.002	1.361
Percent at bottom pay	0.002	1.220	0.003	2.219
# of competitors	0.000	0.053	0.002	0.877
Profit				
Avg. hours PT	0.009	2.546	0.010	3.810
Percent at bottom pay	−0.005	−1.912	−0.006	−3.260
# of competitors	0.002	0.402	0.002	0.589

*System also includes participation equations as reported in table 7.2.

8

Conclusions and Implications

The preceding three chapters presented data from semistructured interviews with former A&P workers who took jobs in the O&O worker buyouts and in the Super Fresh supermarkets, from a survey questionnaire filled out by those workers, and from surveys of shop stewards and managers in their stores. These data provided material for analyses of individual and store processes and outcomes utilizing the theoretical model presented in chapter 2. In this final chapter, we summarize and discuss the findings and draw some conclusions with respect to both that model and policies that might be considered by those interested in job-saving efforts, quality of worklife programs, employee ownership, and related subjects.

The Philadelphia A&P shutdowns and subsequent openings of two job-saving efforts provided a unique opportunity for research. Because the industry, geographic location, previous economic environment, and labor force were common to all stores, we could focus specifically on the relationships among ownership, participation, store functioning, and outcomes. In addition, our use of different methods—surveys and interviews—to look at some of the same phenomena helped to interpret the findings. The consistency of results from these methods gave us confidence in the findings, despite the small sample size.

Though the setting was favorable for research, it had limitations as well. First, with workers in only six stores studied intensively, an overall total of 25 stores for which data on store-level processes and outcomes were collected, and only two of this total being worker buyouts, the sample size requires caution about statistical inferences.

Second, the sample of workers focused on those in the new settings who had formerly been A&P employees and whose jobs were

251

in some way saved. We cannot say much about the effectiveness of the job-saving efforts for those employees who had not experienced the shutdown.

While the Super Fresh supermarket chain or the unions can claim that thousands of jobs were saved which otherwise might have been lost, they cannot claim that thousands of former A&P workers had their working lives and economic fortunes fully restored from the brink of deprivation. Many of those now working for Super Fresh, even at the time of our interviews and surveys, were new to the stores. In an abstract sense, many jobs were saved, but in a real sense most former A&P workers experienced sacrifices. We concentrated on those who had gone through the shutdown so that we could see what happened to the people in these stores, not just what happened to change the stores' functioning.

Third, the study is limited by the very setting that enabled it. That is, the uniqueness of some of the circumstances may reduce the chances that lessons from such bold workplace experiments could be applied elsewhere. Similarly, the controls afforded by the setting over several aspects of potential variation, such as geography, product market, workforce characteristics, and most particularly the focus on one industry, supermarkets, also create potential limits to the generalizability of the findings to other industries, locales, workforces, etc.

With these limits in mind, however, we see much of general interest and importance here. Some of the findings were as hypothesized and some were unexpected. Before we go on to summarize the findings of chapters 5, 6, and 7, we should briefly discuss the hypotheses tested.

Summary of the Theoretical Framework

To understand the potentially wide variation in outcomes in employee-owned and participatory organizations, we developed a multivariate framework. In this framework, we did not assume that outcomes are the direct results of employee ownership and worker participation. Instead, we posited that outcomes are largely functions of organizational processes, which are in turn largely functions of basic input features.

For a graphic representation of the theoretical model, see chapter 2. The framework is also summarized in equation form in chapter 2.

Basic input features are the basic raw ingredients needed to begin employee-owned and participative organizations. They include worker characteristics, organization type, the role of consultants and unions, the business environment, and organizational characteristics.

Organizational processes start to play a role once operations begin. These include the governance of organizational decisionmaking (participativeness) and specific managerial decisions made concerning the deployment of resources (organizational functioning and labor strategy). We hypothesized that these processes play a vital role in translating plans into actions. Participative processes should make employee-owned and participative organizations do things differently from conventional firms.

According to our hypotheses, organizational outcomes, such as viability, productivity, and profitability are influenced by organizational functioning and labor strategy, as well as by the business environment and organizational characteristics. Furthermore, organizational outcomes should directly influence worker outcomes, such as worker income, job security, job and life satisfaction, and family well-being. Worker outcomes should also be independently affected by labor strategy and resource deployment, by the degree of participativeness and by workers' characteristics.

Summary of Findings

To understand the data, we used two statistical methods. First, we looked at the simple mean differences among the three store types—worker-owned, conventional with QWL, and conventional without QWL. These differences told a great deal about the functioning of the stores and their success or failure. Second, we also tried to look at the causal relationships using complex simultaneous-equation modeling. Although we can develop a certain number of conclusions and assertions based on the mean differences among the store types, we felt the need to be more careful in asserting causality; hence the model testing. To a great degree, the mean differences confirm the model hypotheses, but the model testing sometimes confirmed and sometimes contradicted our expectations.

Mean Differences

Store Economic Outcomes

Overall, according to the mean differences, the worker buyouts were successful and effective at saving some jobs. In chapter 7, we found that, compared to the Super Fresh stores, the worker-owned O&O stores had a higher proportion of full-time workers and of workers at the top of the pay scale, better sales growth, and more improvement in labor productivity and unit labor costs when compared with the old A&P performance. The worker-owned stores, which had been among the poorest performing A&P stores, had significantly lower unit labor costs in 1983 than either the QWL or non-QWL Super Fresh stores, despite the fact that they employed a larger proportion of full-time, highly-paid workers. Productivity was also significantly higher in the O&O stores. Moreover, O&O profit margins had improved from lower to higher than those at Super Fresh stores, though that result was not statistically significant.

Worker Characteristics

How did the worker-owned stores achieve these results? To some degree, their success was a function of the special group of former A&P workers that made up their labor forces. In addition, as chapter 5 revealed, staffing patterns of both the O&O and Super Fresh stores affected the implementation of the new systems of worker participation in decisionmaking.

Store Type

The importance of the formal store governance structure was manifested by the rights worker/owners had under their company by-laws compared to rights Super Fresh workers had under the labor agreement. Worker/owners got several things that Super Fresh workers did not—potential returns on their investments in ownership shares, autonomy on the job, self-determination in training, and democratic participation in the entire range of decisionmaking.

In those Super Fresh stores in which QWL programs were fully implemented (more than half in our sample), workers acquired some involvement in decisions through departmental, store, and regional meetings, but their involvement was constrained and limited to short-term decisions. In the other half of Super Fresh stores in the sample, QWL had hardly been implemented. Perhaps some aspects of the QWL program had been put in place in these stores, but few workers were involved.

Participativeness

There was considerable variation in worker involvement among the store types. O&O worker/owners perceived their stores higher than did Super Fresh workers in almost all aspects of participativeness, except, oddly, for the perceived degree of overall worker control. These differences were significant when we compared all the workers in the stores, but full-time workers at Super Fresh tended to be quite similar to the worker/owners in participation in daily decisions and most intermediate ones. Of course, comparatively fewer Super Fresh workers had full-time jobs. And part-time workers, who made up a larger proportion of the workforce at Super Fresh (both in QWL and non-QWL stores), were lower in perceived overall worker control and involvement in daily decisions compared to full-time workers.

All Super Fresh workers, however, reported significantly less worker involvement in long-term decisions than O&O worker/owners. At the non-QWL Super Fresh stores, part-time workers rated worker involvement in long-term decisions even lower than full-timers.

Workers at the QWL stores reported more worker involvement in daily decisions than their counterparts in the non-QWL stores. In long-term decisions and most intermediate decisions, however, both QWL and non-QWL workers reported low worker involvement.

Store Functioning and Labor Strategy

The worker-owned O&Os and the Super Fresh stores also differed in their deployment of labor and other resources. The O&O stores adopted a labor strategy that relied on full-time employment, while the Super Fresh chain relied heavily on part-time workers. The O&O stores had more full-time workers, higher average hours for part-timers, and a smaller percentage of low-paid workers. Turnover and absenteeism were highest for the QWL Super Fresh stores and lowest for the O&Os; however, these differences were usually not statistically significant. The O&O stores emphasized job training for workers significantly more than did Super Fresh. In general, Super Fresh reduced the number of full-time positions, gave part-time jobs with continual reductions in hours per week to most of the former A&P workers, and supplemented these former A&P workers with inexperienced young workers, who were given low wages and part-time jobs.

With respect to other aspects of store functioning, there were fewer differences among the store types. A few findings did, however, point to impacts of worker participation on store operations. In fact, perceptions by workers and shop stewards showed that participation at the QWL Super Fresh stores had significantly more impact on operational practices than in either the O&O stores or the non-QWL stores, though the O&Os were a not-too-distant second. Participation had the effect of slowing down decisionmaking more in the O&Os than the other stores, however.

Worker Outcomes

The main advantage of the O&Os seemed to be that worker/owners worked more hours per week on average. The average annual supermarket income reported by individual worker/owners equalled that reported by QWL workers, but full-time QWL workers reported earning more money from their supermarket jobs in 1983 than full-time O&O worker/owners. Part-time workers at Super Fresh lost out economically, with lower incomes arising from shorter hours and lower-paying positions. An indication that QWL and the labor contract at Super Fresh did indeed work is that QWL workers earned higher bonuses than non-QWL workers. Worker/owners gave themselves bonuses of a size we could not determine and also gained the potential accumulated return (unmeasured here) on the share values of their investments in the stores. Neither the bonuses nor the share appreciation was reflected in their reported annual income.

Worker/owners tended to be satisfied or dissatisfied with different aspects of their jobs compared to QWL and non-QWL workers. For instance, worker/owners were less satisfied with supervision and with co-workers than both QWL and non-QWL Super Fresh workers, but they were more satisfied than non-QWL workers with their job security and their system of decisionmaking. On overall job satisfaction, all three groups tended to score equally. QWL and non-QWL workers tended to be equally satisfied with most aspects of their jobs and lives off the job, however workers/owners were considerably less satisfied with aspects of their lives off the job, particularly with their health, leisure, and family lives.

Simultaneous-Equation Model Testing

In order to go beyond the simple comparisons of mean scores for the different store types, we sought a more precise test of the theoretical framework, through simultaneous-equation modeling, as presented in chapters 6 and 7. First, we looked at which basic input features affected participation. The results indicate that worker characteristics influenced several aspects of participativeness, with workers' educational level, skills, experience, and level of responsibility having the most impact.

Store type was also a significant influence. Worker ownership was a key input to workers' involvement in long-term decisions. Comparing all former A&P workers, worker ownership was associated with perceptions of greater worker involvement in daily decisions, as well. Among full-time workers, however, neither worker ownership nor QWL programs seemed associated with perceptions of higher daily decision involvement.

Comparing shop stewards' perceptions of worker participation in their stores, both worker ownership and QWL seem to increase workers' involvement in daily decisions, but the effect does not appear to be significant. This is probably due to the small number of O&Os in the sample and the wide variation in participativeness among the QWL stores.

Second, with respect to store functioning and labor strategies, the results of the simultaneous equations confirmed what the mean differences and the more qualitative interview data indicated. That is, more worker involvement changes the way labor and time are used, favoring processes that make the organization more cooperative and efficient through the use of more experienced and loyal full-time workers with higher hourly wage rates. Stores that had more worker involvement in long-term decisions (characteristic of worker-owned stores) also had more full-time workers. Stores with more worker involvement in daily decisions had higher average hours for part-timers, more low-paid workers, better interpersonal processes as a result of either QWL or worker ownership, slower decisionmaking, more peer training, higher levels of worker motivation, and more innovations in work processes. Stores with more perceived overall worker control (characteristic of stores with better-educated labor forces) were similar to those with daily decision involvement.

Third, what really accounted for the economic results stores achieved? The labor and resource deployment strategy employed in the O&O and Super Fresh stores had interesting and, to conventional wisdom, unexpected effects. The strategies favoring more full-time workers and more hours for part-timers tended not to increase labor costs and they may have even increased productivity. However, hiring more low-paid workers did not reduce labor costs and did reduce productivity. In general, the common strategy many managers adopt of trying to slash labor costs to increase profits, tended not to work here. Investing in human resources did not endanger profitability.

Furthermore, while improvements in store functioning which resulted from worker participation tended to increase labor costs as a proportion of sales revenue, they also increased productivity. As a result, these changes usually did not reduce profits. In other words, increases in unit labor costs may have been offset by increases in productivity. The bottom line for the store was the same, though of course for workers it makes a big difference to have full-time work, more part-time hours, or more involvement.

Fourth, worker outcomes—including economic outcomes, job satisfaction, and life satisfaction—tended to be influenced most strongly by worker characteristics, participativeness, and store profitability. In general, the more skilled and harmonious the group that was assembled to staff the store, the more overall worker control and involvement in long-term decisions they had, and the more profitable the stores, the better the workers' life satisfaction. On the other hand, higher store profits in 1983 meant less job income and lower satisfaction with pay and benefits. Why? Perhaps this occurred because the worker-owned stores tended to have higher profits, but did not pay the worker/owners as well as full-time workers at QWL Super Fresh stores. Another likely reason might be the rather high expectation some workers, probably worker/owners, seemed to have of rapid riches.

Discussion

A great number of the findings were in line with the hypotheses and the model, particularly on the economic performance of the worker-owned stores, their degree of worker participation, some aspects of their internal functioning, and their labor strategy. Similarly, the QWL Super Fresh stores scored better than the non-QWL stores on workers' involvement in daily decisions and on a few areas of store functioning, but these differences were not reflected in store outcomes.

Many of the results of the model testing also tended to confirm the hypotheses. Worker ownership tended to increase worker involvement in daily and long-term decisions; higher levels of participativeness predicted some improvement in aspects of store functioning and also led to a labor strategy relying on full-time workers; finally, improved store functioning tended to predict improved productivity, even while it increased labor costs.

Some of the findings were not as expected in the theoretical framework, however. The worker-owned stores were not superior to QWL stores in profits or productivity. According to shop steward perceptions, the O&O stores did not differ from QWL stores in worker involvement in daily decisions. In job income, O&O workers were equal to Super Fresh workers, but full-time O&O workers were actually worse off in job income even though they worked longer weekly hours than full-time Super Fresh workers. O&O workers were also equal or lower on most measures of satisfaction, especially satisfaction with leisure and health.

Similarly, unexpected findings cropped up in the model testing. At the store level of analysis, while long-term decision involvement led to a full-time labor strategy, it did not affect measures of store functioning. Surprisingly, improved store functioning led to increased labor costs and did not help profits. Labor strategy did not affect profit, productivity, or labor costs. At the worker level of analysis, measures of participation had surprising effects on job income and work hours per week, while more worker involvement in long-term decisions led to lower satisfaction with leisure.

Despite the surprises, there was considerable support for the theoretical model, particularly in looking at the store level results. That different labor strategies adopted by the stores did not ultimately affect store outcomes is certainly noteworthy. It means that perhaps several ways exist to make stores profitable. Choosing a way that maximizes worker input, relies on full-time workers, and improves intragroup relationships in the store does not reduce the emphasis on viability and success.

Certainly, the multiple objectives of worker-owned enterprises—including steady, high-paying employment as well as profit—did not of necessity sacrifice conventional objectives of efficiency and effectiveness. On the contrary, the ability to raise productivity and efficiency allowed them to meet several goals simultaneously.

Individual worker/owners did benefit from the job-saving efforts, but not in as clear a fashion as the theoretical framework suggested. Yet even though worker/owners were not earning as much as full-time Super Fresh workers, they were much more likely to be full time, and they had other unmeasured financial benefits. We were not able to measure the increase in value of their ownership shares. Also, worker/owners mostly did not reveal to us their bonuses and many even would not reveal their job incomes.

The seemingly surprising finding on worker/owners' lack of psychological benefits in their new situation is very much in line with the mixed findings in the literature reported in chapter 2. Quite possibly, the increased time demands (reflected in work hours) and the entrepreneurial responsibilities they were feeling for the first time are part of the price they pay—the "sweat equity" investment—for becoming owners. Apparently, the strain of becoming a worker/owner was considerable. Perhaps this strain derived in part from higher initial expectations, from self-comparisons with friends and relatives who had full-time jobs at Super Fresh, and from the unexpected burdens of worker ownership.

Nevertheless, despite the fact that O&O worker/owners were not attracted to worker ownership for ideological reasons, and despite the fact that many social and power relationships established in the old A&P system persisted, the O&O workers established effective mechanisms for collective decisionmaking. On the other hand, the QWL program at Super Fresh had limited effects on participation, store functioning, labor strategy, and outcomes, both for workers and for stores. Where QWL did improve store functioning, it improved productivity, increased labor costs, and did not endanger profits.

As discussed in chapter 5 the primary problems at Super Fresh in increasing worker involvement stem from the limits placed by the labor contract and by the autonomy of the management in staffing and operational decisions. In the worker-owned stores, these decisions are made by the worker/owners. The Super Fresh union contract created pressures for management to hire few full-time workers, reduce part-timer hours, and encourage turnover. Workers' resentment over management's unilateral rights, combined with bad feelings about wage and benefit concessions, made QWL unpopular, while increases in the number of part-timers not only made their involvement in QWL impossible, but also led to hostility between full-timers and part-timers.

Where QWL seemed to work best was in providing gripe sessions. Attendance at QWL meetings dropped off, however, when they were held on workers' own time, not paid time. In non-QWL stores, the system did not spread beyond the planning board members, who are department heads, often the only full-time workers. Apparently store managers did not see QWL as a human resource investment for all workers.

Improvements in the quality of work—more full-time jobs, more hours of work for part-timers, more peer training, improved interpersonal interactions, more worker satisfaction with participation, and a better atmosphere for increased effort and effectiveness—tended to raise labor costs as a proportion of sales. These improvements also made it possible for workers to do their jobs better and to have a positive effect on productivity, however. As a result, profit was not jeopardized when better jobs and working condition were provided, despite higher labor costs.

We may conclude that, at least for individual workers, worker ownership was not only a viable way to save jobs, but also gave the average worker a chance at a full-time job with a future. Joint labor-management concessions also worked to save jobs, but at Super Fresh resulted in benefits for a minority of workers, those who got full-time jobs. Both worker ownership and worker participation were effective in making firms profitable and saving jobs, but it may be necessary to combine them to ensure their full benefits to workers and firms.

Broader Issues in Worker Ownership and Participation

To the degree that the O&O stores are representative of worker buyouts—in the initial feasibility of their survival, in the use of an experienced and motivated workforce, in the establishment of egalitarian structures of ownership and participation, in the key involvement of the workers' union—then worker buyouts are indeed a good and effective method of saving jobs. The O&O example shows, moreover, that it was possible even in a competitive environment to save jobs in a way that simultaneously ensured the quality of work and the effectiveness of the firm.

Ownership brought the incentive to increase profits, while participation provided the means to deploy labor and other resources to accomplish workers' goals. Rather than cut their own earnings, worker/owners opted to enhance organizational functioning through means which increase revenues and labor productivity. Such choices may lead to some burdens typical of entrepreneurship: harder work, worrisome responsibilities, and less time with family. Worker/owners hoped that along with these hardships went the rewards they would share.

The establishment of worker participation and bonuses for cutting costs saved jobs at Super Fresh and enhanced the firms' effectiveness. Thousands of jobs (mostly part-time) were saved, labor costs declined, and store profitability increased. Furthermore, as the findings indicate, QWL has been a positive factor where implemented, even despite worker unhappiness over wage, benefit, and work-rule concessions.

Some observers, like Bernstein (1976), argue that participation is most important, not ownership. Worker ownership, they say, may not even be needed. What they advocate is setting up worker participation programs that assure workers a return on their involvement, not on their capital. Ellerman (1982) argues that ownership is simply a bundle of rights that can be arranged in different ways. Thus, the active (to control the business) and passive (to receive the profits) ownership rights can be, and are, split up in various ways in various business forms (Perry and Davis 1985). In employee-owned firms, participation may not accompany ownership or may even be abandoned as worker-owned firms "degenerate" (Russell 1985). It is the right to participate in control that assumes theoretical and practical importance.

On the other hand, participative structures may be incomplete and may degenerate without worker ownership. Workers may have neither the incentive nor the means to control key decisions. Fully implemented QWL at Super Fresh has not been more profitable than either worker ownership at the O&Os or non-QWL at other Super Fresh stores. Furthermore, the incentive to continue it seems diminished. At Super Fresh, worker participation through QWL has been imperfectly implemented. Perhaps QWL and financial incentives could be combined to better advantage, if the bonus were tied to profits or productivity and not to labor costs. Still, it is doubtful that control over long-term decisionmaking would be ceded to workers without some substantial degree of employee ownership.

Employee ownership as a structure, however, even combined with substantial worker participation as in the O&Os, is no guarantee of success. Workers' characteristics and the social composition of the stores, i.e., the processes of recruitment, self-selection, and staffing, were major ingredients that contributed both to participativeness in the stores and to their outcomes. Similarly, at Super Fresh, the ability of store directors to pick their workforce contributed greatly to the success or failure to implement QWL. Participative structures seem to require workers who are experienced, committed, and loyal to co-workers and to store goals.

Besides worker characteristics, however, other factors which we did not observe but only heard about may have affected the way worker ownership came to be practiced. For instance, in the O&O stores, the need to operate and compete in a business environment influenced worker/owners' choices and behavior. The new worker/owners may have been experienced and largely elite workers in their former lives with A&P, but they were novices at running businesses, and especially in running democratic workplaces, which A&P had never been. The stores became very dependent on the IGA, the supply, warehousing, and advertising group to which they and other nonchain stores belonged. IGA gave them financial help and business advice, which they readily adopted. IGA's conventional approach to supermarket operations made sense, but it often drove the notion of running a different, democratic cooperative from conscious awareness.

Such ideological hegemony may be an important contributing factor to so-called degeneration, which is of such great concern to theorists. To develop worker-owned businesses with the inherent goal structure the O&Os have demonstrated, worker/owners and potential worker/owners need more training in dealing with the business environment. They need to be prepared for potential contradictions between economic democracy in the firm and the need for approval from conventional firms who supply them, support them, or compete with them.

In Philadelphia, the development of a critical mass of successful worker-owned supermarkets may give the O&Os the ability to co-opt and influence the business environment. A third store, not named O&O, was opened by one of the groups of worker/owners (see chapter 4). A fourth store, also an O&O, was opened in 1985 in an inner-city neighborhood of Philadelphia with support from the city, UFCW local 1357, and community organizations. PACE, the main consultant to the original O&Os, was a prime mover in the development of the fourth store. In addition, PACE oversaw the conversion of two more supermarkets in the suburbs from private ownership to reopening as O&O stores. The main supplier to IGA has taken increased interest in the O&O model and worked closely with PACE to develop these suburban stores. Soon, PACE hopes, the increased penetration of O&Os in the grocery market will encourage closer ties among the O&Os, which could lead not only to increased market clout, but also to mutual reinforcement of their internal cooperative structures. Besides, with a number of O&Os operating, a training ground for new worker/owners will be available. With these developments, perhaps the worker-owned stores can have a more general acceptance in the business environment as well as impact on the consciousness of other managers and workers.

Implications

Before drawing out lessons from these findings for other job-saving situations, there are some questions to answer. Was the setting unique and not replicable elsewhere? One of the favorable conditions here was the unusual flexibility of the union leadership in accepting unconventional and innovative solutions. Similarly, trying two job-saving strategies at once may have spurred both the worker/owners and the Super Fresh management to greater efforts or to adopt new ideas. While two simultaneous methods might be unusual, the level of local union support was not unlike that found elsewhere, e.g., at the Rath Packing or Hyatt-Clark worker buyouts and at many plants trying QWL programs in the early 1980s.

Were the conditions faced in the A&P shutdown typical of shutdowns? Many of the Philadelphia-area A&P stores threatened with shutdown in 1982 would, in fact, have been viable with few changes in any case. Nevertheless, A&P's corporate strategy, which shut down entire regions, was not an overreaction to the 1981-82 recession; it was a long-term response to chronic decline in A&P's position in the national supermarket industry. Besides, current economic restructuring has closed many potentially profitable plants in many industries.

Perhaps the most atypical feature of the A&P shutdown is its industry. Supermarkets are small, have localized customer bases, and are not interdependent. Many shutdowns, especially the well-publicized ones, in which worker buyouts have been considered have been in large, complex firms involved in national markets. Perhaps buyouts are more appropriate in industries more similar to supermarkets and less appropriate to so-called typical industrial shutdown situations.

To what degree are our results skewed by self-selection of a group of about 40 workers into the worker-owned stores? Without question, this was a special group. It seems that without the Super Fresh option for many workers, there would likely have been more worker buyouts, given the 600 workers who initially made pledges to become worker/owners. Perhaps many of these might-have-been worker buyouts would have had less success than the O&Os.

We have to remember several facts, however. First, A&P stores converted into O&Os were among the lower performers before the shutdown, so the odds were against them, even with a special group to run them. Second, worker/owners generally did not differ demographically from other former A&P workers.

Third, the Super Fresh workers and stores in the samples were largely picked by Super Fresh management. Presumably we were comparing the O&O workers and stores to the best of Super Fresh. At the least, the four Super Fresh stores studied intensively were to some extent showcases. While self-selection operated at the O&O stores, the entire research situation was somewhat skewed, and there is little reason to believe it to be worse for the O&Os.

Fourth, and most important, the simultaneous-equation modeling took into account worker characteristics. They were, in statistical terms, held constant when we looked at the impacts of other factors. In fact, the theoretical framework considers self-selection and staffing as key contributors to the success or failure of employee ownership and worker participation programs.

In the final analysis, we must be cautious, particularly about the small size of our sample, both of workers and of stores. Twenty-two worker/owner respondents and two worker-owned stores limit our ability to make strong generalizations, regardless of our high degree of confidence that the findings accurately describe these job-saving experiments in the Philadelphia area.

Similarly, the observations cover primarily the 1982-84 period. Changes may have taken place since then or may take place in the future which would call the framework and findings into question. We hope that it will be possible to check out these possibilities empirically. Perhaps even more important, however, would be for the hypotheses to be tested elsewhere, under other circumstances.

Theoretical Implications

The findings have a number of implications for employee ownership and worker participation. First, the importance of worker characteristics leads us to conclude that successful and effective buyouts and participation programs do not occur in a vacuum. That is, the effectiveness of employee ownership and involvement depend to a great degree on the education and previous work experience of the workers who use them.

Second, to be truly effective, forms of worker participation, such as QWL programs, should involve genuine redistribution of power. The constraints under which worker involvement is placed in many organizations may become self-defeating and may lead researchers, managers, and workers to the conclusion that it does not work or is not worth the effort. Worker participation programs apparently need to be consistent with other human resource programs in regard to practices such as staffing, scheduling, and economic incentives.

Third, labor strategies and ways of operating, such as investing in workers, hiring higher quality labor, and combining incentives to motivate greater efforts, need more attention. They may be the key link from employee ownership and worker participation to outcomes.

Fourth, the attempt by worker-owned and participatory firms to achieve multiple objectives may explain why these firms sometimes do not appear as profitable as might be hoped for them. Perhaps they are focused on other objectives, such as high pay or secure employment.

Fifth, multiple measures and multiple methods may be necessary to give a comprehensive and consistent picture of organization effectiveness.

Finally, we have to take account of the entrepreneurial headaches involved in worker buyouts and to take into account worker/owners' expectations of reward. It may be more difficult and frustrating to own and manage within a group. These constraints may be felt by workers on a daily basis, while the rewards may be less frequent.

Pragmatic Implications

How does the O&O case compare to other examples, particularly the well-publicized failures? Specifically, why did worker buyouts at firms such as Rath Packing and Hyatt Clark Industries (HCI) fail while the O&Os succeeded?

At least three factors may be involved. One factor may be management style and structure. The larger the firm, the more important is a competent and cooperative management staff, something workers at both Rath and HCI feel was lacking (Redmon, Mueller, and

Daniels 1985; May 1985). At the O&Os, though worker/owners tended to lack direct management experience, the managers hired from outside were easier to monitor because of the smallness and flat hierarchy of supermarkets.

Second, a good part of the answer might lie in factors outside the scope of this single-industry study, in the nature of the industries and product markets in which these firms operate. As Clarke (1984, p. 124) points out, "the producer co-operative form seems uniquely suited for small-scale, service-based, labour-intensive industries such as agriculture, crafts, retailing, printing, construction, media and the arts." To become successful worker buyouts, supermarkets, with a local selling area and a relatively inelastic demand for their products, would have an advantage over companies in more capital-intensive industries with national product markets dominated by huge corporations, such as meatpacking (Rath) and engine bearings (HCI). An interesting exception to this rule, however, is Weirton Steel, which was bought out in 1983 and has since become one of the few profitable major steel companies in the United States.

Third, the other opportunities laid off A&P workers had, both in Super Fresh and in the large metropolitan economy, afforded both job-saving experiments the leeway for selective staffing. The O&Os and Super Fresh might not function as well if staffed with workers inexperienced in performing the basic job functions of workers in the industry. In fact, a study of the new O&O store started from the ground up in Philadelphia indicates some of the difficulties (Granrose, Simon, and Coker 1986). Not only does an inexperienced workforce complicate the start-up process, but it may also threaten the viability of the firm in its initial operations.

Nevertheless, saving the jobs of experienced workers has potential drawbacks for some groups of workers, particularly women and minorities. In these supermarkets, staffing new, participative ventures meant excluding those who were traditionally excluded from the elite. In industries with strong, white-male-dominated internal labor markets, this could perpetuate discriminatory practices in what are supposed to be democratic structures.

Union Involvement

O&O and Super Fresh might not exist were it not for the union's extraordinary initiative. UFCW local 1357 took swift action to put forth a plan for worker buyouts. Still, it took from February until October for the first O&O store to open. It seems imperative for union leadership to consider the buyout option well before the real threat of a plant shutdown is announced. Local 1357 had already done some feasibility studies when A&P announced the closing. The union put forth its buyout proposal with some confidence that it would be accepted by workers and could succeed.

The union may have been better prepared for worker buyouts than for the concessionary agreement which set up Super Fresh. The union leadership may have been prepared for wage, benefit, and work-rule givebacks, but did not accurately predict how the bonus fund would affect workers.

Tying worker bonuses to reductions in labor costs tended to undermine some of the positive effects of QWL. Cost-cutting led management to emphasize part-time work. Worker solidarity, always fragile in an industry in which part-time workers were historically a large part of the workforce, was further undermined. Besides, saving part-time jobs did not effectively meet the long-term needs of the majority of former A&P workers. Those who received part-time jobs at Super Fresh were, in effect, displaced from their jobs anyway.

To counter these effects, perhaps bonuses should be directly tied to productivity improvements or to profits. Similarly, saving fewer full-time jobs may be preferable to saving more part-time jobs for making worker participation work better.

Management Strategy

Management, in order to save jobs and restore or improve profitability, can consider several alternatives to plant shutdowns. Reducing unit labor cost may be an obvious choice, is directly under management's control, and is clearly calculable on a spreadsheet. This strategy may also reduce productivity and ultimately not improve profits, however.

Managers may want to reconsider labor's demand for guaranteed job security. Treating labor as a quasi-fixed cost instead of a totally variable cost may not put management in a straight jacket. Organizations that innovate in the deployment of human resources can become more effective, but it may take substantial amounts of employee ownership and worker participation to motivate managers to look at employees this way in the American context. Changing corporate strategy from its focus on restructuring and financial manipulation for improving balance sheet performance to a focus on human resources could prove very difficult.

Public Policy

The findings of this study may be useful in shaping aspects of public policy with respect to job-saving. First, keeping the workforce of threatened firms together may provide the skills needed to effect a turnaround or a worker buyout. How can that be done? Federal and local government can help by mandating advance notice by companies of impending shutdown. Six months advance notice seems minimal to establish buyouts, and even innovative labor-management agreements take time to negotiate. Similarly, government-mandated or government-provided severance benefits would not only give laid off workers more time to establish a worker buyout but would also enable them to make the necessary personal investments that could leverage other sources of capital needed to run businesses.

Second, government officials trying to save jobs should consider the quality of the jobs saved. Can the jobs saved provide steady employment and income to support families?

Third, incentive for the establishment of worker participation as a way of meeting both workers' and firms' goals might be considered as part of federal and local government loan and technical assistance programs for reversing industrial decline, saving jobs, and promoting employee ownership. Current federal policies concerning employee ownership focus on tax treatment for ESOPs and stock distribution for employee/owners. Presumably, these policies reflect the assumption that stock ownership is somehow by itself a motivator of greater performance in the organization and that employees need only be spurred to greater efforts and loyalty by a new form of compensation, namely the benefit program known as ESOP. Worker participation in decisions, particularly those crucial to the firm's long-term future and direction, may also enhance the effectiveness of employee ownership for meeting economic and social goals. Public policy can encourage employee-owned firms to give active as well as passive ownership rights to employees.

A Practical Caveat

As a by-product of this research, we found out something we had not explicitly set out to study. It seemed that the more success the worker/owners had with their O&O stores, the less willing they were to accept advice from outside the store. PACE, though it had been a prime mover in setting up the stores and training the worker/owners, found its advice less and less sought after. This insular tendency extended to this research project, in that there was less cooperation in giving out store financial information in one of the O&Os and a lower response rate to the interviews and survey questionnaires by worker/owners than by the groups of Super Fresh workers.

Very likely, part of this self-imposed seclusion stems from the new proprietary feelings stirring in the O&O worker/owners about what is now their own enterprise. In any case, it seems an indication of workers taking to heart an important implication of worker control. Researchers and technical assistance providers should take note of this phenomenon and be sensitive to attitudinal and class differences in their work with worker/owners.

Overall Implications

We started in chapter 1 discussing worker buyouts to save jobs in the context of experimentation to find new ways to work, and in an economy undergoing rapid structural change. The 1982 Philadelphia-area A&P shutdown spawned a unique set of responses, which by their exceptional natures focus attention on crucial issues about saving jobs and restructuring workplaces.

The O&O stores, while precious few in number, show that worker buyouts can be effective for job-saving. In fact, they may even have some advantages over other methods, at least to the extent that the Super Fresh stores, with their QWL programs, can represent other methods. That is, the O&O stores seem genuinely to have saved jobs of good quality which will likely last for the long term. Super Fresh saved a larger number of lower-quality jobs, but these jobs will not necessarily be filled by former A&P workers over the long term.

Both innovative responses to the shutdown opened up new sources of organizational effectiveness through worker participation and management flexibility. In both cases, this effectiveness came to some degree at the workers' expense. While the O&O worker/owners made sacrifices, they could consider them as investments or sweat equity. Nevertheless, they traded new responsibilities and worries for the opportunity to share greater control over their fates and fortunes.

Even in its newspaper display ads, Super Fresh used the theme of workers making an "investment" to create the new entity. (These ads successfully fooled many Philadelphians into believing that Super Fresh is employee-owned, rather than an A&P subsidiary.) But the Super Fresh workers' "investment" of wage and benefit concessions, along with reduced hours for part-time workers, earned profits for the stores, in which only a relative few workers shared indirectly. Super Fresh workers are still heard to grumble about recent improvements to their stores as having been financed by the 20 percent wage cut they had to take in order to keep their jobs.

Aside from workers' sacrifices, the key element in both job-saving innovations was increased worker involvement in decisions. Do these examples mean that in saving jobs there should be a restructuring of responsibilities in the workplace and a greater emphasis on human resources and the quality of working life? A report of a recent study of the economic performance of employee-owned firms stated, "Participation is the key" (NCEO 1986). Compared to a matched sample of 164 conventional companies, a sample of 30 employee-owned firms not only performed better, but job-level worker participation was the explanatory factor most consistently significant. Similarly, a study of 43 General Motors plants found significant impacts on economic performance from worker participation through QWL programs (Katz 1985). That is, all other things equal, improved plant economic performance was predicted by improved labor-management relations at the plant, which in turn resulted from greater levels of worker involvement in the QWL programs. Neither study focused on job-saving efforts, however.

Of course, the O&O and Super Fresh job-saving innovations emerged from a particular situation, so we cannot make too strong a case about their generalizability to other circumstances. But both O&O and Super Fresh have been successful and profitable concepts. It would seem to be a good idea to consider the sources of their success—particularly the contribution of employee ownership and worker participation—in other job-saving situations.

After all, the A&P shutdown was really neither peculiar nor unrepresentative. The O&O buyouts and the establishment of Super Fresh with its QWL programs, though geographically circumscribed, are part of broader trends reshaping the economy and the place of workers in firms. The A&P shutdown came about from many of the common circumstances in which corporations and workers find themselves in this society. Rapid structural change and shifting corporate strategies result in economic dislocation.

In this new economic context of the past decade, the rediscovery of employee ownership as a worker response to dislocation has not come about from nostalgic longing for a failed anticapitalist strategy. Nor has involvement of workers in workplace decisionmaking stemmed solely from modern personnel textbook prescriptions for maintaining or creating "union free" environments. Worker buyouts are not inherently inefficient, isolated, economically marginal, or anachronistic sidetracks for labor or management. In fact, the O&O worker/owners and, especially, their union and technical consultants took advantage of the accumulated knowledge of past failures and of theoretical controversies. Moreover, the union put itself in a position to demand management concessions in Super Fresh when it was called upon to concede cuts in wages and benefits.

Both the O&O stores and Super Fresh are examples of forms of economic democracy, in that they involve workers in decisionmaking and, to some, extent, in control of their workplaces. This particular case illustrates the possibility of unions working innovatively with management in workplace restructuring and of unions taking initiative rather than passively accepting management demands for concessions or joint problemsolving. In general, however, such innovations require some significant changes in the behavior and thinking of both managers and unions.

Whether economic democracy is something workers themselves want will be determined by how attractive examples like the O&O stores are to them. Perhaps they will wait until a crisis, such as a plant shutdown, presents them with an opportunity. We have tried to present the facts clearly and fairly. It will be up to other victims of plant closings to build upon these lessons to improve their outcomes in their particular circumstances.

Appendix A

Excerpts From Agreement Between UFCW 1357
and Roslyn O&O (1982-1985)

Article XXIII

The following is intended to explain the O and O concept of cooperative enterprise and is not subject to the arbitration provisions of this agreement for any reason whatsoever.

Employer is structured as a worker cooperative. Under this structure each shareholder must be a worker. Upon voluntary or involuntary termination of employment of a shareholder, his or her share is deemed transferred back to the corporation. Each shareholder is entitled to one, and only one, share.

Major decisions affecting large numbers of workers, large expenditures of money, or impacting on the corporation for a long period of time are made by the worker-owners on a one worker/one vote basis. Other corporate decisions are made by the Board of Directors, a twelve member body, composed of nine workers-owners and three community representatives, all elected by the entire body of worker-owners on a one worker/one vote basis.

. . .

The fee for purchasing a share of the corporation's stock is $5,000 and remains constant throughout the corporate existence. Profits and losses are allocated, in fixed percentages, to an unindividuated collective account, and to internal capital accounts provided for each shareholder. A portion of the profit distributed to the individual shareholder is based on a percentage of his or her capital investment. The remainder is based on his or her labor participation; that is, his or her hours worked as a percentage of total hours worked during the relevant period.

In order to meet outstanding debt obligations during the terms of this Agreement, profit allocations to each worker-owner will equal approximately $1,000 per year. As the profitability of the corporation increases, the profit allocation to each worker-owner increases accordingly.

. . .

Article XXVII
Subsection 3

3. Employer agrees to encourage certain other supermarket entities with the characteristics listed below, created during the term of this Agreement, to join

with it in coalition bargaining with the Union and to utilize this Agreement as a guidepost in its effort to reach agreement with the Union:

a. A worker cooperative structure in which:

(1)   All owners are workers;

(2)   Each worker-owner has one and only one share;

(3)   Upon voluntary or involuntary termination of employment, the share is deemed transferred back to the corporation;

(4)   Corporate decision-making is on a one worker-owner/one vote basis;

(5)   A portion of profit distribution is based on patronage defined as labor participation.

b. Acceptance into membership of O&O Supermarket, Inc., a second-level cooperative which has supermarket worker cooperative members and which provides a variety of business and other support services to them and/or receipt of financial or other technical assistance from O and O Investment Fund, Inc., a non-profit Pennsylvania Corporation providing assistance to worker cooperatives in certain industries including the supermarket industry.

Appendix B

Excerpts from Roslyn O&O Supermarket, Inc.
Cooperative Handbook & Cooperative Charter (1982)

We the Worker-Owners are a group of dedicated supermarket workers, intent on altering the workplace to gain high productivity and profitability levels, and to provide better service to the consumer. At the same time, we will be operating within an organizational structure which serves to perpetuate a much more personally satisfying, fulfilling atmosphere in which to work.

We expect to achieve this by having all our members actively involved in all aspects of the business. This will include sharing in decision-making, helping to determine store policy, having an input in operations, and generally contributing to all areas of our business. By following our cooperative philosophy, we will treat each other with more respect and trust, thereby assuring a workplace with less pressure and bringing out the full potential of all our members. We expect to expand on this ideal to include the consumer, no longer treating the customer only as a dollar sign but as an individual.

We will treat the customers fairly, with the courtesy and respect for which they are entitled. Since our establishment is part of the community, it will also become our goal to work within the communityin order to learn its needs and to do whatever is within our power to help meet these needs.

We ask all our members to contribute a membership fee in order to receive a voting share in the corporation. Upon achieving membership, all members will be entitled to work in our business, take active part in its operation, share in the profits or losses, and have access to all information, both financial and operational. The share received will be symbolic of their membership and cannot be transferred or sold. This voting share will revert back to the cooperative upon a worker owner's termination of their job, for any reason.

To achieve a better working environment, we will have no outside supervision and the manager's duties and responsibilities will be outlined. There will be no breakdown of jobs into simple tasks, no narrow job classifications with restrictive detailed procedures, and finally no formal controls. We will rely strictly on the trust, experience, and knowledge of all members to perform their duties promptly, productively, and with the best interest of the cooperative. As one fares so does the other.

Philosophically, cooperative members want all major decisions made on the basis of consensus, which mandates general agreement by the group members. We want all profits and losses to be equally shared and the format for distribution to be self-determined as set up in the By-Laws. We would like to see trust among all members. TOGETHERNESS TO GET THE JOB DONE. Communications will be open among all members at all times in order to alleviate problems and reach better decisions. We demand that there be respect for all members and their opinions; that all members treat each other with appropriate courtesy at all times. There will be a sharing of knowledge and ideas in all job classifications in order to utilize the ability of all members to the fullest extent.

In order to attain greater knowledge, we want all members to be able to receive all information concerning the business. This includes ordering, functions of other jobs, and information about all financial data (i.e., costs of goods, suppliers' costs, sales volume, and profits). We want all interested members to have the ability to train for any position in the operation of the store, and to have time allocated in which to gain this training.

To reach a higher degree of profitability in our enterprise, we will have store meetings as often as needed in order to keep all members properly informed. We expect to have input by all members in the conservation of costs—bags, care of equipment, and promptness on the job—in order to minimize the cost of operations. We will also make retraining available whenever necessary in any position to make a member more productive and/or satisfied. Workers will have less restrictive job descriptions to alleviate boredom and make full use of individual skills.

As a group, we expect to conduct ourselves with courtesy, friendliness, and professionalism in order to gain confidence and respect from our customers and the business community. We understand the importance of good conduct in our enterprise, which will mean achieving a better working place and a stimulation of business.

Internally, it is the objective of our group to improve the marketplace conditions in order to make our jobs more rewarding and have a more pleasant atmosphere in which to perform our duties.

Externally, the intent of this organization will be to achieve, for the first time, a truly community-oriented store. Lower and fair pricing, group discounts, and hiring within the community when non-member positions become available will all help to benefit the economics of the community. We hope to respond to the needs of the community and to participate in efforts to upgrade conditions wherever possible, whatever form that takes. We intend to not just make the workplace, but also the community, a better place to live.

The Worker Cooperative Defined

A worker cooperative—the legal and organizational structure used for our supermarket—is a firm controlled and operated by the members who work in it. It is a self-governing corporation, characterized by a corporate legal structure with a cooperative set of by-laws. The by-laws assign certain rights to cooperative members, based on their functional work role within the store. To become a member of the cooperative a person is required to make a financial contribution—in this case $5,000.00 as a fee for cooperative membership. (The store manager is not a member of the cooperative and is not required to make any financial contribution.)

In general, the rights attached to cooperative membership are as follows:

- *One worker=one vote.* This allows members an equal voice in the election of the Board of Directors and in determination of major decisions affecting the cooperative.
- *Profit-sharing.* Members will receive patronage dividends, based on the number of hours worked, as specified by the by-laws.

Within the cooperative structure, all members share in the decision-making process, as well as share in the profits; decisions will be made in a democratic way, on the basis of consensus (general agreement by all group members), that is compatible with worker ownership functions.

The cooperative structure positively impacts on four areas of concern for a retail business: business operations, the worker, the consumer, and the community. First, the business itself benefits through the active participation and involvement, on all operational levels, of those maintaining the store on a daily basis. Through a sharing of information and expertise, worker-owners are able to respond quickly to problems which affect the ability of a store to be successful. The flexibility of members in terms of allocation of tasks and each member's knowledge of multiple jobs enable members to meet changing staffing needs, thereby better meeting the business' need to adequately service the customer.

Second, by reopening a store, a primary consumer need is kept in the neighborhood. As a group who realizes the importance of neighborhood-oriented service, store personnel cater to a specific need by supplying products common to the consumer group(s). The consumer, by always being in contact with an owner at any level of store operations, benefits from more individualized service and a quick response to problems or criticisms. By virtue of the increased interaction of owner and customer, the business can address changing store requirements, customer requests, and be more on-target with respect to policy-making.

Third, the cooperative structure benefits the worker by giving people more control over their workplace. It allows a forum for an individual's expression of ideas, concerns, and/or problems and also provides for operational input regarding business planning. The cooperative structure serves the workers' interests as well as those of the business, through the understanding that the workers are the business; when people have control over their work environment personal productivity, quality of work life, and profits to be gained from the business increase.

The fourth and final area to be served by the cooperative is that of the community-at-large. Cooperatives provide an alternative means of maintaining an area's prosperity: the cooperative provides jobs and services, and in this way helps keep neighborhoods intact. Loss of business services negatively affects an area's prosperity and its ability to attract new business and the subsequent influx of jobs, people, and money.

Responsibilities of a Worker in a Worker Cooperative

The responsibilities of the individual worker in a traditional workplace include job performance, neat appearance, and promptness. In a worker cooperative store these responsibilities remain the same, but are expanded to include the increased participation that the cooperative model demands. It is not just important for the individual to perform his duties well, but also to try and gain as much knowledge as possible of the entire operation so that better decisions can be made concerning the business as a whole. Neat appearance is necessary now, not just to please an employer, but also to please the customer. It becomes important to be prompt because (s)he now realizes that when someone has to cover for him/her, it costs the organization productivity and money; this now means that it costs him/her personally.

In order for our system to work, all workers, members and non-members alike, must cooperate with each other. Since the goals are the same, it becomes necessary to be as agreeable, courteous, and respectful as possible to one another.

It is the responsibility of an individual that if he/she sees something in the operation of the business which isn't right, it should be brought to the attention of the group in order to bring about change that will (a) make operations more profitable, or (b) improve working conditions.

Responsibilities of an Owner in a Worker Cooperative

In a worker cooperative grocery store a member has basically the same responsibilities of a conventional market owner; for instance, (s)he has to negotiate a contract with the union, deal with the suppliers, and work with other service agents. An owner must make up company policy, oversee the hiring, firing, and performance of workers, and protect the future of the business through intelligent business planning and formulation of long-range cash flow projections. Further, any decisions for renovations or major changes in the store are made by the owner.

In a worker cooperative these areas are dealt with collectively by all members in one of two ways. They can either decide to deal with every aspect of the business as a full group, or to form separate committees, each with a specific task. The committees would then present their recommendations to the entire group to be collectively approved; this cooperative will utilize the second process, by committee, to conduct their business affairs.

An owner in a conventional business usually has total control over working conditions and personnel policies. In a worker cooperative, while a member will have input into all areas, no one person or body will have unilateral decision-making authority.

As a part-owner in the cooperative there will be times when ease and comfort of the working place might have to give way to the realities of business needs. It is important to remember that there will be times when a member's business nature will have to show precedent over his/her working nature.

The Worker Cooperative Function

The worker cooperative functions on a basis which relates closely to a corporate structure, with the exception that cooperative members have input at all levels of the system. For example, the traditional corporate structure is illustrated by the following diagram:

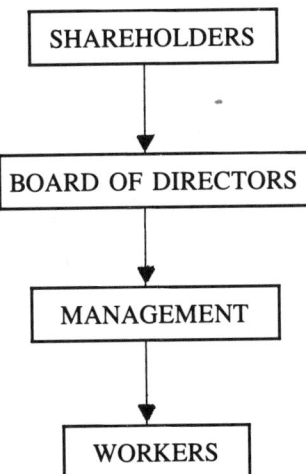

The above reflects an organization in which decision-making comes from the top and flows down through each level. The cooperative structure, illustrated by the diagram below, allows for information and decision-making authority to flow in both directions:

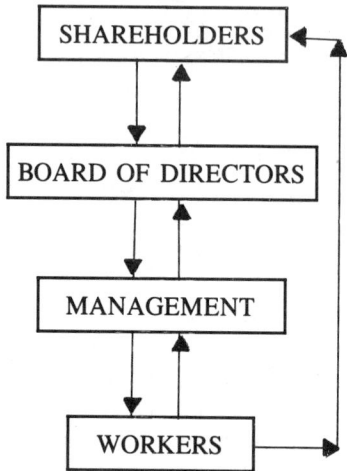

While each level has designated areas of authority and tasks, members and non-members alike have the ability to make input into the system. This allows any group/person to address any other group/person, at designated times, on specific issues; this promotes both the free exchange of ideas, concerns, or problems, and the democratic decision-making process. The primary principle underlying the cooperative model is that each member has the ability to participate, as fully as possible, within their workplace.

In a worker cooperative structure, shareholding is conducted on an equal basis; one member holds one share and is entitled to one vote. In this way, power is equally distributed throughout the membership. Upon termination, a member's share immediately reverts back to the cooperative; members are unable to sell or otherwise transfer their share to any other party.

Governance

The membership elects the Board of Directors as a representative governing body, with the primary function of setting and implementing short-term policies for the cooperative. The board is composed of nine (9) members and three (3) non-members. Within the board there are four offices; that of President, Vice-President, Secretary, and Treasurer. Each officer, along with two other board members, is responsible for specific committee tasks: President—

Executive Committee; Vice-President—Governance Committee; Secretary—Education Committee; Treasurer—Financial Committee. The board president presides at all meetings concerning the cooperative including, but not limited to: the annual General Assembly, monthly board meetings, and special meetings called on an as-needed basis. The members, non-members, and management are directly accountable to the policies set by the Board of Directors, which is in turn accountable to the entire membership.

In a worker cooperative, decision-making authority is allocated among three governing bodies: (1) the General Assembly of Members, (2) the Board of Directors, and (3) the Manager.

Governance
General Guidelines

Membership Decision-Making Authority

Membership review will be required before any of the following matters may be finalized:

(1) Amendments to the articles of incorporation (and initial ratification).
(2) Enlarging the Board of Directors.
(3) Merger or dissolution of the corporation.
(4) Election of directors.
(5) Changes in long or short term goals.
(6) The yearly business plan.
(7) Hiring and firing policies.
(8) Expansion or remodeling of physical plant.
(9) Initiation, modification, or termination of affiliation with suppliers.
(10) Purchase or sale of substantial assets.
(11) Further decision-making authority is established by the *Time Line, Money Line,* and *Member Line.*

Board Decision-Making Authority

(1) Set yearly goals and policies necessary for their implementation.
(2) Select manager, define duties, set salary.
(3) Evalute performance of manager.
(4) Control finances.
(5) Approve all personnel policies. (In the case of hiring, firing, and lay-off policies, membership approval is also necessary.)
(6) Further decision-making authority is established by the *Time Line, Money Line,* and *Member Line.*

Management Decision-Making Authority

The Manager is responsible for day-to-day operational decisions for the cooperative, as defined by the Board of Directors. Further decision-making authority is established by the *Time Line, Money Line,* and *Member Line.*

Time Line

	Manager		Board	Members	
1 day		1 year			3 years
	Decides		Decides	Decide	

Money Line

	Manager		Board	Members	
$1		$3,000.00			$10,000.00
	Decides		Decides	Decide	

Member Line

	Manager		Board	Members	
1 Member		7 Members			50% of Members
	Decides		Decides	Decide	

Articles of Incorporation

Article III
The Treatment of Net Worth and Net Income

1. NET WORTH – There shall be an INDIVIDUAL INTERNAL CAPITAL ACCOUNT in the name of each member and one COLLECTIVE INTERNAL CAPITAL ACCOUNT that in unindividuated. The sum of the balances of the individual accounts plus the balance in the collective account shall equal the Net Worth (=Assets minus Liabilities) of the cooperative.

The membership fee, whether paid in cash or payroll deductions, shall be the initial balance in each member's account. Any gifts or grants to the cooperative shall be credited to the collective account.

The individual capital accounts shall accrue interest at the highest rate not to exceed 12 percent, as determined by the Board of Directors.

Appendix C

Excerpts From Agreement (1982)
between
The Great Atlantic & Pacific Tea Company, Inc. ("A&P")
and
The United Foods & Commercial Workers Union
Locals No. 56 & 1357 ("UNION")

WHEREAS, A&P found it necessary to close its Philadelphia and Scranton Divisions due to business and economic reasons, and

WHEREAS, A&P closed or otherwise disposed of its stores and warehouses in these divisions, and

WHEREAS, those employees in the Union were terminated when the stores closed by the rules of seniority, and

WHEREAS, those stores transferred to other divisions could be closed due to the resulting detrimental impact of those stores closed, and

WHEREAS, the employees in these stores who are members of the Union face termination.

NOW, THEREFORE, the company and the Union agree to:

1. Through their joint efforts strive to reopen as many closed stores as possible, on a guaranteed profitable basis offering eventual re-employment to former A&P employees presently on layoff of December, 1981.

2. Apply this understanding to the employees of all existing operating stores within the jurisdiction of the Union so as to preserve the jobs of such employees which it is agreed are seriously jeopardized by economic circumstances affecting A&P.

3. A&P will establish a new subsidiary which will have separate and independent management and which will be charged only for its own management services (not for the management services generally charged to divisions of A&P). However, non-management overhead, such as overhead related to accounting and MIS services, will be charged to the new subsidiary.

4. The new subsidiary referred to in "3" above will in turn establish subsidiaries or other separate entities, for each store to be reopened, or for each operating store to be operated, all pursuant to the terms of this understanding. Each such store will be a separate enterprise.

. . .

12. Create a mechanism providing for the purchase of the New Entity Store in the following instances:

A. A store owned by the new Entity is to be closed and transferred to a third party.

B. The A&P employees of a store located within the jurisdiction of the Union do not elect to affiliate with the New Entity; and as a result thereof, the store is to be closed and transferred to a third party.

C. The New Entity elects to franchise the store or to enter into a joint venture.

If an event set forth in item 1 above occurs, then the employees of the store to be closed (the "Affected Employees") or the Employee Association ("Pace") shall have the right to purchase said store at a fair price (the "Fair Price"). The mechanism for determination of the Fair Price shall be the subject to further negotiations between the parties. The option to purchase may be exercised only within the ninety (90) day period commencing upon the date that the Fair Price shall have been determined.

· · ·

ADDENDUM
Employees Incentive and Investment Fund

· · ·

4. The amount of Employer contribution for each store shall be one percent (1%) of the store's total sales for the contract year, subject to adjustments as follows: If the store's labor rate for the corresponding period is below nine percent (9%), the contribution rate shall be adjusted upward by one-twentieth of a percentage point (.05%) for each full one-tenth of a percentage point (0.1%) reduction below nine percent (9%). If the store's labor rate for the corresponding period is above ten percent (10%), the contribution rate shall be adjusted downward by one-twentieth of a percentage point (0.05%) for each full one-tenth of a percentage point (0.1%) increase above ten percent (10%). For example, if the labor rate is 8.3%, the contribution rate is 1.35%; if the labor rate is 11.1%, the contribution rate is 0.45%. Under no circumstances shall the Fund be required to reimburse the Employer based on the store's labor rate.

Appendix D

Excerpts From Agreement Between Super Fresh and UFCW 1357 and 56
(1982-1985)

ARTICLE VI
Union Activities

6.1 It is agreed by and between the parties hereto that the Union shall have the opportunity to investigate and resolve problems, to discuss problems with the Employer in an effort to reach a resolution, and to communicate with its members during the term of this Agreement.

. . .

ARTICLE VIII
Seniority

8.2 Seniority for all employees shall be based upon continuous service from the last employment date with Employer within the store location. All new employees shall be on probation for a trial period of sixty (60) days, except as provided in Article XXII, Section 22.2, after which they shall be placed on the seniority roster and their seniority shall date from date of hire.

. . .

ARTICLE IX
Employees Incentive and Investment Fund

9.1 The Employer shall contribute to an Employee Incentive and Investment Fund, which shall be established in accordance with the specifications set forth on the Addendum hereto.

9.2 The establishment and maintenance of the Employee Incentive and Investment Fund shall be conditional upon the approval of the Internal Revenue Service or a court of competent jurisdiction, if applicable, that the plan and any accompanying trust are exempt from taxation under the Internal Revenue Code, and the Employer's obligation to contribute shall be conditional upon the deductibility of such contributions for income tax purposes.

9.3 In the event that, for any reason, the Fund cannot receive the continuing approval of the IRS with respect to the deductibility as an item of business expense of the employer contribution thereunder, the amount of the employer contribution for the period of which such contribution is required under this

Agreement shall be paid directly to the employees in cash, as an employee benefit, by a formula to be mutually determined by the Employer and the Union.

.   .   .

ARTICLE XIII
Quality of Work Life

13.1 The Union and the Employer agree to utilize a Quality of Work Life (QWL) structure to provide a mutual basis for problem solving. It is further agreed to utilize outside (neutral) sources to provide guidance and advice to increase the effectiveness of this program. Such QWL program shall be implemented with the opening of the store.

The resulting QWL program will not become involved in disputes covered under the Grievance & Arbitration Procedure and will not conflict with any terms or conditions of this collective bargaining agreement and will not reduce any rights or privileges of the employee or Employer.

Appendix E

Excerpts from Quality of Work Life for United Food & Commercial Workers Local 56 and Local 1357 with Super Fresh Food Markets (1982)

. . .

III. Organizational Design

6. Overview

Super Fresh will be organized as a two/three level structure. The first level will be that of the corporation itself, which will incorporate five different dimensions:
- Output Units (stores)
- Input Units (service functions)
- Environmental Unit (marketing/advocacy)
- Planning Boards (policy making bodies)
- Management Support System (control)

The second level will be the internal structure of the store itself, which will be organized along the same concept as the corporation, having the five dimensions as does the larger system.
- Output Units (departments)
- Input Units (front end; receiving)
- Environmental Unit (local business development and advocacy)
- Planning Boards (policy making bodies)
- Management Support System (control)

As Super Fresh increases the number of stores it operates, a three level structure will be created that groups the stores into regional units.

6.1 Output Units. Achievement of the organizational ends and objectives (outputs) will be the responsibility of the output units (stores) of the system. The other units are created in order to facilitate the operation of these units. These units will be self-sufficient and autonomous to the degree that the integrity of the whole system is not compromised.

6.2 Input Units. Inputs are the services required to support the output units. Because of economies of scale, technology and geographic dispersion inputs can best be realized at the corporate level. These units will also be semi-autonomous.

6.3 **Environmental Units.** The interaction of the system with its environment is facilitated by the environmental units. The two main functions of these units are marketing and advocacy, that is, attracting the customers, making contact with the external stakeholders and advocating their point of view within the system.

6.4 **Planning Board.** Planning is a process that provides the overall coordinating and integrating funtion for the input, output and environmental units. Planning boards are the main policy making body of the organization and at all levels serve as the vehicle for the participative management style of Super Fresh. This enables the information, judgments and concerns of subordinates to influence the decisions that affect them. One of the key functions of the planning boards is to constantly re-assess the progress the corporation, store, or department is making toward its goals (via feedback from the management support system) and to chart new objectives when necessary. Planning at the store level is directed to those matters affecting the store. Planning affecting more than one store is done at the corporate level.

6.5 **Management Support System.** The management support system is responsible for the comparison of the actual outcomes versus expected outcomes based on the plans and policies set by the planning boards. This provides the means for learning and adaptation.

. . .

7 Components of the System
7.1 Stores (Output units)

7.1.1 The stores will produce the outputs of Super Fresh. Therefore, those activities which are directly compatible with the mission of the "whole," and are necessary for the production of outputs will be considered in this dimension.

7.1.2 Each store will be responsible for the management of its resources and will have an organizational structure very similar to the larger system of which it is a part.

7.1.3 Each store will operate as a semi-autonomous performance center. Financial contributions of each store to Super Fresh will reflect sales minus direct costs and will not have corporate indirect costs charged against it.

7.1.4 Each store will be allowed to retain a percentage of its contributions above a minimum level determined by the corporate planning board. These funds will be used for internal development and local business development by the store consistent with corporate board policies.

7.1.5 Each store will be responsible for making those decisions which affect only its operations. Decisions which impact on the other stores and the corporation as a whole will be made at the corporate level with participation from the Store Director.

7.1.6 Each Store Director will report directly to the Office of the President of Super Fresh.

7.1.7 Each store and department will have a planning board of its own.

7.1.8 At the store level each output department will be headed by a manager who reports directly to the Store Director. These output departments will be as follows:
- Grocery
- Meat
- Produce
- Deli/Bakery

7.1.9 The Store Director will be responsible for general store orientation for all new associates. This orientation will be assessed by the department managers.

7.1.10 The Store Directors in conjunction with department managers will develop departmental cross familiarization programs which will be assessed by the Store Director and those who participate in the program.

. . .

7.4 Planning Boards

7.4.1 There will be planning boards at all levels, including the corporation as a whole, support service units, marketing units, and stores.

7.4.2 In general, each board will consist of (1) the manager of the unit whose board it is, (2) his/her immediate superior, (3) his/her immediate subordinates, and (4) representatives of the associates on higher level boards. The specific membership will be identified in sections 7.4.11 through 7.4.15.

7.4.3 The planning boards will be engaged in continuous interactive planning and reserch to redesign the system as needed.

7.4.4 The planning boards will be policy making bodies and not merely advisory committees, however executive decisions will be left to the respective managers.

7.4.5 Organizational strategies, policies and procedure will be formulated by the planning boards.

7.4.6 The planning boards will explicitly specify the objective and consequences of the plans and policies designed by the board. These objectives and their attainment will be assessed on a regular basis by the management support system.

7.4.7 The planning boards will utilize the information generated by all the units.

7.4.8 Decisions will be made by a consensus of the board members. If consensus cannot be reached as to a course of action, the board will resolve the differences by research and experimentation done by special project committees.

7.4.9 Those holding management positions will be appointed by their immediate higher level manager, however they will have to maintain the confidence of their respective planning boards.

7.4.10 The corporate planning board will make available through Human Resources information and sources on internal and external training on the operation of the food retailing business and its environment. This information will be available to all associates.

7.4.11 At the corporate level the board will meet on a regular basis and will have the following members:
- The President of Super Fresh
- The Director of each store
- Representatives of associates-at-large selected by store planning boards
- The Support Service and the Marketing Unit Directors
- The Presidents of the two Unions
- The responsible manager of A&P or his/her representative
- External stakeholders, if the issue warrants it.

7.4.12 When the number of stores increases the corporate board will be divided into sub-corporate boards, meeting regionally. No more than fifteen stores will be included in a sub-corporate board. The sub-corporate board will have the following members:
- The Vice-President of Retail Operations (representing the President) and his/her assistants (who may function as regional managers)
- The Director of each store (maximum 15)
- An associate from each of the stores to be chosen by each store planning board on a rotational basis.
- The Support Services and the Marketing Unit Directors
- The representatives of the two Unions' management

7.4.13   Coordination of the sub-corporate boards will be done in a special meeting of the corporate planning board at which time an overall corporate plan will be formulated. The following will attend:
- The President
- The Vice-President of Retail Operations and his/her regional assistants
- One Store Director and one associate from each region selected by the sub-corporate planning board on a rotational basis
- Support Services and Marketing Directors
- The Presidents of each of the two Unions or their representatives
- A responsible manager of A&P or his/her representatives

7.4.14   At a store level the board will meet on a regular basis and will have the following members:
- The Store Director and his/her assistants
- The Manager of each department and an associate to be chosen by the department planning board
    - Grocery
    - Meat
    - Produce
    - Deli/Bakery
- The Front End Manager and a cashier
- The representatives of the two Unions
- A representative of the President of Super Fresh

7.4.15   At the department level the board will meet on a regular basis and will include all the associates of that department.

. . .

8.2 Incentive Systems

8.2.1   Each store will contribute a percentage of its sales depending upon total labor cost percentage to an associate investment/incentive fund. The decisions regarding allocation, investment and disbursement of this fund are the right of the associates. The Unions will facilitate the forming of an advisory committee to make these decisions (outside the Super Fresh QWL effort).

8.2.2   Super Fresh will establish a management incentive fund in which each Store Director will participate. The incentive will be paid based on performance in the following areas:
- Sales

– Employee satisfaction
– Store contribution

8.3 Hiring

8.3.1   Former A&P employees will be given preference in hiring at the store level. Placement of these individuals will be done by a hiring committee made up of:
- Director of Human Resources
- The Vice-Presidents of the two Unions
- The store Director will be consulted on the list of Department Managers being considered for his store. This procedure will operate as long as there is a list of former A&P or Super Fresh employees.

Appendix F

[Worker Survey]
Social Innovations at Work Project of Temple University
Study of Philadelphia Supermarkets in Transition

Please answer the following questions either by circling the number most closely corresponding to your personal opinion or situation or by filling in any blanks. Remember, the answers you give will be kept completely confidential. No individual responses will be given to anyone in the store, the union, or anywhere else. A summary of the combined responses of everyone who returns a questionnaire will be available after the study is completed but these will be average answers of the group as a whole, *NOT* your personal response.

DO NOT WRITE
IN THIS
COLUMN
CARD #1
COLUMN #1
ID 1–10

I. JOB EXPERIENCE
1. What is your current position?

   1. ASSISTANT MANAGER
   2. FROZEN FOOD DEPARTMENT MANAGER
   3. DELI DEPARTMENT MANAGER
   4. PRODUCE DEPARTMENT MANAGER
   5. DAIRY DEPARTMENT MANAGER
   6. GROCERY DEPARTMENT MANAGER
   7. OFFICER PERSONNEL
   8. HEAD CASHIER
   9. CASHIER
   10. NIGHT CREW

   11. FROZEN FOOD CLERK
   12. DELI CLERK
   13. PRODUCE CLERK
   14. DAIRY CLERK
   15. GROCERY CLERK
   16. MEAT CUTTER
   17. MEAT WRAPPER
   18. RECEIVER
   19. OTHER:

   _____ 11
   (please identify)

2. On average, how many hours per week do you work in this store?
   _____ HOURS PER WEEK   12–13

3. How long have you worked at this job in this store?   14–15
   _____ YEARS and _____ MONTHS   16–17

4. How many years have you worked in any kind of supermarket, not counting interruptions like child bearing or military service but counting your current job?
   _____ YEARS IN ALL   18–19

II. TRAINING
5. How many years of schooling have you had? (High school graduation =12; college graduation=16)
   _____ YEARS   20–21

297

6. How much job-related training have you received since you
started working here?

1	2	3	4	5
NONE			A GREAT DEAL		22

7. Please circle a "YES" response beside every job you know how to perform.

		NO	YES
a.	Assistant Manager.....................................	1	2
b.	Frozen Food Department Manager.....................	1	2
c.	Deli Department Manager............................	1	2
d.	Produce Department Manager.........................	1	2
e.	Dairy Department Manager...........................	1	2
f.	Grocery Department Manager.........................	1	2
g.	Office Personnel.....................................	1	2
h.	Head Cashier..	1	2
i.	Cashier	1	2
j.	Night Crew..	1	2
k.	Frozen Food Clerk...................................	1	2
l.	Deli Clerk...	1	2
m.	Produce Clerk.......................................	1	2
n.	Dairy Clerk..	1	2
o.	Grocery Clerk..	1	2
p.	Meat Cutter...	1	2
q.	Meat Wrapper.......................................	1	2
r.	Receiver	1	2
s.	Other_____	1	2

(Please Identify) 23

8. How many new *jobs* have you learned since coming to work here?

_____# NEW JOBS LEARNED 24

9. Other than whole new jobs, how many new *skills* have you learned since
coming to work here? (For example: pricing, advertising, display,
scheduling, buying, bookkeeping, supervising, staffing, etc.)

_____# NEW SKILLS 25-26

10. How much have you learned about each of the following things since
coming to work here?

		NOTHING			A GREAT DEAL		
a.	Confidence in handling problems that arise in the store	1	2	3	4	5	27
b.	Willingness to speak up in meetings	1	2	3	4	5	28
c.	How to work on a team	1	2	3	4	5	29
d.	How to influence others	1	2	3	4	5	30
e.	Feeling responsible for your work	1	2	3	4	5	31
f.	How to supervise others	1	2	3	4	5	32
g.	How to listen to others' opinions	1	2	3	4	5	33

III. PARTICIPATION

11. How much are workers' opinions taken into account when decisions are made in your store?

1	2	3	4	5	
NONE			A GREAT	DEAL	34

12. How mucy "say" or influence do each of the following have on what goes on in the store?

	VERY LITTLE 'SAY"			VERY MUCH "SAY"		
a. Workers as a group	1	2	3	4	5	35
b. Department heads	1	2	3	4	5	36
c. Store Director (for O&O—Store Manager)	1	2	3	4	5	37
d. Corporate Planning Board (for O&O—Board of Directors)	1	2	3	4	5	38

13. How much "say" or influence SHOULD each of the following have on what goes on in the store?

	VERY LITTLE "SAY"			VERY MUCH "SAY"		
a. Worker as a group	1	2	3	4	5	39
b. Department heads	1	2	3	4	5	40
c. Store Director (for O&O—Store Manager)	1	2	3	4	5	41
d. Corporate Planning Board (for O&O—Board of Directors)	1	2	3	4	5	42

14. How much involvement do you have in each of the following kinds of decisions?

	I AM NOT IN- VOLVED	I AM IN- FORMED BEFORE- HAND	I CAN GIVE MY OPINION	MY OPINION IS TAKEN INTO ACCOUNT	I SHARE EQUALLY IN DE- CISIONS	I CAN DECIDE ON MY OWN	
a. Improvement in working conditions	1	2	3	4	5	6	43
b. Appointment of a new department head	1	2	3	4	5	6	44
c. Hiring new employees	1	2	3	4	5	6	45
d. Making a major capital investment	1	2	3	4	5	6	46
e. Having more training programs during work time	1	2	3	4	5	6	47

f. Assigning tasks that have to be done	1	2	3	4	5	6 48
g. Changing the vendors or displays	1	2	3	4	5	6 49
h. Their working hours	1	2	3	4	5	6 50
i. Shutting down the store	1	2	3	4	5	6 51

15. How much involvement DO YOU WANT in each of the following kinds of decisions?

	I DON'T WANT TO BE IN-VOLVED	I WANT TO BE IN-FORMED BEFORE-HAND	I WANT TO GIVE MY OPINION	I WANT MY OPINION TO BE TAKEN INTO ACCOUNT	I WANT TO SHARE EQUALLY IN DECISIONS	I WANT TO DE-CIDE ON MY OWN
a. Improvement in working conditions	1	2	3	4	5	6 52
b. Appointment of a new department head	1	2	3	4	5	6 53
c. Hiring new employees	1	2	3	4	5	6 54
d. Making a major capital investment	1	2	3	4	5	6 55
e. Having more training programs during work time	1	2	3	4	5	6 56
f. Assigning tasks that have to be done	1	2	3	4	5	6 57
g. Changing the vendors or displays	1	2	3	4	5	6 58
h. Their working hours	1	2	3	4	5	6 59
i. Shutting down the store	1	2	3	4	5	6 60

16. How much does the opportunity to contribute to decision making influence the amount of extra effort you put into your job?

     1   2   3   4   5

NONE AT ALL   A GREAT DEAL   61

17. How much does the opportunity to contribute to decision making influence how effectively you are able to do your job?

     1   2   3   4   5

NONE AT ALL   A GREAT DEAL   62

18. How much extra effort do you actually put into doing a good job?

     1   2   3   4   5

NONE AT ALL   A GREAT DEAL   63

19. How often is it true for you personally that working hard leads to high productivity?

     1   2   3   4   5

NEVER   ALMOST ALWAYS   64

20. How often is it true for you personally that working hard leads to doing your job well?

     1   2   3   4   5

NEVER   ALMOST ALWAYS   65

IV. STORE FUNCTIONING

21. Which of these consequences have occurred because of your QWL (for O&O—O&O) system of decision making?

	DEFINITELY NOT			DEFINITELY YES		
a. People know more about what goes on here	1	2	3	4	5	66
b. People are more willing to accept decisions	1	2	3	4	5	67
c. The quality of decisions has increased	1	2	3	4	5	68
d. It takes longer to make decisions	1	2	3	4	5	69
e. There is more trust between the manager and the employees	1	2	3	4	5	70
f. Disagreements are talked about more openly	1	2	3	4	5	71
g. Disagreements are more easily resolved	1	2	3	4	5	72

Card #77-78-79

V. VALUES AND SATISFACTION

23. Here is a list of things a person could have on his or her job. How important is each of the following to you?

	MODERATELY IMPORTANT			EXTREMELY IMPORTANT	
a. A feeling of accomplishment	1	2	3	4	5	11
b. Personal growth and development	1	2	3	4	5	12
c. Having a good relationship with co-workers	1	2	3	4	5	13
d. Pay and fringe benefits	1	2	3	4	5	14
e. QWL (For O&O— Worker Ownership	1	2	3	4	5	15
f. Job security	1	2	3	4	5	16
g. Independence	1	2	3	4	5	17
h. Getting a promotion or a better job	1	2	3	4	5	18
i. Having a good relationship with your boss	1	2	3	4	5	19

24. How satisfied are you with each of the following aspects of your job?

	VERY SATISFIED			VERY DISSATISFIED	
a. The feeling of accomplishment it gives you	1	2	3	4	5	20
b. The amount of personal growth it offers	1	2	3	4	5	21
c. Your relationship with co-workers	1	2	3	4	5	22
d. Your pay and fringe benefits	1	2	3	4	5	23
e. QWL (For O&O— Worker Ownership)	1	2	3	4	5	24
f. Your job security	1	2	3	4	5	25
g. Your independence	1	2	3	4	5	26
h. Your change to get promoted or a better job	1	2	3	4	5	27
i. Your relationship with your boss	1	2	3	4	5	28

25. How satisfied are you with each of the following aspects of your life?

	VERY SATISFIED				VERY DISSATISFIED	
a. Your family life	1	2	3	4	5	29
b. Your leisure life	1	2	3	4	5	30
c. Your job, overall	1	2	3	4	5	31
d. Your career	1	2	3	4	5	32
e. Your feelings about yourself as a person	1	2	3	4	5	33
f. Your economic situation	1	2	3	4	5	34
g. Your life, in general	1	2	3	4	5	35
h. Your health	1	2	3	4	5	36

VI. HOUSEHOLD SITUATION

26. What is your marital status?

1	2	3	4	5	
SINGLE	MARRIED	SEPARATED	DIVORCED	WIDOWED	37

27. What is your age? _____ YEARS   38-39

28. What is your race? 1. WHITE   2. BLACK   3. OTHER   40

29. What is your sex? 1. FEMALE   2. MALE   41

30. What is your religion?

1	2	3	4	
CATHOLIC	PROTESTANT	JEWISH	OTHER	42

31. Do you:
    1. OWN YOUR OWN HOUSE FREE AND CLEAR?   43
    2. OWN YOUR OWN HOUSE, MORTGAGED?
    3. RENT?
    4. LIVE WITH RELATIVES/PAY SOME ROOM AND BOARD?
    5. LIVE WITH RELATIVES/PAY NOTHING?

32. What is the total number of people living in your household?   44-45
    _____ PEOPLE

33. How many of these people are under 18? _____   46-47

34. How many people are economically dependent upon you for at least
some of their support? (Count both those living in your household
and those living elsewhere.)
    _____ TOTAL DEPENDENTS   48-49

35. What is your usual hourly wage for this job?
    _____ DOLLARS PER HOUR   50-51

36. What is your total annual income from this job? (Not counting
your bonus.)
    _____ DOLLARS PER YEAR   52-56

37. What was the amount of your most recent bonus?

      _____ DOLLARS   57-61

38. What is the total annual income for everyone in your household combined? (Include any other income you have.)

      _____ DOLLARS PER YEAR   62-67

39. What was your total personal income on your A&P (or previous) job?

      _____ DOLLARS PER YEAR   68-72

40. How many months were you laid off altogether since A&P announced its shutdown in March of 1982?

      _____ MONTHS   73-74

41. As far as savings are concerned, how are your savings now compared to before the shutdown?

     1   2   3   4   5

MUCH WORSE   THE SAME   MUCH BETTER   75

42. As far as debt is concerned, how much do you owe now compared to before the shutdown?

     1   2   3   4   5

MUCH MORE   MUCH LESS   76

                                             Card #77-78-79

                                             CARD#3

                                         COLUMN #

                                             ID 1-10

43. During the past two years, did changes in your financial situation make it harder or easier for your family to do any of the following things?

		HARDER		SAME		EASIER	
a.	Buying a house	1	2	3	4	5	11
b.	Having a wedding, etc.	1	2	3	4	5	12
c.	Buying a car	1	2	3	4	5	13
d.	Paying school tuition	1	2	3	4	5	14
e.	Having a baby	1	2	3	4	5	15
f.	Retiring	1	2	3	4	5	16
g.	Buying a stereo, boat or other leisure purchase	1	2	3	4	5	17
h.	Keeping something you were making payments on	1	2	3	4	5	18
i.	Having a vacation	1	2	3	4	5	19
j.	Moving out on own	1	2	3	4	5	20

44. How have any changes in your income affected your day to day budget?

		LESS IN BUDGET		SAME		MORE IN BUDGET	
a.	For food.............	1	2	3	4	5	21
b.	For clothing..........	1	2	3	4	5	22
c.	For transportation......	1	2	3	4	5	23
d.	For leisure...........	1	2	3	4	5	24
e.	For housing...........	1	2	3	4	5	25

45. Have changes in your income led you to seek extra income in any new ways such as the following:

		NO	YES	
a.	Working another job.........................	1	2	26
b.	Having someone else in your family work.........	1	2	27
c.	Getting money from friends/relatives.............	1	2	28
d.	Doing services (i.e., fixing things)...............	1	2	29
e.	Bartering or trading for things..................	1	2	30
f.	Selling things................................	1	2	31
g.	Other_____	1	2	32

(Please Specify)

[Questions 46-51 appeared only on the Super Fresh Survey]

46. At Super Fresh, how much are you getting out of work compared to A&P?

1	2	3	4	5
MUCH LESS		THE SAME		MUCH MORE

33

47. At Super Fresh, how much control do you have over your life compared to A&P?

1	2	3	4	.5
MUCH LESS		THE SAME		MUCH MORE

34

48. Did you ever go to the following meetings?

		NO	YES	
a.	Store (operation or QWL)	1	2	35
b.	QWL Training	1	2	36
c.	Corporate Planning Board	1	2	37
d.	Regional Planning Board	1	2	38

49. What is QWL?

50. Are there separate QWL & operations meetings?

	1	2	
	NO	YES	50

Card #77-78-79

51. How are QWL issues different from operations issues?

Thank you for your participation. Please seal your questionnaire in the envelope provided and return it as directed. If you have a question, call Dr. Judith Goode, 787-7773.

Appendix G

Social Innovations at Work Project of Temple University
Study of Philadelphia Supermarket Transition
Shop Steward Information

Please answer the following questions either by circling the number most closely corresponding to your situation or by filling in any blanks. Remember, the answers you give will be kept completely confidential. No individual responses will be given to anyone in the store, the union, or anywhere else. A summary of the combined responses will be available after the study is completed but these will be average answers of the group as a whole, *NOT* your personal response.

DO NOT WRITE
IN THIS
COLUMN
CARD #1
COLUMN #1
ID 1–10

I. BACKGROUND INFORMATION

1. What is your current position?

1. ASSISTANT MANAGER	11. FROZEN FOOD CLERK
2. FROZEN FOOD DEPARTMENT MANAGER	12. DELI CLERK
3. DELI DEPARTMENT MANAGER	13. PRODUCE CLERK
4. PRODUCE DEPARTMENT MANAGER	14. DAIRY CLERK
5. DAIRY DEPARTMENT MANAGER	15. GROCERY CLERK
6. GROCERY DEPARTMENT MANAGER	16. MEAT CUTTER
7. OFFICER PERSONNEL	17. MEAT WRAPPER
8. HEAD CASHIER	18. RECEIVER
9. CASHIER	19. OTHER:
10. NIGHT CREW	

_____   11-12
(please identify)

2. On average, how many hours per week do you work in this store?
_____ HOURS PER WEEK   13–14

3. How long have you worked at this job in this store?   15–19
_____ YEARS and _____ MONTHS

4. How many years have you worked in any kind of supermarket, not counting interruptions like child bearing or military service but counting your current job?
_____ YEARS IN ALL   20–21

5. How many years of schooling have you had? (High school graduation =12; college graduation=16)
_____ YEARS   22–23

307

6. What is your marital status?

    1   2   3   4   5

SINGLE MARRIED SEPARATED DIVORCED WIDOWED   24

7. What is your age? _____ YEARS   25-26

8. What is your race? 1. WHITE 2. BLACK 3. OTHER   27

9. What is your sex? 1. FEMALE 2. MALE   28

10. What is your religion?

    1   2   3   4

CATHOLIC PROTESTANT JEWISH OTHER   29

11. How many months were you laid off altogether since A&P announced its shut down in March of 1982?

          _____ MONTHS   30-31

12. What is your total annual income from this job? (Not counting your bonus.)

          _____ DOLLARS PER YEAR   32-36

13. What was the amount of your most recent bonus?

          _____ DOLLARS   37-41

14. What is the total annual income for everyone in your household combined? (Include any other income you have.)

          _____ DOLLARS PER YEAR   42-47

15. How many people are economically dependent upon you for at least some of their support? (Count both those living in your household and those living elsewhere.)

          _____ TOTAL DEPENDENTS   48-49

II. PARTICIPATION

16. How much are workers' opinions taken into account when decisions are made in your store?

    1   2   3   4   5

NONE   A GREAT DEAL   50

17. How much "say" or influence *do* each of the following have on what goes on in the store?

	VERY LITTLE "SAY"				VERY MUCH "SAY"	
a. Workers as a group	1	2	3	4	5	52
b. Department heads	1	2	3	4	5	53
c. Store Director (For O&O—Store Manager)	1	2	3	4	5	54
d. Corporate Planning Board (For O&O—Board of Directors)	1	2	3	4	5	55

18. How much "say" or influence *SHOULD* each of the following have on what
goes on in the store?

		VERY LITTLE "SAY"				VERY MUCH "SAY"	
a.	Worker as a group	1	2	3	4	5	56
b.	Department heads	1	2	3	4	5	57
c.	Store Director (For O&O—Store Manager)	1	2	3	4	5	58
d.	Corporate Planning Board (For O&O—Board of Directors)	1	2	3	4	5	59

19. How much does the opportunity to contribute to decision making
influence the amount of extra effort workers in this store put into their jobs?

1	2	3	4	5	
NONE AT ALL				A GREAT DEAL	60

20. How much does the opportunity to contribute to decision making
influence how effectively workers in this store are able to do their jobs?

1	2	3	4	5	
NONE AT ALL				A GREAT DEAL	61

21. How much extra effort do workers in this store actually put into
doing a good job?

1	2	3	4	5	
NONE AT ALL				A GREAT DEAL	62

22. How often is it true for workers in this store that working hard leads
to high productivity?

1	2	3	4	5	
NEVER				ALMOST ALWAYS	63

23. How often is it true for workers in this store that working hard leads
to high productivity?

1	2	3	4	5	
NEVER				ALMOST ALWAYS	64

24. How often is it true for workers in this store that working hard leads
to doing their job well?

1	2	3	4	5	
NEVER				ALMOST ALWAYS	65

25. Which of these consequences have occurred because of your
QWL (For O&O—O&O) system of decision making?

	DEFINITELY NOT				DEFINITELY YES	
a. People know more about what goes on here	1	2	3	4	5	66
b. People are more willing to accept decisions	1	2	3	4	5	67
c. The quality of decisions has increased	1	2	3	4	5	68
d. It takes longer to make decisions	1	2	3	4	5	69

e. There is more trust between the manager and the employees	1	2	3	4	5	70
f. Disagreements are talked about more openly	1	2	3	4	5	71
g. Disagreements are more easily resolved	1	2	3	4	5	72

CODE #77-80

CARD #2
COLUMN #
ID # 1-10

26. How much involvement do *workers* have in each of the following kinds of decisions?

	THEY ARE NOT IN- VOLVED	THEY ARE IN- FORMED BEFORE- HAND	THEY GIVE THEIR OPINION	THEIR OPINIONS ARE TAKEN INTO ACCOUNT	THEY SHARE EQUALLY IN DECISIONS	THEY DECIDE ON THEIR OWN	
a. Improvement in working conditions	1	2	3	4	5	6	11
b. Appointment of a new department head	1	2	3	4	5	6	12
c. Hiring new employees	1	2	3	4	5	6	13
d. Making a major capital investment	1	2	3	4	5	6	14
e. Having more training programs during work time	1	2	3	4	5	6	15
f. Assigning tasks that have to be done	1	2	3	4	5	6	16
g. Changing the ven- dors or displays	1	2	3	4	5	6	17
h. Their working hours	1	2	3	4	5	6	18
i. Shutting down the store	1	2	3	4	5	6	19

27. What percent of workers *actually* participate in decision making in the store?

VERY OFTEN PARTICIPATE	_____%	20-21
OCCASIONALLY PARTICIPATE	_____%	22-23
RARELY PARTICIPATE	_____%	24-25
NEVER PARTICIPATE	_____%	26-27

100%

28. How much involvement do *department heads* have in each of the following kinds of decisions?

	THEY ARE NOT IN-VOLVED	THEY ARE IN-FORMED BEFORE-HAND	THEY GIVE THEIR OPINION	THEIR OPINIONS ARE TAKEN INTO ACCOUNT	THEY SHARE EQUALLY IN DECISIONS	THEY DECIDE ON THEIR OWN	
a. Improvement in working conditions	1	2	3	4	5	6	28
b. Appointment of a new department head	1	2	3	4	5	6	29
c. Hiring new employees	1	2	3	4	5	6	30
d. Making a major capital investment	1	2	3	4	5	6	31
e. Having more training programs during work time	1	2	3	4	5	6	32
f. Assigning tasks that have to be done	1	2	3	4	5	6	33
g. Changing the vendors or displays	1	2	3	4	5	6	34
h. Their working hours	1	2	3	4	5	6	35
i. Shutting down the store	1	2	3	4	5	6	36

29. How much involvement do *store directors* have in each of the following kinds of decisions?

	THEY ARE NOT IN-VOLVED	THEY ARE IN-FORMED BEFORE-HAND	THEY GIVE THEIR OPINION	THEIR OPINIONS ARE TAKEN INTO ACCOUNT	THEY SHARE EQUALLY IN DECISIONS	THEY DECIDE ON THEIR OWN	
a. Improvement in working conditions	1	2	3	4	5	6	37
b. Appointment of a new department head	1	2	3	4	5	6	38
c. Hiring new employees	1	2	3	4	5	6	39
d. Making a major capital investment	1	2	3	4	5	6	40
e. Having more training programs during work time	1	2	3	4	5	6	41
f. Assigning tasks that have to be done	1	2	3	4	5	6	42
g. Changing the vendors or displays	1	2	3	4	5	6	43

h. Their working hours	1	2	3	4	5	6	44
i. Shutting down the store	1	2	3	4	5	6	45

III. TRAINING

30. How many job-related training programs have occurred here since the A&P shutdown?

    1   2   3   4   5

NONE   A GREAT DEAL   46

31. To what extent are workers encouraged to train each other on the job?

    1   2   3   4   5

NONE   A GREAT DEAL   47

32. How much have workers been trained in each of the following things since the A&P shutdown?

	NONE				A GREAT DEAL	
a. Confidence in handling problems that arise in the store	1	2	3	4	5	48
b. Willingness to speak up in meetings	1	2	3	4	5	49
c. How to work on a team	1	2	3	4	5	50
d. How to influence others	1	2	3	4	5	51
e. Feeling responsible for their work	1	2	3	4	5	52
f. How to supervise others	1	2	3	4	5	53
g. How to listen to others' opinions	1	2	3	4	5	54
h. How to perform a new job	1	2	3	4	5	55
i. How to perform new skills for their same job (advertising, pricing, scheduling, etc.)	1	2	3	4	5	56
j. How QWL (for O&O—Worker Ownership) works	1	2	3	4	5	57

33. To what extent has the union been supportive of QWL? (For O&O—Worker Ownership)

      1   2   3   4   5

NOT AT ALL   A GREAT DEAL

34. (#34-39—Not asked at O&O) To what extent have workers been encouraged to go to each of the following kinds of meetings?

	NEVER			ALWAYS		
a. Store operational meetings	1	2	3	4	5	59
b. Store QWL meetings	1	2	3	4	5	60
c. QWL training meetings	1	2	3	4	5	61
d. Corporate Planning Board	1	2	3	4	5	62
e. Regional Planning Board	1	2	3	4	5	63

35. In your estimation, to what extent has QWL been implemented in your store?

    1   2   3   4   5

NONE AT ALL   A GREAT DEAL   64

36. How satisfied are the workers with QWL as it is practices in your store?

      1   2   3   4   5

VERY SATISFIED   VERY DISSATISFIED   65

37. What is QWL?

38. How is QWL different from operations?

39. Are there separate QWL and Operations meetings?

      1   2

    NO   YES

If so, what goes on at each?

Thank you for your participation. Please seal your questionnaire in the envelope provided and return it as directed. If you have a question, call Dr. Judith Goode, 787-7773.

Appendix H

Social Innovations at Work Project of Temple University
Study of Philadelphia Supermarkets in Transition
Store Director (For O&O—Manager) Information

Please answer the following questions either by circling the number most closely corresponding to your situation or by filling in any blanks. Remember, the answers you give will be kept completely confidential. No individual responses will be given to anyone in the store, the union, or anywhere else. A summary of the combined responses will be available after the study is completed but these will be average answers of the group as a whole, *NOT* your personal response.

DO NOT WRITE
IN THIS
COLUMN
CARD #1
COLUMN #1
ID 1-10

I. CHARACTERISTICS OF THE EMPLOYEES IN YOUR STORE

1. What is the total number of people employed in this store?
   _____ TOTAL # OF EMPLOYEES   11-12

2. How many of these employees are Full Time?
   _____ FULL TIMERS   13-14

3. How many are Part Time?
   _____ PART TIMERS   15-16

4. On average, how many hours per week do your Full Timers work?
   _____ HOURS/WEEK FT   17-18

5. On average, how many hours per week do your Part Timers work?
   _____ HOURS/WEEK PT   19-20

6. How many employees quit, were fired, retired or died during the past year?
   _____ # TURNED OVER   21-22

7. In an average week, how many employees are absent?
   _____ # ABSENT   23-24

8. How many of your employees have supervisory responsibilities?
   _____ # SUPERVISORS   25-26

9. How many of your employees (Full and Part Time) are female?
   _____ # FEMALES   27-28

10. How many of your employees are non-white?
   _____ # NON-WHITE   29-30

315

11. How many of your employees have at least a high school diploma or GED?

_____ # H.S. GRADUATES   31-32

12. What percent of your workers are at the top of the pay scale?

_____ %   33-34

13. How much are they paid per hour?

$_____ HOUR   35-39

14. What percent of your workers are at the bottom of the pay scale?

_____ %   40-41

15. How much are they paid per hour?

$_____ HOUR   42-46

16. How many employees can you schedule for more than one job?

_____ EMPLOYEES   47-48

17. How many training programs have been run for your employees during the past year?

_____ # TRAINING PROGRAMS   49-50

18. To what extent are workers encouraged to train each other on the job?

    1   2   3   4   5
  NONE   A GREAT DEAL   51

19. What is the average seniority of workers in your store?

_____ YEARS SENIORITY   52-53

II. CHARACTERISTICS OF YOUR STORE

20. How many square feet of selling area do you have?

_____ THOUSAND SQUARE FEET   54-56

21. How many other food stores compete with you in the neighborhood you serve?

_____ # COMPETITORS   57-58

22. How easy is it for you to obtain credit for the store?

    1   2   3   4   5
VERY DIFFICULT   VERY EASY   59

III. PARTICIPATION

23. How much are workers' opinions taken into account when decisions are made in your store?

    1   2   3   4   5
NOT AT ALL   A GREAT DEAL   60

24. How much "say" or influence *DO* each of the following have on
    what goes on in the store?

	VERY LITTLE "SAY"			VERY MUCH "SAY"		
a. Workers as a group	1	2	3	4	5	61
b. Department heads	1	2	3	4	5	62
c. Store Director (For O&O— Store Manager)	1	2	3	4	5	63
d. Corporate Planning Board (For O&O—Board of Directors)	1	2	3	4	5	64

25. How much "say" or influence *SHOULD* each of the following have on
    what goes on in the store?

	VERY LITTLE "SAY"			VERY MUCH "SAY"		
a. Workers are a group	1	2	3	4	5	65
b. Department heads	1	2	3	4	5	66
c. Store Director (For O&O— Store Manager)	1	2	3	4	5	67
d. Corporate Planning Board (For O&O—Board of Directors)	1	2	3	4	5	68

26. How much involvement do *you* have in each of the following kinds
    of decisions?

	I AM NOT IN-VOLVED	I AM IN-FORMED BEFORE-HAND	I CAN GIVE MY OPINION	MY OPINION IS TAKEN INTO ACCOUNT	I SHARE EQUALLY IN DECISIONS	I CAN DECIDE ON MY OWN	
a. Improvement in working conditions	1	2	3	4	5	6	69
b. Appoint of a new department head	1	2	3	4	5	6	70
c. Hiring new employees	1	2	3	4	5	6	71
d. Making a major capital investment	1	2	3	4	5	6	72
e. Having more training programs during work time	1	2	3	4	5	6	73
f. Assigning tasks that have to be done	1	2	3	4	5	6	74
g. Changing the ven-dors or displays	1	2	3	4	5	6	75
h. Their working hours	1	2	3	4	5	6	76
i. Shutting down the store	1	2	3	4	5	6	77

CODE #78-80

318

27. How much involvement do *department heads* have in each of the
following kinds of decisions?

	THEY ARE NOT IN- VOLVED	THEY ARE IN- FORMED BEFORE- HAND	THEY GIVE THEIR OPINION	THEIR OPINIONS ARE TAKEN INTO ACCOUNT	THEY SHARE EQUALLY IN DECISIONS	THEY DECIDE ON THEIR OWN	
a. Improvement in working conditions	1	2	3	4	5	6	11
b. Appointment of a new department head	1	2	3	4	5	6	12
c. Hiring new employees	1	2	3	4	5	6	13
d. Making a major capital investment	1	2	3	4	5	6	14
e. Having more training programs during work time	1	2	3	4	5	6	15
f. Assigning tasks that have to be done	1	2	3	4	5	6	16
g. Changing the vendors or displays	1	2	3	4	5	6	17
h. Their working hours	1	2	3	4	5	6	18
i. Shutting down the store	1	2	3	4	5	6	19

28. How much involvement do *workers* have in each of the following kinds
of decisions?

	THEY ARE NOT IN- VOLVED	THEY ARE IN- FORMED BEFORE- HAND	THEY GIVE THEIR OPINION	THEIR OPINIONS ARE TAKEN INTO ACCOUNT	THEY SHARE EQUALLY IN DECISIONS	THEY DECIDE ON THEIR OWN	
a. Improvement in working conditions	1	2	3	4	5	6	20
b. Appointment of a new department head	1	2	3	4	5	6	21
c. Hiring new employees	1	2	3	4	5	6	22
d. Making a major capital investment	1	2	3	4	5	6	23
e. Having more training programs during work time	1	2	3	4	5	6	24

f. Assigning tasks that
   have to be done   1   2   3   4   5   6   25

g. Changing the ven-
   dors or displays   1   2   3   4   5   6   26

h. Their working hours   1   2   3   4   5   6   27

i. Shutting down the
   store   1   2   3   4   5   6   28

29. What percent of your workers ACTUALLY participate in decision making
    in the store?

VERY OFTEN PARTICIPATE	_____%	29-30
OCCASIONALLY PARTICIPATE	_____%	31-32
RARELY PARTICIPATE	_____%	33-34
NEVER PARTICIPATE	_____%	35-36
	100%	

30. Which of these consequences have occurred because of your QWL
    (For O&O—O&O) system of decision making?

                      DEFINITELY NOT   DEFINITELY YES

a. People know more about
   what goes on here   1   2   3   4   5   37

b. People are more willing to
   accept decisions   1   2   3   4   5   38

c. The quality of decisions has
   increased   1   2   3   4   5   39

d. It takes longer to make
   decisions   1   2   3   4   5   40

e. There is more trust between
   the manager and the
   employees   1   2   3   4   5   41

f. Disagreements are talked
   about more openly   1   2   3   4   5   42

g. Disagreements are more
   easily resolved   1   2   3   4   5   43

IV. INNOVATIONS

31. To what extent have jobs or duties that people perform changed since 1982?

     1   2   3   4   5

NO CHANGE   A GREAT DEAL

                                 OF CHANGE   44

32. To what extent have new methods for doing things in a supermarket
    been used in this store since 1982?

     1   2   3   4   5

NONE   A GREAT DEAL   45

33. To what extent have new kinds of supermarket equipment been used
    in this store since 1982?

     1   2   3   4   5

NONE   A GREAT DEAL   46

V. STORE FINANCIAL INFORMATION

Please base the first four answers to each question on figures from the most recent four quarters. That is, the data should include October 1, 1983 to September 31, 1984. Remember all of this data will be kept confidential and is intended to *help you*.

	Oct. 1, 1983 to Dec. 31, 1983	Jan. 1, 1984 to March 31, 1984	April1, 1984 to June 30, 1984	July 1, 1984 to Sept. 31, 1984
34. What was your sales volume?	$ _____	$ _____	$ _____	$ _____
35. What was the total cost of goods sold?	$ _____	$ _____	$ _____	$ _____
36. What was your store's net income?	$ _____	$ _____	$ _____	$ _____
37. What were your operating expenses?	$ _____	$ _____	$ _____	$ _____
38. What was your total payroll expenditure?	$ _____	$ _____	$ _____	$ _____
39. What was your total cash flow?	$ _____	$ _____	$ _____	$ _____
40. What was the total value of your assets?	$ _____	$ _____	$ _____	$ _____
41 How much did you spend on capital improvements?	$ _____	$ _____	$ _____	$ _____
42. What was the average TOTAL # of employee hours worker per week?	$ _____	$ _____	$ _____	$ _____

44. If your business should slump temporarily, how likely is it that you would do each of the following things? Please circle 1 number for each statement *then* go back and rank order the top *10* things you would do: 1=the first and 10=the last.

RANK ORDER		EXTREMELY UNLIKELY				EXTREMELY LIKELY	
_____	a. Reduce hours of full time workers	1	2	3	4	5	11
_____	b. Reduce hours of part time workers	1	2	3	4	5	12
_____	c. Reduce the # of full time workers	1	2	3	4	5	13
_____	d. Reduce the # of part time workers	1	2	3	4	5	14
_____	e. Bargain to reduce wages	1	2	3	4	5	15
_____	f. Change product mix	1	2	3	4	5	16
_____	g. Reduce advertising/specials	1	2	3	4	5	17
_____	h. Increase advertising/specials	1	2	3	4	5	18
_____	i. Reduce coupons	1	2	3	4	5	19
_____	j. Draw from savings/checking	1	2	3	4	5	20
_____	k. Sell liquid assets	1	2	3	4	5	21

_____ l. Borrow from the bank	1	2	3	4	5	22
_____ m. Reduce wages of owners	1	2	3	4	5	23
_____ n. Other _____	1	2	3	4	5	24
identify						
_____ o. Other _____	1	2	3	4	5	25
identify						

DID YOU REMEMBER TO RANK YOUR TOP 10?   28-47

VI. CONSULTING

45. Since March 1982, have you ever had a consultant assist you or your employees in improving your store operations?

            1   2
            NO   YES

If so, how many *hours* of consulting time did you receive from each of the following sources in each topic area?

	JOB OR SKILL-TRAIN-ING	QWL TRAIN-ING	GROUP PROCESS TRAIN-ING	STORE OPERAT-ING PRAC-TICES	FINAN-CIAL	LEGAL	OTHER
a. A&P	_____	_____	_____	_____	_____	_____	_____
b. PACE (Sherman Kreiner Andy Lamas)	_____	_____	_____	_____	_____	_____	_____
c. GREY AREAS (Jay Guben & Merry Guben)	_____	_____	_____	_____	_____	_____	_____
d. IGA	_____	_____	_____	_____	_____	_____	_____
e. PALM (John Good)	_____	_____	_____	_____	_____	_____	_____
f. UFCW 1357	_____	_____	_____	_____	_____	_____	_____
g. UFCW 56	_____	_____	_____	_____	_____	_____	_____
h. OTHER	_____	_____	_____	_____	_____	_____	_____
i. OTHER	_____	_____	_____	_____	_____	_____	_____
j. OTHER	_____	_____	_____	_____	_____	_____	_____

(Please specify)

46. How much have workers learned about each of the following things since the A&P shutdown?

	NOTHING				A GREAT DEAL
a. Confidence in handling problems that arise in the store	1	2	3	4	5
b. Willingness to speak up in meetings	1	2	3	4	5
c. How to work on a team	1	2	3	4	5
d. How to influence others	1	2	3	4	5
e. Feeling responsible for their work	1	2	3	4	5
f. How to supervise others	1	2	3	4	5

322

g.	How to listen to others' opinions	1	2	3	4	5
h.	How to perform a new job	1	2	3	4	5
i.	How to perform new skills for their same job (advertising, pricing, scheduling, etc.)	1	2	3	4	5
j.	How QWL (For O&O—Worker Ownership) works	1	2	3	4	5

THANK YOU FOR YOUR PARTICIPATION. PLEASE SEAL YOUR QUESTIONNAIRE IN THE ENVELOPE PROVIDED AND MAIL. IF YOU HAVE ANY QUESTIONS, CALL DR. JUDITH GOODE, 787-7773.

Appendix I

Mean Differences on Major Study Variables Among Store Managers, Shop Stewards, Full-Time Workers, and Part-Time Workers In the Six Stores Studied Intensively

Study variables	Mean responses of				Significant differences (p <.05)
	Store managers	Shop stewards	Full-time workers	Part-time workers	
Workers' Opinions Considered[1]	4.04	3.23	3.53	2.32	a,b,c,d,f
Perceived Degree of Influence:[2]					
Workers as a Group	3.54	2.76	3.09	2.24	a,b,d,e
Department Heads	4.42	3.60	4.17	3.50	a,b
Store Managers	4.65	4.54	4.69	4.3	d
Board	4.46	4.24	4.38	4.09	—
Worker Involvement in:[3]					
Improving Work Conditions	3.72	3.04	4.09	2.19	a,b,d,e,f
Appointing Department Head	1.92	1.96	3.10	1.26	b,c,d,e,f
Hiring Workers	1.84	1.65	3.22	1.30	b,c,e
Making Major Capital Investment	1.28	1.54	2.47	1.25	b,c,e
Having More Work Training	1.14	1.25	1.67	1.19	b,d,e
Assigning Daily Tasks	2.40	1.92	5.14	3.02	b,c,e,f
Changing Vendors or Display	2.36	3.00	3.57	1.75	b,c,e
Setting Working Hours	2.40	2.15	4.21	1.77	b,c,e
Shutting Down the Store	1.48	1.79	2.64	1.30	b,c,e
Consequences of QWL (Worker Ownership):[4]					
People Know More	4.24	3.40	3.75	2.51	a,d,e,f
People Are More Willing to Accept Decisions	3.80	3.28	3.60	2.55	b,d,f
Quality of Decision Increased	4.08	3.12	3.56	2.45	a,b,d,f
Takes Longer to Make Decisions	3.00	2.88	3.22	2.64	b
More Trust Between Manager and Worker	4.44	3.32	3.65	2.61	a,b,c,d,f
Disagreements Are Talked About More Openly	4.28	3.48	4.07	2.75	a,b,d,f
Disagreements Are More Easily Resolved	4.12	3.52	3.60	2.48	b,d,f
Workers Encouraged to Attend Store QWL Meetings[5]	3.76	3.76	3.55	2.57	b,d,f

LEGEND: a=Store Managers vs. Shop Stewards. b=Full-Time vs. Part-Time Workers. c=Store Managers vs. Full-Time Workers. d=Store Managers vs. Part-Time Workers. e=Shop Stewards vs. Full-Time Workers. f=Shop Stewards vs. Part-Time Workers.

NOTES:
1. Responses range from 1 Not At All to 5 A Great Deal.
2. Responses range from 1 Very Little Say to 5 Very Much Say.
3. Responses range from 1 Not Involved to 5 Own Decision.
4. Responses range from 1 Definitely Not to 5 Definitely Yes.
5. Responses range from 1 Never to 5 Always.

Appendix J

Comparison of Mean Responses Between Stores Where Interviews Were Held and Stores Where No Interviews Were Held

	Store managers responses in QWL stores			
	Interviewed	Non-interviewed		
	Stores (n=2)	Stores (n=11)	*t*-value	2-tail P
Actual Say:				
Workers	4.50	2.73	2.81	0.11
Department head	5.00	4.00	5.24	0.00
Store manager	4.50	4.64	0.26	0.84
Corporate board	5.00	4.27	3.07	0.01
Ideal Say:				
Workers	4.50	3.45	1.82	0.21
Department head	5.00	4.27	3.07	0.01
Store manager	4.00	4.82	1.49	0.17
Corporate board	4.00	4.27	0.27	0.83
	Union stewards responses in QWL stores			
	Interviewed	Non-interviewed		
	Stores (n=2)	Stores (n=11)	*t*-value	2-tail P
Actual Say:				
Workers	3.50	3.09	0.27	0.84
Department head	4.50	3.91	1.00	0.42
Store manager	5.00	4.64	1.79	0.10
Corporate board	4.50	4.18	0.55	0.64
Ideal Say:				
Workers	4.00	3.91	0.09	0.94
Department head	4.50	4.45	0.08	0.94
Store manager	5.00	4.82	1.00	0.34
Corporate board	4.50	4.00	0.83	0.49

Appendix J (continued)

| | Store managers responses in non-QWL stores | | | |
| | Interviewed | Non-interviewed | | |
	Stores (n=2)	Stores (n=8)	t-value	2-tail P
Actual Say:				
Workers	4.50	4.00	0.73	0.52
Department head	4.50	4.63	0.22	0.85
Store manager	4.50	4.64	0.22	0.85
Corporate board	4.50	4.38	0.21	0.85
Ideal Say:				
Workers	4.50	4.38	0.22	0.85
Department head	4.50	4.63	0.23	0.85
Store manager	4.50	4.63	0.23	0.85
Corporate board	4.50	3.75	1.03	0.36
	Union stewards responses in non-QWL stores			
	Interviewed	Non-interviewed		
	(n=2)	(n=7)	t-value	2-tail P
Actual Say:				
Workers	2.50	1.86	1.06	0.34
Department head	3.00	2.86	0.13	0.92
Store manager	4.00	4.38	0.37	0.78
Corporate board	5.00	3.86	1.80	0.12
Ideal Say:				
Workers	4.00	4.29	0.79	0.46
Department head	4.00	4.43	1.44	0.20
Store manager	4.00	4.50	1.87	0.10
Corporate board	4.00	4.14	0.35	0.74

REFERENCES

Ackoff, Russell L., Per Broholm and Roberta Snow. "Returning a Troubled Business to Profitability: Case Study of Super Fresh," in Russell L. Ackoff, Per Broholm and Roberta Snow, eds. *Revitalizing Western Economies: A New Agenda for Business and Government.* San Francisco: Jossey-Bass, 1984.

Aldrich, Howard and Robert N. Stern. "Resource Mobilization and the Creation of U.S. Producers' Cooperatives 1835-1935," *Economic and Industrial Democracy* 4 (1983); 371-406.

Argyris, Chris. *Personality and Organization.* New York: Harper, 1957.

"A&P's Busy Boss," *Business Week* 2699 (August 3, 1981): 32.

"A&P Looks Like Tenglemann's Vietnam," *Business Week* 2724 (February 1, 1982):42-44.

Barber, Randy and Andrew R. Banks. "Up Against More Gloom and Doom," *Labor Research Review* 5 (Fall 1984): 95-112.

Barmash, I. "Evolution of a Leaner A&P," *New York Times* (April 27, 1982): D1.

Batstone, Eric. "France," in Frank H. Stephen, ed., *The Performance of Labor-Managed Firms.* New York: St. Martin's Press, 1982.

_____ . "Organization and Orientation: A Life Cycle Model of French Cooperatives," *Economic and Industrial Democracy* 4 (1983): 139-161.

Bellas, Carl J. *Industrial Democracy and the Worker-Owned Firm.* New York: Praeger, 1972.

Berman, Katrina V. *Worker-Owned Plywood Cooperatives: An Economic Analysis.* Pullman, WA: Bureau of Economic and Business Research, 1967.

Bernstein, Paul. *Workplace Democratization: Its Internal Dynamics.* Kent, OH: Kent State University Press, 1976.

Blasi, Joseph R. and William F. Whyte. "Worker Ownership and Public Policy," *Policy Studies Journal* 10 (1981): 320-337.

_____ . Perry Mehrling and William F. Whyte. "The Politics of Worker Ownership in the United States," in Colin Crouch and Frank A. Heller, eds., *International Yearbook of Organizational Democracy, Vol. I: Organizational Democracy and Political Processes.* New York: Wiley, 1983.

_____ , _____ and _____ . "Environmental Influences in the Growth of Worker Ownership and Control," in Bernhard Wilpert and Arndt Sorge, eds., *International Yearbook of Organizational Democracy, Vol. II: International Perspectives on Organizational Democracy.* Chichester: Wiley, 1984.

Blim, Michael L. "The Changing Labor Process in an American Service Industry." Paper presented at the American Anthropological Association Annual Meetings, Washington, DC, December 1985.

Bluestone, Barry and Bennett Harrison. *The Deindustrialization of America.* New York: Basic Books, 1982.

Blumberg, Paul. *Industrial Democracy: The Sociology of Participation.* New York: Schocken Books, 1968.

Bradley, Keith. "A Comparative Analysis of Producer Co-operatives: Some Theoretical and Empirical Implications." *British Journal of Industrial Relations* 18 (1980): 155-168.

_____ and Alan Gelb. "The Mondragon Cooperatives: Guidelines for a Cooperative Economy?" in Derek C. Jones and Jan Svejnar, eds., *Participatory and Self-Managed Firms: Evaluating Economic Performance.* Lexington, MA: Lexington Books, 1982.

_____ and _____. *Worker Capitalism: The New Industrial Relations.* Cambridge, MA: MIT Press, 1983.

Braverman, Harry. *Labor and Monopoly Capital: The Degradation of Work in the Twentieth Century.* New York: Monthly Review Press, 1974.

Bureau of National Affairs. "Two-Tiered Pay Systems." *Collective Bargaining Negotiations and Contracts* 93 (1985a): 121.

_____. "Two-Tiered Wage Plans," *Collective Bargaining: Negotiations and Contracts* 16 (1985b): 991-992.

_____. *Employee Ownership Plans.* Washington, D.C.: Bureau of National Affairs, 1987.

Campbell, Donald T. and Julian C. Stanley. *Experimental and Quasi-Experimental Designs for Research.* Chicago: Rand McNally, 1963.

Clark, Dennis and Merry Guben. *Future Bread: How Retail Workers Ransomed Their Jobs and Lives, With a Guide to Cooperative Ownership.* Philadelphia: O&O Investment Fund, 1983.

Clarke, Tom. "Alternative Modes of Cooperative Production," *Economic and Industrial Democracy* 5 (1984): 97-129.

Compa, Lance and Paul J. Baicich. "Rejoinder," *Labor Research Review* 5 (Fall 1984a): 113-116.

_____. "Model Struggle, Yes. Model Contract, No," *Labor Research Review* 5 (Fall 1984b): 86-94.

"Concessionary Bargaining: Will the New Cooperation Last?" *Business Week* 2743 (June 14, 1982): 66-69.

Conte, Michael. "Participation and Performance in U.S. Labor-Managed Firms," in Derek C. Jones and Jan Svejnar, eds., *Participatory and Self-Managed Firms: Evaluating Economic Performance.* Lexington, MA: Lexington Books, 1982.

_____ and Arnold S. Tannenbaum. "Employe-Owned Companies: Is the Difference Measurable?" *Monthly Labor Review* 101 (July 1978): 23-28.

_____ , _____ and Donna McCulloch. *Employee Ownership.* Ann Arbor: Institute for Social Research, University of Michigan, 1981.

Cornforth, Chris. "Some Factors Affecting the Success or Failure of Worker Cooperatives," *Economic and Industrial Democracy* 4 (1983): 163-190.

Cosyns, Jane and Raymond Loveridge. "The Role of Leadership in the Genesis of Producer Cooperatives." Paper presented at the International Conference on Producer Cooperatives, Gilleleje, Denmark, June 1981.

Curl, John. *History of Work Cooperation in America: Cooperatives, Cooperative Movements, Collectivity and Communalism From Early American to the Present.* Berkeley, CA: Homeward Press, 1980.

Dachler, H. Peter and Bernhard Wilpert. "Conceptual Dimensions and Boundaries of Participation in Organizations: A Critical Evaluation," *Administrative Science Quarterly* 23 (1978): 1-39.

Derber, Milton. *The American Idea of Industrial Democracy, 1865-1965.* Urbana, IL: University of Illinois Press, 1970.

Diamond, David J. "A&P's Worker Managers," *New York Times* (May 21, 1983): 37.

Dirlam, Joel B. "The Food Distribution Industry," in Walter Adams, ed., *The Structure of American Industry* 5 ed. New York: Macmillan, 1977.

Doeringer, Peter and Michael Piore. *Internal Labor Markets and Manpower Analysis.* Lexington, MA: D.C. Heath, 1971.

Ellerman, David P. "On the Legal Structure of Workers' Cooperatives," in Frank Lindenfeld and Joyce Rothschild-Whitt, eds., *Workplace Democracy and Social Change.* Boston: Porter Sargent, 1982.

_____ . "ESOPs and Coops: Worker Capitalism and Worker Democracy," *Labor Research Review* 6 (Spring 1985): 55-69.

Espinosa, Juan G. "On the Problems of Estimating the Relative Efficiency of Participatory and Self-Managed Enterprises in Developing Countries: Some Illustrations from the Case of Chile," in Derek C. Jones and Jan Svejnar, eds., *Participatory and Self-Managed Firms: Evaluating Economic Performance.* Lexington, MA: Lexington Books, 1982.

_____ and Andrew S. Zimbalist. *Economic Democracy: Workers' Participation in Chilean Industry 1970-1973.* New York: Academic Press, 1978.

European Economic Commission (EEC). *Prospects for Workers' Cooperatives in Western Europe,* 3 Vols. Brussels: European Economic Commission, 1981.

Fleeson, Lucinda. "An Experiment By Owner-Workers Celebrates Year 1," *Philadelphia Inquirer* (October 16, 1983): D1.

330

Freeman, B.M. "Why Employee Buyouts Often Fall Short of Hopes," *Wall*

Freeman, Richard B. and James R. Medoff. *What Do Unions Do?* New York: Basic Books, 1984.

Freund, William C. and Eugene Epstein. *People and Productivity: The New York Stock Exchange Guide to Financial Incentives and the Quality of Work Life.* Homewood, IL: Dow Jones-Irwin, 1984.

Gordus, Jeanne P., Paul Jarley and Louis Ferman. *Plant Closings and Economic Dislocation.* Kalamazoo, MI: W.E. Upjohn Institute for Employment Research, 1981.

Granrose, Cherlyn S. and Arthur Hochner. "Are Women Interested in Saving Their Jobs Through Employee Ownership?" *Economic and Industrial Democracy* 6 (1985): 299-324.

_____, Elaine Simon and Cynthia Coker. "Job Creation in North Philadelphia: The Strawberry Mansion O&O Supermarket." Working paper, Department of Human Resource Administration, Temple University, 1986.

Greenberg, Edward S. "Participation in Industrial Decision Making and Work Satisfaction: The Case of Producer Cooperatives," *Social Science Quarterly* 60 (1980): 551-569.

_____. "Producer Cooperatives and Democratic Theory: The Case of the Plywood Firms," in Robert Jackall and Henry M. Levin, eds., *Worker Cooperatives in America.* Berkeley: University of California Press, 1984.

Hammer, Tove Helland and Robert N. Stern. "Employee Ownership: Implications for the Organizational Distribution of Power," *Academy of Management Journal* 23 (1980): 78-100.

_____, Jacqueline C. Landau and Robert N. Stern. "Absenteeism When Workers Have a Voice: The Case of Employee Ownership," *Journal of Applied Psychology* 66 (1981): 561-573.

Hartley, Robert F. *Management Mistakes.* Columbus, OH: GRID, 1983.

Hochner, Arthur. "Worker Ownership and the Theory of Participation." Ph.D. dissertation, Harvard University, 1978.

_____. "Worker Ownership, Community Ownership, and Labor Unions: Two Examples," *Economic and Industrial Democracy* 4 (1983a): 345-369.

_____. "Worker Ownership and Reindustrialization: A Guide for Workers," in Donald Kennedy, ed., *Labor and Reindustrialization: Workers and Corporate Change.* University Park, PA: Dept. of Labor Studies, Pennsylvania State University, 1983b.

_____ and Douglas Bennett. "Reversing Store Closings Through Worker Ownership and Participation: Impacts on Organization, Employees and Labor Relations." Application for Research Incentive Fund, Temple University, 1982.

_____ and Cherlyn S. Granrose. "Sources of Motivation to Choose Employee Ownership as an Alternative to Job Loss," *Academy of Management Journal* 28 (1985): 860-875.

Industrial Democracy in Europe International Research Group (IDE). *Industrial Democracy in Europe*. Oxford: Clarendon Press, 1981.

Jackall, Robert and Joyce Crain. "The Shape of the Small Worker Cooperative Movement," in Robert Jackall and Henry M. Levin, eds., *Worker Cooperatives in America*. Berkeley: University of California Press, 1984.

_____ and Henry M. Levin, eds. *Worker Cooperatives in America*. Berkeley: University of California Press, 1984.

Jick, Todd. "Mixing Qualitative and Quantitative Methods: Triangulation in Action," *Administrative Science Quarterly* 24 (1979): 602-611.

Jones, Derek C. "American Producer Cooperatives and Employee-Owned Firms: A Historical Perspective," in Robert Jackall and Henry M. Levin, eds., *Worker Cooperatives in America*. Berkeley: University of California Press, 1984.

_____ and Jan Svejnar. "The Economic Performance of Participatory and Self-Managed Firms: A Historical Perspective," in Derek C. Jones and Jan Svejnar, eds., *Participatory and Self-Managed Firms: Evaluating Economic Performance*. Lexington, MA: Lexington Books, 1982.

Kanter, Rosabeth Moss. *The Change Masters: Innovation for Productivity in the American Corporation*. New York: Simon and Schuster, 1983.

Katz, Harry C. *Shifting Gears: Changing Labor Relations in the U.S. Automobile Industry*. Cambridge: MIT Press, 1985.

_____ , Thomas A. Kochan and Mark R. Weber. "Assessing the Effects of Industrial Relations Systems and Efforts to Improve the Quality of Working Life on Organizational Effectiveness," *Academy of Management Journal* 28 (1985): 509-526.

Kelso, Louis and Mortimer Adler. *The Capitalist Manifesto*. New York: Random House, 1958.

_____ and Patricia Hetter. *Two Factor Theory: The Economics of Reality*. New York: Random House, 1967.

Kochan, Thomas A., ed. *Challenges and Choices Facing American Labor*. Cambridge: MIT Press, 1986.

Kochan, Thomas A., Harry C. Katz and Nancy R. Mower. *Worker Participation and American Unions: Threat or Opportunity?* Kalamazoo, MI: W.E. Upjohn Institute for Employment Research, 1984.

Kreiner, Sherman and Andrew Lamas. "Worker Ownership: Keeping APACE," *WIN Magazine* 7/8 (1983): 4-8.

Kruse, Douglas. *Employee Ownership and Employee Attitudes: Two Case Studies*. Norwood, PA: Norwood, 1984.

Lammers, Cornelius J. "Power and Participation in Decision-Making in Formal Organizations," *American Journal of Sociology* 73 (1967): 201-216.

Lawler, Edward E., III, Stanley E. Seashore and Cortland Cammann. *Michigan Organizational Assessment Package.* Ann Arbor: Survey Research Center, University of Michigan, 1975.

Leroy, Greg. "Mismanagement: Labor's Rightful Cause," *Labor Research Review* 6, 1 (1987): 1-11.

Levin, Henry M. "Issues in Assessing the Comparative Productivity of Worker-Managed and Participatory Forms in Capitalist Societies," in Derek C. Jones and Jan Svejnar, eds., *Participatory and Self-Managed Firms: Evaluating Economic Performance.* Lexington, MA: Lexington Books, 1982.

_____ . "Employment and Productivity of Producer Cooperatives," in Robert Jackall and Henry M. Levin, eds., *Worker Cooperatives in America.* Berkeley: University of California Press, 1984.

Likert, Rensis. *New Patterns of Management.* New York: McGraw-Hill, 1961.

Lin, Jennifer. "Super Fresh Clerks Rethinking Union's Investment," *Philadelphia Inquirer* (October 6, 1983): 15C.

Livingston, Craig. "Lessons from Three UAW Locals," *Labor Research Review* 6 (Spring 1985): 35-39.

"Local Unions May Give A&P Its Best Bargains," *Business Week* 2737 (May 3, 1982): 31-32.

Locke, Edwin A. and David M. Schweiger. "Participation in Decision-Making: One More Look," *Research in Organizational Behavior* 1 (1979): 265-339.

Long, Richard J. "The Effects of Employee Ownership on Job Attitudes and Organizational Performance: An Exploratory Study," Ph.D. dissertation, New York State School of Industrial and Labor Relations, Cornell University, 1977.

_____ . "The Effects of Employee Ownership on Organizational Identification, Employee Job Attitudes, and Organizational Performance: A Tentative Framework and Empirical Findings," *Human Relations* 31 (1978a): 29-49.

_____ . "The Relative Effects of Share Ownership vs. Control on Job Attitudes in an Employee-Owned Company," *Human Relations* 31 (1978b): 753-763.

_____ . "Desires for and Patterns of Worker Participation in Decision Making After Conversion to Employee Ownership," *Academy of Management Journal* 22 (1979): 611-617.

_____ . "Worker Ownership and Job Attitudes: A Field Study," *Industrial Relations* 21 (1982): 196-215.

Lowin, Aaron. "Participative Decision-Making: A Model, Literature Critique, and Prescriptions for Research," *Organizational Behavior and Human Performance* 3 (1968): 68-106.

Lynd, Staughton. "Why We Opposed the Buy-out at Weirton Steel," *Labor Research Review* 6 (Spring 1985): 41-51.

Macy, Barry A. "The Bolivar Quality of Work Life Program: A Longitudinal Behavioral and Performance Assessment." Paper presented at 32nd Annual Meeting of the Industrial Relations Research Association, Atlanta, 1979.

_____. "The Bolivar Quality of Work Life Program: Success or Failure?" in Robert Zager and Michael Rosow, eds., *The Innovative Organization: Productivity Programs in Action.* New York: Pergamon Press, 1982.

_____ and Phillip H. Mirvis. "A Methodology for Assessment of Quality of Work Life and Organizational Effectiveness in Behavioral-Economic Terms," *Administrative Science Quarterly* 21 (1976): 212-226.

Marsh, Thomas R. and Dale McAllister. "ESOPs Tables: A Survey of Companies with Employee Stock Ownership Plans," *Journal of Corporation Law* 6 (1981): 551-623.

May, Jim. "The Hyatt-Clark ESOP," *Labor Research Review* (Spring 1985): 25-33.

McCain, Roger. "Empirical Implications of Worker Participation in Management," in Derek C. Jones and Jan Svejnar, eds., *Participatory and Self-Managed Firms.* Lexington, MA: Lexington Books, 1982.

Meade, J.E. "The Theory of Labour-Managed Firms and Profit Sharing," *Economic Journal* 82 (1972): 402-428.

Metzgar, Jack. "Introduction," *Labor Research Review* (Fall 1984): 81-85.

Mintzberg, Henry. *The Structuring of Organizations.* Englewood Cliffs, NJ: Prentice Hall, 1979.

Moberg, David. "A Big Step Toward Worker Ownership," *In These Times* (June 2-15, 1982): 2.

National Center for Employee Ownership (NCEO). "Participation is the Key," *Employee Ownership* VI, 3 (1986): 1.

Nicholson, Margaret M. "The Management of Participation: A Comparison of Work Environments in Participatory and Traditional Management Systems in the Retail Food Industry." Ph.D. dissertation, University of Pennsylvania, 1985.

Nie, Norman W., C.H. Hull, J.G. Jenkins, Karen Steinbrenner and D.H. Bent. *Statistical Package for the Social Sciences,* 2d ed. New York: McGraw-Hill, 1975.

Nightingale, Donald V. *Workplace Democracy: An Inquiry into Employee Participation in Canadian Work Organizations.* Toronto: University of Toronto, 1982.

334

Oliver, Nick. "An Examination of Organizational Commitment in Six Workers' Cooperatives in Scotland," *Human Relations* 37 (1984): 29-45.

Olson, Deborah G. "Union Experiences With Worker Ownership," *Wisconsin Law Review* 5 (1982): 729-823.

O'Toole, James. "The Uneven Record of Employee Ownership: Is Worker Capitalism a Fruitful Opportunity or an Impractical Idea?" *Harvard Business Review* 57 (November-December 1979): 185-197.

Ouchi, William. *Theory Z: How American Business Can Meet the Japanese Challenge.* Reading, MA: Addison-Wesley, 1981.

PACE News. Philadelphia: Philadelphia Association for Cooperative Enterprise, 1982.

Palley, Robin. "For Markets, a Super Compliment," *Philadelphia Daily News* (July 10, 1987): 31.

Parker, Mike. *Inside the Circle: A Union Guide to QWL.* Boston: South End Press, 1985.

Parzen, J., Catherine Squire and Michael Kieschnick. *Buyout: A Guide for Workers Facing Plant Closures.* San Francisco: California Office of Economic Policy, Planning, and Research, 1982.

Patard, Richard. "Employee Stock Ownership in the 1920s," *Employee Ownership* 2 (1982): 4-5.

Perrow, Charles. *Complex Organizations: A Critical Essay.* Glenview, IL: Scott Foresman, 1972.

Perry, Stewart E. *San Francisco Scavengers: Dirty Work and the Pride of Ownership.* Berkeley: University of California Press, 1978.

_____ and Davis Hunt. "The Worker-Owned Firm: The Idea and Its Conceptual Limits," *Economic and Industrial Democracy* 6 (1985): 275-296.

Peters, Thomas J. and Robert H. Waterman, Jr. *In Search of Excellence: Lessons from America's Best-Run Companies.* New York: Warner Books, 1982.

Pryor, Frederic L. "The Economics of Production Cooperatives: A Reader's Guide," *Annals of Public and Cooperative Economy* 54 (1983): 133-171.

Quinn, Robert P. and Graham H. Staines. *The 1977 Quality of Employment Survey.* Ann Arbor: Institute for Social Research, University of Michigan, 1977.

Redmon, Gene, Chuck Mueller and Gene Daniels. "Worker Control at Rath Packing," *Labor Research Review* 6 (Spring 1985): 5-24.

Rhodes, Susan R. and Richard M. Steers. "Conventional vs. Worker-Owned Organizations," *Human Relations* 34 (1981): 1013-1035.

Rosen, Corey. *Employee Ownership: Issues, Resources, and Legislation.* Washington, DC: National Center for Employee Ownership, 1981.

_____ and Katherine Klein. "Job Creating Performance of Employee-owned Firms," *Monthly Labor Review* 106 (January 1983): 15-19.

_____ , _____ and Karen Young. *Employee Ownership in America: The Equity Solution.* Lexington, MA: Lexington Books, 1985.

_____ . "The Future of Employee Stock Ownership Plans," *Pension Briefings* 87-4 (1987).

Rosow, Jerome M., ed. *Teamwork: Joint Labor-Management Programs in America.* New York: Pergamon Press, 1985.

Ross, Irwin. "Employers Win Big in the Move to Two-Tier Contracts," *Fortune* (April 29, 1985): 82.

Rothschild-Whitt, Joyce. "The Collectivist Organization: An Alternative to Rational-Bureaucratic Models," *American Sociological Review* 44 (1979): 509-527.

_____ . "Who Will Benefit from ESOPS?" *Labor Research Review* (Spring 1985): 71-80.

Ruben, George. "Collective Bargaining in 1982: Results Dictated by Economy," *Monthly Labor Review* 106 (January 1983): 28-37.

Russell, Raymond. *Sharing Ownership in the Workplace.* Albany: State University of New York Press, 1985.

_____ , Arthur Hochner and Stewart E. Perry. "Participation, Influence, and Worker-Ownership," *Industrial Relations* 18 (1979): 330-341.

Salpukis, Agis. "The Two-Tier Wage Impact," *New York Times* (October 30, 1985): 01.

Schaffer, Jan. "Last 11 A&Ps in Philadelphia Will Be Closed," *Philadelphia Inquirer* (March 2, 1982a): 1A.

_____ . "Union Bids for 21 Closed A&P Stores," *Philadelphia Inquirer* (March 5, 1982b): 1A.

_____ . "Competitors Cry Foul at Success of Super Fresh," *Philadelphia Inquirer* (April 3, 1983): 1D.

Schuster, Michael. *Union-Management Cooperation: Structure, Process, Impact.* Kalamazoo, MI: W.E. Upjohn Institute for Employment Research, 1984.

Sertel, Murat R., ed. *Workers and Incentives.* New York: North-Holland, 1982.

Shirom, Arie. "The Industrial Relations Systems of Industrial Cooperatives in the United States, 1880-1935," *Labor History* 13 (1972): 533-551.

Siegel, Irving H. and Edgar Weinberg. *Labor-Management Cooperation: The American Experience.* Kalamazoo, MI: W.E. Upjohn Institute for Employment Research, 1982.

Singer, Jack N. "Participative Decision-Making About Work: An Overdue Look at Variables Which Mediate Its Effects," *Sociology of Work and Occupations* 1 (1974): 347-371.

336

"Slim Packings for Supermarket Workers," *Business Week* 2857 (August 27, 1984): 26.

Slott, Mike. "The Case Against Worker Ownership," *Labor Research Review* 6 (Spring 1985a): 83-97.

————. "Reply to Swinney." *Labor Research Review* 6 (Spring 1985b): 113-114.

Sockell, Donna R. "The Union's Role Under Employee Ownership: Stability or Change?" Ph.D. dissertation, New York State School of Industrial Labor Relations, Cornell University, 1982.

Steiner, Robert. "123 Years of A&P: From Unprecedented Growth to Radical Corporate Surgery." B.A. thesis, Temple University, 1982.

Stern, Robert N. and Tove Helland Hammer. "Buying Your Job: Factors Affecting the Success or Failure of Employee Acquisition Attempts," *Human Relations* 31 (1978): 1101-1117.

————, K. Haydn Wood and Tove Helland Hammer. *Employee Ownership in Plant Shutdowns*. Kalamazoo, MI: W.E. Upjohn Institute for Employment Research, 1979.

————and R.A. O'Brien. "National Unions and Employee Ownership." Working paper, New York State School of Industrial and Labor Relations, Cornell University, 1977.

Stephen, Frank H. "The Economic Theory of the Labour-Managed Firm," in Frank H. Stephen, ed., *The Performance of Labor-Managed Firms*. New York: St. Martin's Press, 1982.

Strauss, George. "Some Notes on Power Equalization," in Harold Leavitt, ed., *The Social Science of Organizations: Four Perspectives*. Englewood Cliffs, NJ: Prentice Hall, 1963.

————. "Workers' Participation in Management: An International Perspective," *Research in Organizational Behavior* 4 (1982): 173-265.

Supermarket News Distribution Study of Grocery Store Sales. New York: Fairchild Publications, 1981.

Supermarket News Distribution Study of Grocery Store Sales. New York: Fairchild Publications, 1983.

Swinney, Dan. "Worker Ownership: A Tactic for Labor," *Labor Research Review* 6 (Spring 1985): 99-112.

Tannenbaum, Arnold S. *Social Psychology of the Work Organizations*. Belmont, CA: Brooks/Cole, 1966.

————. *Control in Organizations*. New York: McGraw-Hill, 1968.

————. "Employee-Owned Companies," *Research in Organizational Behavior* 5 (1983): 235-268.

————, Harold Cook and Jack Lohmann. *Research Report: The Relationship of Employee Ownership to the Technological Adaptiveness and Performance of Companies*. Ann Arbor: Survey Research Center, University of Michigan, 1984.

_____ , Bogdan Kavcic, Menachem Rosner, Mino Vianello and Georg Weiser. *Hierarchy in Organizations: An International Comparison.* San Francisco: Jossey-Bass, 1974.

Thomas, Hendrik. "The Performance of the Mondragon Cooperatives in Spain," in Derek C. Jones and Jan Svejnar, eds., *Participatory and Self-Managed Firms: Evaluating Economic Performance.* Lexington, MA: Lexington Books, 1982.

_____ and Chris Logan. *Mondragon: An Economic Analysis.* London: Allen and Unwin, 1982.

Toscano, David. *Property and Participation: Employee Ownership and Workplace Democracy in Three New England Firms.* New York: Irvington, 1983a.

_____ . "Toward A Typology of Employee Ownership," *Human Relations* 36 (1983b): 581-602.

U.S. Congress. House. Committee on Banking, Finance and Urban Affairs. Subcommittee on Economic Stabilization. *Hearings on Employee Stock Ownership Plans.* 96th Cong., 1st sess., 1979.

U.S. Congress. Joint Economic Committee. *Hearings on Employee Stock Ownership Plans (ESOPs).* 94th Cong., 1st sess., 1975. Pts 1 and 2.

U.S. Congress. Joint Economic Committee. *Broadening the Ownership of New Capital: ESOPs and Other Alternatives.* 94th Cong., 2nd sess., 1976.

U.S. Congress. Senate. Select Committee on Small Business. *Role of the Federal Government in Employee Ownership of Business.* 96th Cong., 2nd sess., 1980.

U.S. Department of Labor. Bureau of Labor Statistics. Mideast Region. *Philadelphia Employment Trends,* 1982.

U.S. General Accounting Office. *Employee Stock Ownership Plans: Benefits and Costs of ESOP Tax Incentives for Broadening Stock Ownership.* Washington, DC: Government Printing Office, 1986.

U.S. General Accounting Office. *Employee Stock Ownership Plans: Little Evidence of Effects on Corporate Performance.* Washington, DC: Government Printing Office, 1987.

Vanek, Jaroslav. *The General Theory of Labor-Managed Market Economies.* Ithaca, NY: Cornell University Press, 1970.

Vroom, Victor H. "Some Personality Determinants of the Effects of Participation," *Journal of Abnormal and Social Psychology* 59 (1959): 322-327.

Walton, John. "A Systematic Survey of Community Power Research," in Michael Aiken and Paul E. Mott, eds., *The Structure of Community Power.* New York: Random House, 1970.

Ward, Benjamin N. "The Firm in Illyria: Market Syndicalism," *American Economic Review* 48 (1958): 566-689.

Webb, Sidney and Beatrice Webb. *A Constitution for the Socialist Common Wealth of Great Britain.* London: Longmans, 1920.

Whyte, William F. "Confronting the Conglomerate Merger Menace." Statement prepared for the Subcommittee on Antitrust and Restraint of Trade Activities Affecting Small Business of the House Committee on Small Business. *Conglomerate Mergers—Their Effects on Small Business and Local Communities.* 96th Cong., 2nd sess., 1984. H. Doc. 96-393.

————. "Employee Ownership: Lessons Learned." Paper presented at 37th Annual Meeting of the Industrial Relations Research Association, Dallas, Texas, 1984.

————. "Philadelphia Story," *Society* 23 (March-April 1986): 36-43.

————. "Philadelphia Worker Ownership and Worker Participation Program." New York State School of Industrial Labor Relations, Cornell University, 1983. Photocopy.

————, Tove H. Hammer, Chris B. Meek, Reed Nelson and Robert N. Stern. *Worker Participation and Ownership.* Ithaca, NY: ILR Press, 1983.

Williamson, Oliver. *Markets and Hierarchies.* New York: Free Press, 1975.

Wintner, Linda. *Employee Buyouts: An Alternative to Plant Closings.* Research Bulletin #140, The Conference Board, 1983.

Woodworth, Warner. "Collective Power and Liberation of Work." Paper presented at the Tenth World Congress of Sociology, Mexico City, August 1982a.

————. "Worker Takeover of a General Motors Plant: Toward a Robin Hood Theory of Change." Paper presented at Third International Conference of the International Association for the Economics of Self-Management, Mexico City, August 1982b.

Work in America: Report of a Special Task Force to the Secretary of Health, Education, and Welfare. Cambridge, MA: MIT Press, 1973.

"Worker Ownership May Save Some A&Ps," *Business Week* (June 28, 1982): 44-45.

Young, Wendell. "The Implementation of Super Fresh's Nontraditional Responses to Traditional Problems." Address to the Industrial Relations Research Association, Philadelphia Chapter, December 11, 1984.

Zager, Michael P. and Jerome M. Rosow, eds. *The Innovative Organization: Productivity Programs in Action.* New York: Pergamon Press, 1982.

INDEX